Decide

Decide
Better ways of making better decisions

DAVID WETHEY

KoganPage

LONDON PHILADELPHIA NEW DELHI

First published in Great Britain and the United States in 2013 by Kogan Page Limited

120 Pentonville Road	1518 Walnut Street, Suite 1100	4737/23 Ansari Road
London N1 9JN	Philadelphia PA 19102	Daryaganj
United Kingdom	USA	New Delhi 110002
www.koganpage.com		India

© David Wethey, 2013

The right of David Wethey to be identified as the author of this work has been asserted by him in accordance with the Copyright, Designs and Patents Act 1988.

ISBN   978 0 7494 6629 9
E-ISBN   978 0 7494 6630 5

British Library Cataloguing-in-Publication Data

A CIP record for this book is available from the British Library.

Library of Congress Cataloging-in-Publication Data

Wethey, David, 1944-
  Decide : better ways of making better decisions / David Wethey.
     p. cm.
  ISBN 978-0-7494-6629-9 – ISBN 978-0-7494-6630-5   1. Decision making.   I. Title.
  HD30.23.W48 2013
  658.4′03–dc23
                                                                        2012032992

Typeset by Graphicraft Limited, Hong Kong
Print production managed by Jellyfish
Printed and bound by CPI Group (UK) Ltd, Croydon, CR0 4YY

Contents

**05   It's a matter of time: the magic number 60:
It's vital to know how long you have got** 132

06 The people factor: Personality profiling creates teams that work, and helps us all understand ourselves – and one another 161

My story
How I came to write this book

I first became fascinated by the subject of decision making 10 years ago, for reasons I will explain. I had started a company called Agency Assessments International (AAI) in 1988, having worked in advertising for 20 years before that. The main business of AAI (and happily it is still flourishing) is advising advertisers – in our case, mainly large global corporates – on choosing and getting peak performance out of their advertising and communications agencies.

So I have earned a living helping big companies make important decisions in one key area: their marketing and advertising. My partners and I have been privileged to see the world's most talented advertising agencies use all their creativity to try to win multi-million-pound accounts in some titanic pitch battles. In facilitating pitches, we have developed sophisticated criteria and subcriteria and a whole range of scoring systems. To make the final selection we have used every permutation of logic and emotion, evidence and chemistry.

My interest has stemmed directly from organizing countless pitches around the world, and attending both the agency presentations and the subsequent selection meetings. It has been endlessly fascinating watching agencies deciding to pitch this way or that. Equally so to watch clients deciding on their new agency. The experience has opened my eyes.

1992 (the year of my decisions epiphany) was a highly significant year in my family life, as I shall explain shortly. Maybe this would be the moment to share with you some personal details, starting with what I call the first journey. Everyone's first journey is a learning journey. It lasts from learning to crawl up to the point where someone hires you because of what you know, and the value you can add. My first journey took just over 30 years. It started in the West Midlands, where I was born just before the end of the Second World War in 1944, moved to Oxford, where I was brought up and educated, and ended in Lisbon at the start of the portuguese counter-revolution in November 1975. I studied politics at Oxford University, which was academic, and in Lisbon which was not. I also studied philosophy and economics – both of which came in handy later on.

After three fascinating years in marketing research at the AC Nielsen Company finding out why some companies and brands are winners, while others aren't, I was persuaded to enter the bad, bold, brash world of advertising, where I worked in agencies around the world for 20 years, trying to find creative solutions for client problems.

I started at an agency called Pritchard Wood & Partners (PWP) in London. It was 1988, towards the end of the Mad Men era. PWP was a very creative agency owned by the American giant Interpublic. It was the place where account planning was invented by Stanley Pollitt. I replaced a man called Frank Lowe as Account Executive on a disinfectant brand. This was after a traumatic year attempting to hang on to our clients after Pollitt, American Creative Director Gabe Massimi, and the man who had hired me, Martin Boase, broke away from PWP to form the legendary Boase Massimi Pollitt.

We were later merged with Erwin Wasey, also owned by Interpublic. The merger was good for me. I entered it in 1969 as an account manager with just one year's experience in advertising. My new chairman, Dennis Reader, invited me to become his personal assistant with a brief to market the agency. When I moved on four years later I was a board Director, with a track record across clients such as British Leyland, Cadbury, Carnation, the *Sunday Telegraph* and Unilever. Coincidentally, Waseys was the agency into which much later on Frank (now Sir Frank Lowe) reversed to set Lowe Howard Spink on course to become the most creative of all the global agencies.

After my first overseas adventure at Waseys based in Madrid and Valencia (and staying for a year at the Ritz in Madrid!) launching the Spania orange brand across Europe, I was transferred to big sister McCann-Erickson to head up its joint venture in Portugal. My predecessor had left to play piano in the bar frequented by most of his former clients. I learned Portuguese and a great deal about hanging on to clients. My 30th birthday party on the Estoril coast where we lived took place almost exactly a year after arriving in Lisbon. Early next morning my hangover was interrupted by the Carnation Revolution. I have no difficulty in remembering that significant date: 25 de Abril 1974, the day the tanks rolled into Lisbon. The revolution taught me a lot: survival, keeping a business going under very difficult circumstances and, importantly, taking one decision after another under pressure. My Portuguese skills improved dramatically to the point of being able to sing (in private, naturally) the revolutionary songs. But still it was fun – enjoying one of the world's most balmy climates, golf, a great social life, drinking excellent wine, eating *bacalhau*, listening to Fado.

I was transferred to Kuala Lumpur (KL), Malaysia in November 1975 to run McCann's business there. The learning journey was over, and the second journey had begun. I call the second journey 'putting the learning to use'. Not that I stopped learning. You never do that. But your second agency management job is definitely the moment to start putting the learning into practice. I loved Malaysia. It is a great place to live. Hot, tropical, exciting and very different from anywhere I had been before. Asia was already becoming the most dynamic part of the world. So after backs to the wall in Portugal, it was exhilarating to work in a country where all the economic indicators were positive, as prices for oil, rubber, palm oil and minerals pushed inexorably upwards. At the office it was stimulating too. We had a talented mix of expats and Malaysians, and most of our international clients were sending stars of the future to South East Asia.

After three terrific years in KL I returned with McCann to the United Kingdom in 1978, as Deputy Managing Director of Harrison McCann. A year later I was headhunted to leave the Interpublic world after 11 years to run a big local agency, Royds. The London of 1979 (with Thatcher elected as Prime Minister) was a very different place from the city I had left in 1973 (with the three-day week). Budgets were rising, creativity was on fire, and I found my overseas experience invaluable. After two years at Royds, I did what all admen dream of: started my own agency, Wethey Scott Pocock (WSP), with Stuart Pocock and Gavin Scott.

WSP had trendy offices in a private cobbled mews in Pimlico. It was a good time. We had a great team of nearly 40 people. We won some big clients, including Honda Cars, Loctite, Whyte & Mackay, Rothmans and Oral B. We developed something of a 'specialism' in travel and leisure products, which was enjoyable. Eventually we took advantage of the marketability of small creative agencies, and sold the business to a group with advertising and recruitment agencies all over the country. For 18 months I worked for the new owners, as Chairman of their London businesses, and a main board Director. I loved having a company Jaguar and not having my house on the line – but hated being told what to do. I suppose it was inevitable that one day I was going to walk out – which I did after a really spectacular row with the Group Chief Executive Officer (CEO) in the best hotel in Glasgow. I gave the Jaguar back and planned a summer off. It was 1988 and I hadn't had more than three weeks away from work since I had left university more than 20 years before.

Well, the summer off never happened. The very first Monday of my new life Ben Allen phoned. He was the Managing Director (MD) of a bank I had pitched for unsuccessfully two years before.

'I called the office, David, and they said you were at home. I need to talk to you because we've fired our agency and I have told the board we are going to appoint you without any further pitch.'

So I explained to Ben what had happened. I didn't have an agency any more.

Ben said: 'That gives us a big problem. What are we going to do about it?'.

I told him that it presented me with a problem too, but offered to meet him that day to give him whatever advice and help I could. The meeting took an hour, but I stayed for five months, having agreed to help him find a new agency. Agency Assessments International (AAI) was born.

The second journey continued right on into the years building up AAI; up to July 2002 in fact. That was the month in which Saffy, my fourth child and younger daughter, had a very serious horse riding accident. She was in a coma for a month, then in hospital for a long time with no definite hope of recovery. Life for the family simply stopped. I didn't go to the office for weeks. My team coped brilliantly. The story has a happy ending: Saffy has made a full recovery. And I had time to think. I started to see life differently. It was time to start the third journey – which I call 'sharing the learning'.

I had always written a lot of articles in the trade press, spoken at workshops, seminars and conference, drawing on my consulting work to comment on the client–agency relationship, pitches, agency remuneration and so on. But now I decided to use the learning and experience I had accumulated over the first two journeys to predict the future for agencies and clients.

I didn't like what I saw. The client–agency relationship was nothing like as strong as it used to be. The agency business model was under threat. The pitch was getting out of control. I decided to put together a suggested programme for radical change. I produced a conference programme called 'Sea Changes', which I presented to clients, agency gatherings and mixed industry audiences some 30 times on both sides of the Atlantic.

I also started to promote the third journey. Not just my third journey, but the third journey for countless talented and experienced people who have learned, put their learning to use, and then found themselves 'too old', redundant, retired, surplus to requirements. I realized that there was a tremendous talent pool in every industry and profession still able to work and contribute, but apparently not wanted any more. It is worse than that. Every year brings more redundancies, more retirements, more waste. It means that more people are in a position to share their learning, but not asked.

I am on a mission – not least with this book – to give these people the belief that there is a third journey for them. The third journey was a key decision for me. It was as important as earlier decisions to leave the respectability of research for advertising, to seek my fortune overseas, to start my own agency, and to leave the familiar agency life for the uncharted waters of client-side consulting.

I have carried out client projects or worked with the advertising industry in some 38 countries. There has been every chance to witness how decision making is done differently in different countries and cultures, as well as in a wide spectrum of diverse companies and organizations. Nor do you need me to explain that men and women do not necessarily perform in the same way. We have also seen big teams, small teams, democratic teams, and rule by diktat from above. I have had many insights into corporate decision taking, and into the way leaders, individuals and teams operate.

I have to be honest. The experience has not left me in thrall to the twenty-first-century corporate world. I am not exactly a fan of the way many companies make decisions, or of the way many managers, executives and directors are supposed to operate. Do I think the talent well has dried up? Quite the reverse is true. All over the world companies can choose from the most educated, qualified, diverse and gifted management pool in history. In turn these men and women can call on technological support that would have been inconceivable even in the year 2000. They can also look forward to an exponential increase in both information and technology. So why am I being critical?

I think we have got it wrong. I have wanted to write a book about decision making for a long while now, because I think it is one of the most crucial life skills, and at the same time one of the least understood, and least well executed. Comb the shelves at Waterstones or WH Smith, at Blackwell's or Barnes & Noble, and you will find scores of titles on leadership, and very few on decisions. It is the same on Amazon. It is the same at airport and station bookstalls.

My experience working with large corporates is that many have consciously or subconsciously adopted a culture of push back and delay. It seems to be quite acceptable to be sceptical about even obviously good ideas, and only to move forward cautiously with a devil's advocate stance. This is delay of one kind. More insidious still is the painstaking (some would call it painful) evaluation process that seems to be the fate of so many promising projects for change. Not only does this cause delay of itself; worse still, governance in many organizations has created obstacles to progress in terms of having to wait for the next meeting of this board, that board or the management leadership team. The whole shebang often makes passport control and security at the slowest airport look like open sesame.

Are most of us not interested in decision making? Or is it that we don't think about it much? Or do we think we are pretty good at it? Maybe it is because everyone is confident about small decisions, while big decisions are seen as something only to be attempted by the very powerful.

Or is it because we haven't seen evidence of what the decision-maker equivalents of the sportsmen Woods, Messi, Federer and Usain Bolt can achieve? Is it because decision making has played second fiddle to leadership?

Decision science is a complex and rich academic area, quite apart from its importance in every aspect of human life. It is vital that political and business leaders not only make winning decisions, but also adopt robust process. This is no less important for key players in fields as diverse as the military, the emergency services, medicine, sport and investment (from hedge funds to racehorses).

We all juggle our lives, so decision making is a crucial skill in everything from choosing a career to choosing a partner, from deciding on a house to deciding on a holiday.

But why did I become involved? First it was to learn more. Years of first-hand experience of the choosing and selection process at AAI have given me some unique insights into what works and what is most unlikely to. But I was keen to understand more about decision making on a wider front. I started reading voraciously to make sure I understood the academics, the consultants and the behavioural economics populists.

By early 2011 I had definitely decided to write this book. In February I was very lucky that the Institute of Practitioners in Advertising (IPA) offered to put on a seminar about decision making at its expense as a thank you for my work on the client–agency relationship, and my membership of its Behavioural Economics Taskforce with the then President Rory Sutherland. My ambition was already to share my insights on decision making with the widest possible audience. The event went well, beyond both the IPA's expectations and mine, and gave me my first significant public exposure as a decisions 'expert'.

I was persuaded to run a Twitter feed at the event, and to start blogging about decisions. There were important developments, as it has turned out. My dedicated site **www.makingbetterdecisions better.com** has won a following, and it has given me a platform to share a great deal of topical and hopefully innovative comments. I use Twitter shamelessly to promote those blog posts and the ones I do monthly on the Marketing Society blogsite: **http://blog.marketing-soc.org.uk/tag/david-wethey/**.

I have reproduced quite a few of the blog posts here – for two reasons: firstly, they mostly relate to a specific event or controversy, which will hopefully make them sharper and more relevant than mere theory; and secondly, they are easy to read at around 400–500 words! I have updated some of the blogs, but left others as they were to give you more of an idea of the specific decision dilemma I was writing about.

If the blogging has provided a platform, the interviews with 'famous deciders' have given me priceless inputs. My debt to this inspiring group of individuals is immense. I learned so much from these people – not least about how generous they were prepared to be in sharing experiences and ideas, as well as giving me their time. As I in turn share the anecdotes, examples and learning with you in the course of this book, you will spot inevitable differences between how these people choose and decide. But I am confident you will also see the similarities and common factors.

For many of the people I interviewed, dreams and ambitions arrived at a very early age – often before their tenth birthday. They were able to articulate clearly what they were thinking as well as what they were doing. Several have also had the courage to make radical life changes later in life, often for far more hours, and far less money.

My interviewees could all identify the particular opportunity, challenge or problem that represented an opportunity to make a really big decision. Almost all gave gut feel as their main driver in making decisions, having gone through looking at options and doing risk assessment. The interviews gave me a profound respect not just for their decisions, but also for the way those decisions were made.

Since completing the book I've made the biggest decision of my business career: to turn my back on 75 per cent of my revenue by refusing to run any more pitches asking agencies for free goods – and aiming to convert the whole industry to a better way. Scary, but the right thing to do. An instinctive decision with rational back-up. And yes, I slept on it before pressing the button!

Acknowledgements

My heartfelt thanks go to all those people who have kindly helped and encouraged me along the way, and without whom this book could not have been written. I have received advice and assistance beyond measure. But no one who knows me well will be surprised that I have not always taken the advice I have received, and I bear sole responsibility for the book's contents.

I am exceedingly grateful to all those who agreed to be interviewed, my Great Deciders: Simon Calver, Barbara Cassani, Ellis Downes, Paddy Eckersley, Sir Jeremy Greenstock, Karl Gregory, Randy Haynes, Vanburn Holder, Sir Tom Hughes-Hallett, General Sir Mike Jackson, David Jones, Nigel Jones, Ray Julian, Dame Ellen McArthur, Lord Moynihan, Paddy O'Brien, David Snelson, Charles Spence, Daniel Topolski, Bishop David Urquhart, Vitaly Vasiliev, and Sir Nick Young.

The amount of knowledge passed on to me directly and indirectly by this group is incalculable.

A warm thank you also to those who introduced me to some members of my 'star panel'. I would particularly like to mention Kevin Murray (who has been a great encourager from the beginning), Neil Dawson, Mark Williams, Hamish Pringle, Chris Rea, Peter Cowie, John Goodwin, Bryn Snelson, Christophe Cauvy and John Rudaizky.

I have also huge admiration for the outstanding researchers, authors and pioneers in this exciting decision making landscape, many of whom I have referenced in this book. Thank you all.

It was Professor Bob Shaw who first opened my eyes to the academic world of decision science on a flight to Manchester more than ten years ago, and I have learned a lot from him over the years.

Few admen have a fraction of the knowledge of Mike Longhurst in the area of personality profiling agency and client people. He has been a particular support.

Talking of admen, the incomparable Rory Sutherland inspired me, and countless others, to take an interest in Behavioural Economics.

There is another group of friends, clients and colleagues whose counsel has always been available to me when I asked for it – I would like to say how much I appreciate their support: Chris Satterthwaite, Lotta Malm-Hallqvist, Celia Couchman, Kevin Allen, Murray Chick, Paul Bainsfair, Fernanda Romano, Martin Riley, Moray MacLennan, Nick Brien, Sergio Guerreiro, Peter Kirby, John Russell, Janet Hull, Brett Gosper, Massimo Costa, Chris Macdonald, Serge Nicholls, Johan Fourie, Simon White, Laura Holme, Laurence Green, Philip Purdon, Ian Millner, Nick Hurrell, Stephen Maher, Fred Prego, Andrea Messa, Helen Weisinger, Neil Hughston, Anna Maria Clarke, Tim Brooks, Paolo Torchetti, Simon Hall, Peter Cundall, and, of course, John Tylee.

Thank you also to my business partners Brian Sparks and Russel Wohlwerth, and my foursomes partner Steve Parrott, who have always been prepared to help me with an aspect of decision making, when it probably distracted from the pitch or putt at hand.

My publisher Matthew Smith has simply been outstanding – as a guide to the tyro author, as a skilled editor, and above all as chief cheerleader for this project. The work of everyone on the Kogan Page team has been of the utmost professionalism, with special mention going to Nancy Wallace in taking the book from script to beautiful book.

Without the loyal support at every turn of my remarkable assistant Tania Zimmerman, the book would probably still be several months away.

Above all I treasure the love and unwavering encouragement from Sue and the rest of the family – and their forgiveness for all the time I have spent away from what a husband and father should be doing.

Introduction
A better way to make better decisions

In any moment of decision, the best thing you can do is the right thing. The worst thing you can do is nothing.

(THEODORE ROOSEVELT, 26TH US PRESIDENT, 1858–1919)

Decision making isn't just a now-and-then transactional thing. It is also the way we manage ambitions and achieve goals. Decision making is the navigation system of choice for ambitious people and organizations. The word 'ambitious' is chosen deliberately. We humans are an optimistic species. It was optimism that inspired our forebears to travel out of Africa and populate the planet. It was optimism that fuelled man's exploration of space. It is optimism that gets us up in the morning.

Antonio Damasio said in *Self Comes to Mind: Constructing the Conscious Brain* (2010), 'We all woke up this morning and we had with it the amazing return of our conscious mind. We recovered minds with a complete sense of self and a complete sense of our own existence – yet we hardly ever pause to consider this wonder.'

If you buy a book on a big subject like decision making, you want there to be a big idea in there somewhere – some new thinking, a theory, a process, a reason why, probably supported by breathtaking statistics. But in truth this is a 'how' book more than a 'wow' book. I would love to have discovered the formula for successful decisions. That would be a tall order, not least because it often takes time to find out if a decision has been a success. What I have focused on is helping the reader find a better way of making decisions. I have also tried to explain why skilled practitioners succeed, and why others fail. But as Teddy Roosevelt said a hundred years ago, it is really important to make decisions, not duck them, and to get in the habit of doing so. To make successful decisions all the time is a pious hope. No one can achieve that. But to approach decision making in a *better way* is a completely attainable goal.

Let's take golf as a parallel. Golf is a gentle and ancient pastime, with a simple principle – the golfer who gets the ball in the cup in the fewest number of strokes wins. To play you need to have sufficient skill to swing the club so as to hit the ball. You also need to be able to walk, pull a trolley or drive a buggy so as to get round 9, 18, 36, 72 or however many holes constitute the match or competition you are playing. And you need to understand the scoring system and the rules. That combination of skills doesn't add up to a big idea. Rather, it is *the idea* of golf. To play like a champion requires altogether more knowledge and skill. That's why our instructional book of golf needs chapters on the grip, developing a repeating and effective swing, using the various different clubs, playing in the wind, getting out of hazards and so on. It may well also include tips on course management, optimum preparation and practice techniques, and how to win against better players. There will almost certainly be a section on common mistakes, and how to correct them. Is there one Big Idea that will help the tyro golfer become a winner? As a keen golfer of more than 50 years experience, I will let you into a secret: there isn't one! If you like, the Big Idea in golf is not to have a big idea. It is more about taking on board a host of small ideas, and understanding enough of the context and background of the activity to be able to make sense of these thoughts, ideas and techniques, and put them to good use.

Chapter 1 of this book is called 'Dreams and determination'. It tells the stories of some remarkable people I have interviewed. I am sure that there is a clear correlation between success and decision-making ability, and hopefully the interviews with my 'great deciders' will inspire in terms of the determination, dreams and readiness to change course that these people have shown in their lives. There is also an obvious implication that if readers acquire better decision technique, that will lead to more success. The interviewees are a mixture of business people and outstanding individuals from disparate fields including the armed forces, politics, law, medicine, academia, the charity sector, sport, gambling and dating. Hopefully this will be both more interesting and appealing than a 100 per cent concentration on the 'business section'.

Chapter 2, 'Nightmares', by contrast, is about what can go wrong, and why. No one said decision making is easy, and some degree of error is inevitable. This chapter is not meant to induce fear of failure; rather to point out the well-chronicled pitfalls, the infamous decision traps that have caught out people and organizations throughout history, and still do today. Being wrong now and then is part and parcel of being human. But avoiding serious disaster is as important as pursuing success.

All decisions are a journey – not a single step. The decision journey effectively starts in Chapter 3 ('Opportunities and problems'). This chapter emphasizes the importance of opportunities – identifying them and exploiting them. Recognizing an opportunity is often the first step to making a great decision – particularly in longer-term decision making. We also see that solving problems and making decisions are two different things. Remember that it has to happen in that order. A decision made before a problem has been solved (an 'early decision') is likely to fail. We live in a data-rich world, with the information and intelligence we need to analyse opportunities and solve problems and readily available as never before. Deciding to decide, when we are looking at considered decision making, will almost invariably involve dealing with opportunities and problems.

Chapter 4 is called 'Smart decision making' – the practical system I set out to look for. Decision making is no different from any other skill area. Good method and technique is essential. We can always power it up and fall back on it. But it is not just about logic and reason; they will only take us so far. Academics have made great progress over recent years in understanding how our brains work. Our conscious mind can only cope with a tiny fraction of what we see and experience. The subconscious brain is so much more than the unconscious mind of Freud and Jung. So far from being a sort of 'dark side' taken up with dreaming and suppressed desire, our subconscious brain is a formidable processing and control unit where we hold our attitudes, beliefs, habits and perceptions. It is also a computerized factory controlling our physical skills, motor functions, heartbeat, breathing, digestion and so much more.

Smart decision making is a mixture of good thinking and harnessing the power of the subconscious brain. This formula will help us rise to most challenges. This chapter is not only about building up to a decision, making it, and ensuring that we have buy-in, so that the decision is effectively a mutual one: we also look at the vital importance of communicating the decision – often the moment when a decision goes live – and implementing it. We also need learning and feedback skills.

The time available to make a decision is a focal point of this book. It is vital to know how long we have got. We do best if we pace ourselves, and adjust our analysis, judgement and action to the time available. In Chapter 5, 'It's a matter of time: the magic number 60', we start with sixty seconds or less. The faster we have to make any one decision, the more instinctively we have to act. The subconscious brain can manage quite a lot of these challenges on its own. Fast decision making is a function of the training and experience which has preconditioned how specialist performers decide and react – whether it's a matter of life and death, or just routine. Interestingly, much of the motivation in these stressful circumstances is defensive: staying alive, helping others, saving lives, avoiding danger. In emergency situations, people can be confident in their ability and the decision they make, but at the same time cautious, careful and considered. We used to think it was only people like fighter pilots, firefighters, soldiers and referees who had to make very fast decisions. But now we realize that we all have a host of 'autopilot skills' from driving a car, and coping with crowded streets and stations in the rush hour, to cooking, playing football and using a computer or smartphone. There is usually no time at all for detailed analysis. Hang around and you'll lose out.

Something else has changed. The power of social media has been demonstrated graphically by the role it played in the Arab Spring.

Its influence is everywhere, giving us access to all areas. But all areas can access us. Lightning-speed communications and social media have therefore irrevocably changed the rules of engagement for everyone in the public eye. When beset by controversy or scandal it is no longer an option for politicians, business leaders and even football managers to keep their heads down and make no comment. As David Jones, Chief Executive Officer (CEO) of French communications giant Havas, put it to me: 'Make every decision as if the world knows about it. Because they will.'

Sixty minutes is the average time for a meeting. Our diaries are full of meetings. The one-hour meeting has become the base unit of time. The meeting is the best and worst element in the business process; best, because teamwork cannot flourish without bringing people together; worst, because meetings can become a contagious, infectious blight on progress. The crucial start point is to reposition the meeting as a forum for decision making. We need to streamline business decision making by making meetings super-productive.

Next we look at managing the decision journey for longer-term decision making. Sixty hours (briefing Monday, response Thursday, or over a weekend) provide time to think, plan and rehearse. Sixty days are enough for a quite ambitious project. Sixty weeks provide time for not just one decision, but a complete feasibility study. Most change management stories in business, government and other large organizations will involve one of these time frames, or more likely a combination. In all these cases serious teamwork will have been the order of the day. But what works on the grand scale will also work for individuals faced with opportunities, problems and significant decisions to take. If you have time, use it.

We have looked at how we all have conscious minds and subconscious brains. We also know how very different we are from each other – and that is obviously going to affect our decision making. I have called Chapter 6 'The people factor'. All decision making is determined by the people who make the decisions, and all the people they affect. To understand what makes a person tick, we have to profile their personality. It is a vital tool. It helps us to understand ourselves, and each other. It enables the creation of teams that work. Profiling is fascinating, useful and fun.

Choosing (Chapter 7, 'Choice is three-dimensional decision making') is a special kind of decision making. Decision making normally consists of looking at a series of options. Do we act now, or not? If we are going to decide, do we say yes or no? If there are a number of options on the table, which one are we going to go with? Decision making is about ranking options. Before we can select or choose, we need to have searched for possible candidates. With choosing there is a vital preliminary phase: whittling the candidates or options down to a number we can handle. How do we do that? It has to be by elimination, not ranking. We look at three aspects of choice. We start with life choices, some of which we make for ourselves, while others are made for us. Then we look at choosing in the sense of searching and selecting – the niche I have inhabited for nearly a quarter of a century. Finally I turn to consumer choice, the world where, directly or indirectly, I have spent my whole working life. Thanks to two major advances – the consumer revolution, with the consumer now firmly in charge of the dialogue after years of being target practice, and neuromarketing – this has become an exciting and very different place.

I have picked some broad arenas for special treatment. Chapter 8 is about 'War'. This is decision making at the macro level. War is terrifyingly different in the world of decision making. War brutally turns the value system upside down, by making life cheap, and infrastructure, property and heritage destructible. It is because the stakes in wartime decision making are so high that military history is so compelling.

Chapter 9 is called 'Sport and other games'. Britain is crazy about sport. It is not that we use our popular sports as analogues for the real world: for so many people, sport *is* the real world. Decision making is controversial, and everywhere – with players on the field, with coaches, with administrators, and of course with referees and umpires. But there are less physical games, like chess, from which we can learn; and then there is gambling, the second-biggest investment medium.

Finally, in Chapter 10, we turn to the most intimate choosing and decision making zone – 'Love', and the search for a partner. There is something of the 'how to' about *Decide*, and Chapter 11 is 'My 20 best decision tips'.

Perhaps it is easier to explain what the Big Idea in decision making is not. It is not just about confidence and decisiveness, although they are vital in emergency situations, where you have less than sixty seconds to make up your mind. But gung-ho firefighters and combat pilots may not live to fight another day. Overconfident triage nurses and lifeguards risk as many lives as they save. Soldiers who shoot before they think and referees who whistle before they engage their brain are a liability. Yet semantically we refer to decisiveness as a virtue, when we consider longer-term decision making. Whereas being considered and methodical is probably a higher-order characteristic.

Maybe the biggest idea in decision making is being adaptable. As in golf it depends on a mixture of rational thinking and technique. But of equal importance are emotional intelligence, psychology and managing people, and getting the most out of them. Forward planning is essential, but it is also vital to be able to work backwards in time by postulating different courses of action and assessing back-to-front scenarios. To be a good decision maker you have to be a good decision planner. Decision planning can be significantly enhanced by using a team, and in companies and organizations there is no choice. Organization charts predicate a kind of obligatory democracy. So it pays to understand team-building technique and how to profile personalities and thinking styles. We need to understand the power of 'groupthink', but it is also really important to realize its limitations, and I cover a range of possible problem solving techniques at the end of Chapter 3. I talk extensively about that familiar corporate device 'the meeting' in Chapter 5.

In a real sense decision making is a misnomer – or to put it another way, it scarcely does justice to the activity as far as considered decision making is concerned. When you have enough time, decision making consists of several vital ingredients, among which making the decision (like hitting the ball at golf) is just one. In contrast, the more we know about the ability of our subconscious brain to see us through, the more readily we can use its phenomenal capacity, and relax in the knowledge that we are doing the right thing.

I believe that to be a positive decision maker is an indispensable skill. In every field success comes from grasping opportunities and solving problems, yet the seized opportunity and the solved problem do not turn into beneficial change without a top-quality decision-making process, and the flair and confidence to implement it. The aim of this book is to help you sharpen your technique, and develop the confidence to decide rationally and instinctively. Everyone needs a balance of both.

It is an urban myth that with important decisions, the only way forward is to concentrate on logical process, to agonize over information, and to rationally compute a solution. There is an academic history behind this, and the management consultancy industry has perpetuated it, with something of a vested interest in longer, more complicated solutions. There is overwhelming evidence that the subconscious (some call it gut feel) plays a part in almost everyone's decision-making mechanism. In the interviews I conducted for this book, this was very clear. It was also clear from the books and papers I read. As Jonah Lehrer wrote in *How We Decide* (2009):

> When we make decisions, we are supposed to consciously analyse the alternatives and carefully weigh the pros and cons. In other words, we are deliberate and logical creatures. This simple idea underlies the philosophy of Plato and Descartes; it forms the foundation of modern economics; it drove decades of research in cognitive science. Over time, our rationality came to define us. It was, simply put, what made us human. There's only one problem with this assumption of human rationality: it's wrong. It's not how the brain works.

Decide is obviously about decision science. It is about how we think. It is about how we approach, define and solve problems. It is about what we do. It is also very much about how other people think and behave. So many fields come together in decision making: mental agility, physiology, psychology, neurology, game theory and more.

When decisions are being made, how do we know that the evidence is any good? The word 'evidence' smacks of the court room. Everyone (police, witnesses, defendant and victim) has to swear that the evidence they give is true. But a lot of important decisions are made on the basis of information, data, analysis and interpretation that no one of sound mind could or would swear to. Where does this evidence come from? There's a long list: colleagues, advisers, experts, friends, family, members of the public, academics, journalists, editors. How do we know the evidence is reliable? Is it factually correct? Has it been analysed and interpreted objectively? Or is it dodgy? Is it biased? Whether decisions are primarily conscious or subconscious, it is still critical to be able to call on the best intelligence, information and data. My motivation in writing *Decide* is to help readers develop good decision habits. I sincerely want to help you use the best techniques. I want you to achieve consistently good results. Decision-making can be incredibly difficult. Or at least it's difficult to do it consistently well. It is a lesson I have learned over the course of my life – in work and outside.

Decide is a vital book for everyone whose life depends on successful decision making. Many people make decisions without properly considering the context, options and implications of their actions. Or worse still they simply manage the consequences of avoiding taking decisions. The difference between winning and losing in business, and often in life, hangs on getting it right. This book proves that decision making does not have to be a long-drawn-out process, as long as it is approached with a mixture of rational and lateral thinking.

Business people and companies that don't make decisions – or that make bad ones – will die. Woolworth, Enron, Worldcom, Arthur Andersen and numerous airlines all provide object lessons in the perils of flawed decision making. It is possible in each case to trace key moments where decisions were made – often by one individual – with no attempt to mutualize or ratify the decision.

It has also been painful to read about the rise and fall of former 'crown jewel' British companies such as Marconi and Cable & Wireless, where managements prided themselves on strong decision making, but decided to focus on a future which never came and to abandon a present which was real and profitable. Governments too tend to make policy on the hoof, announce their decisions, and then live to rue the consequences.

Decision making isn't easy, but there are rules that work – and this book emphasizes the importance of both creative problem solving and managing decisions through. *Decide* is aimed at both a broad business and professional audience, and at the general reader. It is not filled with jargon or complicated business models. It uses as many interesting examples as I could find. I have tried to make decision making an accessible subject.

The breadth of appeal is in the subject matter itself. Everybody has to make decisions. In companies, everyone from the CEO downwards is paid to make decisions, but there is little specific training on how to make them. There are plenty of courses in financial management, man management, supply chain management and negotiation skills – but what about decision-making skills? As individuals we also face important decisions through our lives, and can benefit from understanding what works and what is less likely to.

As well as being thought-provoking, *Decide* is practical in its approach and sets out a clear approach to decision making, that if properly followed will enable the reader to make or contribute to effective decisions, whatever the time available. This book highlights both the importance of good decision making and the sometimes fatal consequences of getting it wrong – particularly if a decision has been made (and announced) before the problem has been solved. It shows that decision making does not benefit from a macho style, and should ideally involve team participation. You need a properly constructed decision-making approach, which needs to be in place for the whole 'journey'. But there is no substitute for creativity and ideas.

To be a good decision maker, you also have to recognize your own profile, and how you think, as well as how colleagues on a team or friends or family members operate. Hopefully after reading this book, the reader will understand how to balance optimism and pessimism, data and intuition, and importantly how to approach future decision challenges with greater confidence. Most of all I hope very sincerely that you will be far more interested in decision making, and engaged with it, than you were before.

Chapter One
Dreams and determination
What drives great deciders

> *Every journey I've made has been about the journey, not the destination. For some racers, their whole reason for doing that race is to be at the finish line. My goal was to get to the finish line as fast as possible but I wanted to be out there. I loved being out there.*

(ELLEN MACARTHUR, RECORD-BREAKING ROUND-THE-WORLD SAILOR, AND ECO-WARRIOR)

Early years

The careers of many of the people I interviewed – and Ellen MacArthur is a classic example – have been heavily influenced by significant events in their childhood, or aspects of their young lives. Let me tell you about some of them.

For Ellen, dreams and ambitions arrived at a very early age. As she said to me:

> There've been two big decisions in my life. The first was when I was given an opportunity to go sailing for the first time on my Aunty Thea's boat. I was only four. I remember the journey down there, sitting and looking out of my aunt's car window as we drove through the low flatlands of Essex going to the boat.

I'd never been to Essex before; I'd never seen anywhere flat like that before because I was from Derbyshire. I remember seeing the boat for the first time, instinctively knowing which boat it was sitting on a mooring in the river. And the most amazing feeling was actually climbing on board because it was like stepping into a new world. I was so excited, I tried to go underneath the guard wires which you'd normally climb over and I got stuck because I had a big lifejacket on. I went on board and I remember just looking up and looking down, looking round. And then my Aunty opened the doors and I remember looking in there thinking that's all you need; that is a little home which can go anywhere. The most amazing feeling of all was the first time we hoisted the sails. To a four year old it was the greatest feeling of freedom that could ever be experienced. It was that feeling that we could go anywhere in the world. And it was almost in that second, the sky is the limit. This just opened up a world of opportunity and adventure and learning.

Ellen's excitement at her aunt's boat made her desperate for one of her own, but geography and her family's limited means were just two of the obstacles. I asked her if her parents understood the depth of her passion for boats, and how she eventually raised the money. Did her parents understand?

At that stage, I don't know. They grew to understand for sure. Some of it they were unaware of. The financial side's quite interesting because I had no money. We never got pocket money as kids, so I would ask for birthday and Christmas money – we used to get, I think, £15 when I was little and then £20 for birthday and Christmas so that used to go in the Building Society. When I started going to secondary school I got control of my dinner money so I got it every day rather than having to pay it in once a week, which is what you have to at junior school. So every single day right through school, I'd either have nothing for lunch or I would have baked beans and mashed potato, which was four pence each, and then I would pile the plate with gravy which was free and that would be my lunch. The rest of the change I saved every day from the age of 11 till

17. It was the only way I could do it because that was the only way I could save. I couldn't go and work locally as we lived in the middle of no where. I worked at home, but we never got given spending money for that. It just wasn't the way we were brought up. So I saved right through school. I'm not sure they knew just how keen I was, because I never told them about that. In fact, they didn't know about it till I was 18 when I set off on my first solo trip round Britain. And someone asked me in an interview, so Ellen, how did you save up for your first boat, you know? Did your parents buy you it, kind of thing? And that shocked me because that wasn't how it was at all, you know, I'd had to save every single penny. I said on the radio that I had mashed potato and baked beans every day at school, or I'd take bread out the cupboard and a banana or something, and then mum and dad reacted quite badly to that because they thought that it made them out to be quite bad parents. But the reality was that was the only way that I could achieve it. The first boat was £535, which was a lot of money.

When I was going through school, I absolutely wanted to sail around the world. I read everything I could. I read everything from Swallows and Amazons to Sir Francis Chichester to Robin Knox-Johnston, Naomi James – I read everything I could possibly get my hands on to learn. And I would just sit in my bedroom for hours reading these books, learning, trying to understand, trying to learn as much as I could about navigation; just hanging on to the one week I got to sail every summer with my Aunty Thea, because that was it. It was the family holiday and seven of us and the dog would go down to the East Coast!

Ellen's determination was extraordinary. Between races she lived off £10 a week and lived in a Portakabin. When she realized she needed a sponsor, she wrote 2,500 letters before she found one. We will catch up with some of the remarkable decisions she made – first to realize her sailing ambitions; later to abandon the sea for her pioneering work on sustainability and the circular economy.

Paddy Eckersley, later famous as the airline captain whose heroism and cool decision making was to save hundreds of passengers in a 747 with two blazing port engines on take-off from Jeddah, Saudi Arabia, grew up in Zululand in the 1940s. He told me:

> I was born in a tiny village way up in northern Natal. It was very rural, very basic. You know, outdoor loos, things like that. My grandfather was English, came to Africa, and married a local girl. He and his brother were advisors to one of the rebel Zulu pretenders to the throne. This was the late 1890s.
>
> I was always interested in flying, for some reason or other. I hardly saw any airplanes, living out in the country, but we had a flying doctor to look after the villages. He had a tiny little aircraft, a two-seater, and every chance I got I'd run up to the little airstrip. Growing up in South Africa, of course, flying was an impossible dream, because of the Apartheid laws and so on. There's no way in which I could get anywhere near learning how to fly or becoming a pilot, as such. Anyhow, I went through high school and went to college in Durban. I came back as a teacher. Everything else was a sort of closed door, except teaching. I thought I might become a doctor, but there was a quota of how many of us could become doctors, from different racial groups, because we were classed as coloureds, and only so many a year were allowed to become doctors. I spent just less than a year teaching in South Africa, and then I decided to leave and go to Rhodesia, because they were recruiting teachers, and they were gradually getting rid of the Apartheid type of government. I had just turned 21. They gave me a job and posted me to what was then Nyasaland (part of the then Federation of Rhodesia and Nyasaland). I thought, well, here's a country which is more receptive to new ideas, and I tried to join the local flying club, because that was the only way to get into aviation at my age. But there were still a lot of South African types in Nyasaland and Rhodesia. Their clubs were a sort of closed shop – very difficult to get into them. But fortunately for me there was an English guy who was working as an air traffic controller in Blantyre. He tried to help me get into flying, but met up with a whole lot of obstacles, and that was a failure. I left and went to Northern Rhodesia (later

Zambia), with the break-up of federation. Fortunately for me, the same chap also transferred himself to Northern Rhodesia, and we met up there again. We went through a lot of problems, but eventually I was successful, and had the dubious honour of being the first non-white in the flying club. I started flying, did the training, got a private licence, and flew.

Karl Gregory is the Managing Director (MD) of the successful dating site Match.com. Karl comes from Malta, as he explained to me:

Tourists used to stop off in Malta and buy handmade sweaters. My dad supplied all the wool to the people who created those sweaters. Selling wool in Malta, in a hot Mediterranean country, is like selling ice to the Eskimos; difficult task. But they did quite well from that. I was interested in business even when I was young, but whenever I went and offered ideas to him or his brothers, they were so dismissive and so old fashioned that I knew fairly early on that I wasn't going to be able to operate, live and do business in Malta. At which point, and I was about 12, one of my first decisions was that I would have to study abroad. So, later when I had got my first degree, my second big decision was, I'm leaving to go and study at Strathclyde – where I got a Master's in International Marketing.

Colin, Lord Moynihan is Chairman of the British Olympic Association. When I interviewed him, Colin told me that his childhood had been far from plain sailing, and that he felt he had a lot to live up to:

The catalyst for ambition and direction in my life was unquestionably the loss of my father when I was ten. From that moment onwards there was the added responsibility for a young man to ensure that my mother and my younger sister were looked after and that my life had direction. And I was fully aware even then of an extraordinary family background, where, after twelve generations of Moynihan's serving in the army, my great-grandfather was the only non-officer to get Victoria Cross on the first day they were awarded by Queen Victoria in the Crimea. Andrew Moynihan VC at that time had absolutely no money and he came from a family that was sharing a small house in Leeds. He was informed by the Duke of Cambridge that because of his gallantry, the Duke would educate his son, should he ever have one. He did, and the promise was duly honoured, and Berkeley Moynihan, my grandfather, after generations in the army, decided that his life should be dedicated to healing people. He walked past the Leeds Infirmary and said the Moynihans have done enough fighting, it's time now to start healing, and he eventually became the leading surgeon of his day, surgeon to the King, and Surgeon General in the First World War. He gained a hereditary peerage for his services to medicine, but wouldn't move from Leeds. Leeds Infirmary was very much his home. I grew up with this family history, and even more extraordinary, there had been four Moynihan brothers from Tipperary, all killed on the same day in the Battle of Malplaquet (1709). So I suppose I was very conscious, as a young boy, that there was a great deal to live up to now that Dad had died young, following very severe injuries suffered in India in the Second World War. All the money in the Moynihan family from my grandfather was locked into trust, and the trust therefore went directly to my half-brother Anthony (the notorious playboy). He took all the money and everything else, and therefore we moved to the gardener's bungalow where in a small two-bedroom property we relied on my godparents to fund us. Mum went out to work, and it was the complete opposite of the lifestyle we had at Ashtead. The Haberdashers Company, unbeknown to me, paid for my education at Monmouth School.

Nigel Jones is the CEO of Publicis London, the advertising agency, and a former youth prodigy at chess. Nigel told me:

> I've got lots of theories and thoughts about chess, because literally I've been playing it all my life. I started when I was about six, and played almost continually till I was 24, and I mean literally two to three hours per day, including 48 hours over the weekend. So it was a massive part of my youth, really, and I can't really remember a time when I didn't play chess seriously.

Nigel was one of the Jones Boys – three brothers all playing professional chess.

"I'm the eldest, then there's Chris, and then there's Patrick. We were very different players – Chris was literally born as a chess player, so he was taught to play chess when he was five. When he was five and one day, he was a brilliant chess player. He was as good as Nigel Short, and he is exactly the same age. When they were both 17, I think Chris was ranked something like the third best under 18 year old in the world.

Patrick, on the other hand, was always a little dyslexic, he's amazingly bright and now has a PhD but he hasn't got English O-level, and he needed to work incredibly hard at becoming a great chess player, probably practised four or five hours a day and he eventually became a really good player as well – almost through sheer desire. I was somewhere in the middle. They have both said to me that they thought my main characteristic was that I was the most competitive person they'd ever met, and I was just never going to let anyone beat me at chess, and that's what drove me.

I'll tell you something else which is a big driver in my life, I mean, so fundamental to my life that it has been an influence on practically every decision I make. I had cancer that was supposed to be terminal when I was 19, between school and university. I then had three years of treatment, over 200 doses of radiotherapy, a year of chemotherapy, five or six operations, was down to about six stone, and lost my hair. Anyway, it didn't kill me. It turned out not to be terminal, obviously, or I still wouldn't be here. I think am one of the longest-surviving Hodgkin's Lymphoma 4B patients in Britain. I've lived now longer without it than I did before, in fact. And it's got quite interesting consequences. It means I'm one of the few people in Britain who's had radiotherapy over 25 years ago, actually, and they don't really know what happens to you after 25 years of radiotherapy. So I'm sort of an experiment in what happens, and they now seem to think that 20 years is a key time for radiotherapy – some kind of fundamental half-life, after which bits of your body that haven't worked for 20 years suddenly start working again. Which is interesting.

David Jones (another advertising Jones, but no relation), the Global CEO of Havas Group, grew up in affluent circumstances in Cheshire.

My dad was the Managing Director of a big textile company up there, and I had it incredibly happy and easy, and wanted for nothing as a child. Despite that, I was a complete git, and a real rebel. My older sister was a genius, straight A's at everything. To give you an example, she was second in the country in her chartered accountancy exams. Most people fail these exams the first time, and she was the number two in Britain, and was disappointed because she was only number two!

I think I probably decided that the only way that I could actually make my mark was by being a rebel. So I was often in trouble and my parents sent me off at the age of 16 to India for three months, to stay with my godmother, who was over there.

We travelled in second and third class trains around India, nearly being kidnapped, getting stuck in the Himalayas in mudslides, getting a very serious illness with a 98 per cent mortality rate and being hospitalised. I think it really opened my eyes to what a complete idiot I'd been. That was probably the first stage of actually becoming a decent person.

I was really into business and into languages, but the problem was, all the university courses combining business and languages at the time offered just one year overseas as a language assistant.

I didn't want that. Then a brilliant new course came along where I could do two years at business school in the UK but also two years in a German business school, studying alongside German students, in German. All the exams were in German and they made no exceptions for the fact that you were not German. It was the first business degree to be sponsored by the European Union. I was only 18.

That was very good for me on a couple of levels. In today's world, if you go overseas, you're very connected. You have mobile phones, email and so on. But at that time, letters were the only way you kept in touch with your family and friends plus one phone call every two weeks from a phone booth, which cost in modern-day terms about $200. So you're alone in the middle of Southern Germany, you're not going home for six months. You don't know anyone and you're completely cut off, and have to fend for yourself.

Not only was it an amazing degree, because the quality of the business school in Germany and education was just superb, but it was a great experience from that perspective. The other thing it did; it meant that when I moved back to the UK, and was suddenly writing exams in English again, it felt incredibly easy.

Vitaly Vasiliev is the CEO of Gazprom Marketing and Trading, based in London. He grew up in a very different environment. As he told me:

"I was born in Moscow. It was a very interesting time. When the Soviet Union collapsed I was at university age. Funny thing, it was a great school. There was a lot of positive stuff in terms of education, and fundamental knowledge. It was interesting also from the point of adaptability. You can be rebellious. And you can always find a way even if something is forbidden, or not allowed. You can always find a way. If you can't change something you need to lead something to change it. And I decided to talk to my people, and eventually became the leader of the Young Communist Party at school. I then became the leader of the school itself. As leader of the school I had power. If you want to do something, basically to be somebody or to do something is actually the tool.

I told my friends, please have some dreams. If you want to change something, do something, or build something. And actually then you will think what will help me to do it. There was one particular university I was dreaming to get into. People told me that it's impossible to get into this university because it's the best university and so on. And I just said okay, that's exactly what I want to do. And it took me three years to get in, after graduating from high school. So I studied there and after graduation I joined the Gazprom company in Moscow.

Simon Calver has been CEO of Europe's largest DVD rental business Lovefilm for seven years. In April 2012 he joined Mothercare as CEO. He told me that he grew up surrounded by retail:

> My grandfather set up supermarkets and my middle brother was born above one of the supermarkets, and so from very early days, you know, we were stocking shelves, merchandising, doing stock checks. That was how we grew up. So the shop was the epicentre of a smallish Gloucestershire suburb. And it was also the centre of our lives. For me it was always the shop or the rugby pitch. They were probably the two most defining places where we grew up.

Barbara Cassani, famous for getting off the ground both Go (BA's budget airline) and Great Britain's 2012 Olympic bid, was born in the United States (US). She told me:

> We'll start way, way back. I think it is relevant that I am the youngest of three, because I've always been a kind of peace-maker. My brother, my sister, and me. We were very different. And there were always a lot of arguments. I came from a very stressful, strife-ridden family situation, and so I was always trying to figure out how to make it peaceful at home. So I do not like conflict, and I figured that out a few years ago. I think it was because of my childhood. But having said that, I am naturally a very questioning person. Sometimes people think I am looking for conflict, but actually I'm always looking for resolution and preferably in a way where everyone feels good about an idea. That's the cultural background or baggage that I brought to the working world.

Changing course

Another important characteristic of the accomplished deciders I interviewed is the courage and single-mindedness they showed in changing course. I am not talking here about minor adjustments, but highly significant moves, which in all four cases took them unalterably away from fields where they were familiar and doing very well.

Let me start with Sir Tom Hughes-Hallett, who recently announced his intention to step down as CEO of Marie Curie after more than twelve years at the helm. Tom was for many years a very successful banker. Here is his story:

> Yes, and so I was getting bored, and I opened the appointments section of the Sunday Times. It would have been May 2000. And there was this job, saying, Marie Curie Chief Executive. And I don't know why, but I cut it out, and I put it in my pocket. It was the pocket of a tweed jacket. I remember so well. It wasn't a suit. And I don't wear a tweed jacket very often, you know, once every three months or something. I was trustee, then, of a family trust in Scotland. And, of course, what you wear for a family trust meeting in Scotland, is a tweed jacket. So the tweed jacket went back on, maybe eight weeks later, and I got to Heathrow, when the telephone rang in my pocket. So got the mobile out, and there was this ad.
>
> I looked at it again while I was waiting at the airport, and I thought, do you know what, actually, I'm really interested. And I then made another good decision, which was, don't answer the advertisement. Look on the website. And I saw that the chief executive was Nicholas Fenn. We had judged the Jawaharlal Nehru scholarship together, about a year before. I never really talked to him. Just remembered the name. So I rang him. And I said, look, this is ridiculous, but it's probably too late. He said, on the contrary, we're short-listing tomorrow. And I said, well, I'm in no way qualified. And Nick said, I don't know why. He said, our last two chief executives have been a general and an ambassador, so why not a banker?
>
> I hadn't done any research on the charity. I didn't do any comparative research to see if it was the right one to apply for. But my best mate at Enskilda, who I'd worked with for 12 years, died of cancer when he was 40. And he'd been looked after by Marie Curie. So I rang his widow, Charlotte, and said,

shall I apply? She said, you've got to. It's a wonderful organization. That was the end of research. It's embarrassing, really. But at the same time, Barclays were trying to recruit me to run their private bank, and I went for it. And I went for both in parallel, and I was offered both jobs.

We had a family conference. So this was unusual decision-making, I think. I called the family together, who then were 15, 12, 9, and 47. We had a family meeting in the cottage in Suffolk, and we discussed it, and they voted. It was a hung jury. The girls wanted me to come to Marie Curie. Archie wanted me to go to Barclays because he said that his friends would have heard of it, and no one had ever heard of Flemings, where I was. And my youngest, who is the conservative one, wanted me to stay put. So I thought the ayes had it. The girls had it. And I'd made up my mind anyway, to be honest with you. But I thought it was such a big decision for the family, and financially, it was going to have consequences. I'm so glad I had the family conference, because they've, sort of, been part of my career as a result.

I told Tom that he was the first person I had talked to who described a democratic decision, but went on to explain that I had mainly been talking to alpha males. I'll always remember his reply: 'I do tapestry, and I play the harpsichord, so that should give you a clue.'

I told Tom that academics in America, who write books about decision science, all prescribe almost exactly the kind of decision-making process, favoured by his family. I said, 'This is what you're supposed to do. It isn't seen by American academics, at least, as remotely eccentric. But you're the first person who's done it. Everybody else has made their own decisions.'

I went on to ask Tom how Marie Curie has turned out:

Completely fantastic. I mean, it's been the best 12 years of my life, without any question. I've loved every second of it. I thought I'd come for five years. I'm not very good at long-range planning. I didn't really know what I'd do afterwards. But it's gone like a flash, and it's been a fantastic journey. I've really,

really enjoyed it, and I've made some really good decisions here that I'm really proud of, too.

In many ways Sir Nick Young has a similar story. He was a City solicitor who became a partner of a law firm in Ipswich. Here's Nick's story, in his own words, about how he came to be in the charity sector:

"I was well set up, earning good money, nice bunch of partners. I ran the local solicitors' group. I was also running a church youth group. We were involved in a lovely local community, so leaving would be a big step. I looked at all sorts of options, and then got to thinking more and more about the voluntary sector. I eventually just took the plunge and rang up the nearest charity that I could find to Ipswich, which was the Sue Ryder Foundation, run by Lady Ryder of Warsaw, one of the great philanthropists of our times.

I rang the Sue Ryder Foundation, and was slightly startled to be put straight through to Lady Ryder. Told her that I just wanted to come and talk to somebody about what's it like working in a charity. Lady Ryder replied, Oh, well, you'd better come and see me! What are you doing tomorrow?

So literally the next day I found myself in her office – a tiny, tiny little woman, great big eyes – in her little office in the Sue Ryder Home in Cavendish in Suffolk, surrounded by mounds of paper. People were coming and going, and there was a sense of really being at the hub. We talked the whole afternoon and most of the evening about her work: setting up homes for people with cancer and motor neurone disease, and her work during the Second World War as a member of the SOE – Special Operations Executive. She spent a lot of time in Eastern Europe helping victims of the concentration camps at the end of the War. It was an amazing story, a very moving story, a fascinating, interesting story.

And I'll never forget that afternoon, really, because it was July in Suffolk, and as I drove away there was a great big red sun setting behind a classic Suffolk cornfield. I just had this sense, incredibly strong sense, (it was so strong I had to stop the car) that I had just been picked up and put down in the right place. That's where I'm supposed to be! So I started giving free legal advice to her and her husband, Group Captain Leonard Cheshire, VC, founder of the Cheshire Homes. He really was something, just a fabulous man. He will be a saint one day. I also did bits of fundraising, you know, helping them with their various projects, mostly in and around East Anglia.

They took to phoning me up once a month and saying, come along, Mr Young – we've got a job; you know, when are you going to come and work for us? Well, I was very attracted in theory by that, but you know, they didn't have a bean to bless themselves with. It would mean a 70 per cent drop in salary if I was going to do that. Hence, puffing cigarettes around the park and worrying and fretting about it, until my darling wife Helen said to me one day, oh, for God's sake, you'd love this work, give it a go. We can sell the house, we can get rid of the mortgage; you can always get back to the law if it doesn't work out. So I did, and that's how I ended up going to work for Sue Ryder. The first day I drove with her at dawn up to one of the new acquisitions, a beautiful stately home called Staunton Harold Hall in Leicestershire. My job was to turn that into a Sue Ryder Home. It was the first of about ten million-pound-plus building projects that I managed, from acquisition through design, build, appointment of staff, getting local people involved in the running of the Home, so we could pass it over to them. Each one was a kind of two-year project: I had sort of four or five on the go at any one time, and absolutely adored it from the very word go.

Sir Nick went from Sue Ryder to the British Red Cross, from there to run Macmillan Cancer Support (where he received his knighthood), and finally back to the top job at the Red Cross. Of his current job he says:

> And that's what makes it such fun, and that's why I'm still here eleven years later, because where would I find another more interesting, more challenging, more thrilling job? It is a job where absolutely everybody in the organization passionately believes in

what they're doing, and in the part they have to play in it. I mean, there isn't a better job in the UK – probably not in the world.

David Urquhart is now Bishop of Birmingham, and a member of the House of Lords. He was previously an executive with BP. He told me how the change happened:

I did six wonderful years in BP, and did six different jobs all in either Economic Planning or Marketing, and basically getting rid of the stuff. All downstream, and that was really good. It was going to be my continuing life's work.

Looking forward to my change of direction, I've mostly been influenced, not so much by visions and ideas, but by people. And also, by rehearsing my engagement with Christian faith as an adult. I had a huge amount of knowledge of Bible and things, because that was my education. I hadn't come from a very ardent practising Christian family, but the people in Uganda [where he went during the Idi Amin period on a gap year after school to work in a United Nations project for the disabled] who had time to listen and talk about life and how you get on, particularly if you're physically disabled, were very striking. When it came to a change of direction from a business career, it was the parents of the kids who came to the youth club where I was helping out in the back streets of Middlesbrough that influenced me. Most of them were unemployed steelworkers, and seeing me do voluntary work with young people, they said why didn't I do it full-time? And so the seeds of what I do now were sown while I was in full flow in a completely different way of life. I eventually went off, and did a couple more jobs at BP, then got interviewed by the church, interviewed by a college in Oxford, was told I could study there, and so resigned from BP.

I asked David if there was any fast track into the Anglican priest-hood. There was not. He described his church career as follows:

Give up your job, go back to school for two years, back to university, do a postgraduate course at Oxford. At thirty-two I was ordained in York to work in Hull. It was nearly five years' training and then I went across to Hull, worked in the city for another five years, tried to establish a church in the inner city, and then I went to Coventry as a vicar. I went Birkenhead as a suffragan bishop, and then five years ago I came down to Birmingham to be bishop.

We left Ellen MacArthur having scrimped and saved to buy her first boat, with her extraordinary ocean sailing and record breaking career ahead of her. It is sacrilege not to write about all her achievements and records, but she has done it brilliantly herself in her book *Full Circle* (2010). Let's pick up Ellen's story a bit later, on the cusp of her making her second momentous decision:

It's the biggest decision I've ever made in my life. And I never thought I would stop what I was doing because I loved it. It was my dream from four years old. I was living in this incredible world with incredible people running these projects that were just mind-blowing. We were doing everything that I dreamed of. I could have found any amount of money to do any sailing project – I'd just broken the sailing lifetime Round the World record; it was the point at which you could do anything, literally.

But it was at this point that I realized something for the first time. You sail around the world using the resources you have. You take the minimum because you have to, else you'll never break the record and you'll never win the race. You learn the absolute definition of the word finite. What you have is all you have; at 2,500 miles away from land you cannot stop for more.

And I'd never translated that to land, ever, not once. And I stepped off the boat at the finish line and I started to question whether our world was any different. You know, at the end of my journey I could refuel, I could stop, I could refuel my 475 litres of diesel that power two computers and autopilot quite easily. We only have that stuff once in the history of humanity and that really struck me, and it was a bit like picking up a stone and seeing something and having two choices. I could either ignore it and carry on with my dream job of sailing around the world and just put that stone back down, or I could put it to one side and learn.

And I chose to learn, and began a five-year journey up to the launch of the foundation, talking to scientists, experts, teachers, CEO's, farmers about how we use resources; how resources fuel our economy. From travelling to food production – everything. And it's essential; these resources are absolutely core to everything that we do; from running a hospital to growing food; from building an automobile to fuelling it. I mean, the transport element, the materials element, the energies element – everything's intertwined. I love learning and the more I learned the more involved I became.

I visited power stations, I talked to engineers, I talked to experts. Everything that I found fascinated me. It blew me away and the more I learned, the more I thought to myself we have a massive challenge in front of us. I picked up The International Energy Agency (IEA) report for 2008. It's a report that advises 29 governments across the globe, including the US, Australia, most of the European countries. The report, *World Energy Outlook*, it was called, said we have 'about 40 years of (conventional) oil left'. I read the executive summary and I was absolutely blown away. That's my lifetime. Everything we do uses oil and it just made me realize that, actually, we need to find a different way of operating because the dependence on that material could be 40 years, it could be 80 years, but no one thinks it will be any longer. That was the point, and that's what I'd understood from the boat. Finite means finite – there is no more.

The whole turning point for me was when I was looking into coal. I'd looked into oil, I'd looked into materials, I was starting to look into the whole thing. But I looked into coal and I'd been to one of the big coal fire power stations, stood in the burner and looked up at this 180'-high cathedral of pipes – the burner was being repaired by the engineers. I was there with the engineers and welders who were fixing it – absolutely amazing. It was like going down the mines. It reminded me of my great grandfather who was a miner who spent 50 years of his life down the mines on the Derbyshire/Leicestershire border and he was alive when I was a kid.

I used to sit on his knee; I would listen to his mining stories. He would talk about the pit ponies. When they were withdrawn from the mines and they retired, they would be around the mouth of the pits and the miners would save the crusts of their sandwiches and take them to these horses because they'd worked together. They'd worked underground for years. He told me all these stories.

On the World Coal Association home page when I looked at it that year, it said 118 years of coal left. It's not an exact figure, it can't be. But I thought back to my great grandfather. He was alive until I was 11 years old and he was born exactly 118 years before that year. That was it for me. I'd come across the most important challenge of my life.'

Summing up the interview highlights

Until I did these interviews, I had never associated decision making directly with dreams and determination. I had seen it as more functional and episodic. I now realize how wrong that was. Nor had I understood the relevance to decision making of willpower (look at Ellen MacArthur and Paddy Eckersley) or self-denial (for example Tom Hughes-Hallett, Sir Nicholas Young and Bishop Urquhart).

There's a new book *Willpower. Rediscovering the Greatest Human Strength* (2011) by Baumeister and Tierney, which makes some surprising claims about the degree of character forming that can be achieved by denying yourself all sorts of treats and forbidden fruits. The authors also find a scientific explanation for that feeling of well-being that comes (they claim) from dieting and exercise. Apparently Freud's ego can be depleted by excess and indulgence, but you can build back 'muscular tone' in the ego by doing the right things. Wisely, the book tells you not to try to and give up all your bad habits at once!

As for self-denial, I posted a blog on the subject last year. Not having read Baumeister and Tierney at the time, my view was more compassionate than encouraging.

Blog extract

Giving up – the saddest words

There are many kinds of decision – but giving up is one of the hardest. 'Give up' is what's known to wordsmiths and academics as a phrasal verb. Most phrasal verbs ending in 'up' are highly positive, for example:

- grow up;
- go up;
- change up;
- talk up;
- lighten up;
- make up;
- cheer up;
- warm up.

But giving up itself, in the sense of quitting, and giving up anyone or anything (with notable exceptions like smoking and other vices) carries connotations of loss and deprivation.

Deciding to give up blocks the route to much that we have valued.

Deciding to give up leaves us memories, but no anticipation.

Deciding to give up can be really difficult.

Conceptually it is so much more attractive to decide to do, go, try, experience or see something new. When faced with a number of options (let's say for the sake of argument, it's just two), how much more compelling to contemplate the new, than contemplate the loss of the old. Somehow the reward–risk equation is just not balanced when the choice is between sunny uplands and vowing not to return.

When your partner, friend or colleague next comes down on the side of giving up, please be supportive and understanding.

It's always a tough decision.

Chapter Two
Nightmares

Striking a balance between being tolerant of mistakes, and understanding the danger signs that tell you a decision can go badly wrong

In school we learn that mistakes are bad, and we are punished for making them. Yet, if you look at the way humans are designed to learn, we learn by making mistakes. We learn to walk by falling down. If we never fell down, we would never walk.

(ROBERT T KIYOSAKI, 1945–, AMERICAN INVESTOR AND AUTHOR – CREATOR OF RICH DAD, POOR DAD)

All debacles are caused by one or all of three blunders (Paul Nutt, *Why Decisions Fail*, 2002)

1 Rushing to judgement
2 Misusing resources
3 Applying failure-prone tactics

It's the fear of making a seriously bad decision that inspires so many good ones. This chapter is about the spectre of disastrous decisions. Human behaviour is influenced by many positive motivations, from the promise of paradise, economic advantage and happiness, right down to best practice and survival (which corporate gurus will not bracket together, but let's be honest...). It is also demonstrably spurred by both bad examples of where things have gone wrong, and fear of failure. In the pages that follow I talk about this aspect, using some of my blog posts, and flagging the more obvious decision traps that lurk in wait for us. Mistakes are inevitable. We are human. We are also subject to all manner of vicissitudes and bad luck, which we can do little or nothing about. The problems are needless mistakes (such as falling into a well-known decision trap) and really expensive mistakes.

When I started to write this book, I had to look much more widely than the world of clients and agencies that I know best. To understand the importance of good decision making, it was important to look at *real* nightmares and learn from them. In that context it was natural to look at historic corporate disasters like Enron. I also considered more recent examples: the collapse of Lehman Brothers, and the dominoes of the banking system that were saved from extinction only by government and central bank intervention. Then I considered recent public relations disasters like BP's Deepwater Horizon oil spill in 2010, and the unfolding nightmare of News International.

Academics and journalists have drilled down to find explanations. Was it greed and malice aforethought? (For Enron, or on a smaller scale the Ponzi schemes of Bernard Madoff and Allen Stanford, the answer is almost certainly yes.) You could argue that the systemic phone-hacking at News International was also in that category. Or did these catastrophes stem from poor governance (eg Arthur Andersen, Lehman, the banks)? Or was it largely or partly flawed decision-making technique? BP seems to be a good example of bad decision making, if that isn't a contradiction in terms.

Oil companies have lived with risk and controversy since the days of Rockefeller. Digging for oil, bringing it to the surface or shore, refining it and transporting it are all fraught with difficulty and danger. Also, such is the value of oil to the developed world that all the big players in the petroleum industry are de facto politically powerful and prominent – alternately courted and hated.

Explosions happen on oil rigs unfortunately. The loss of life is tragic, but not completely preventable, even in a safety-conscious era. Pollution was bound to ensue, despite Herculean efforts to cap the well. The affected area in the Gulf of Mexico could hardly have been higher profile, and the environmental damage and the damage to BP's reputation were both very serious. But it can certainly be argued that BP's handling of communications about the crisis left a great deal to be desired, particularly given that they were not the only ones at fault. Transocean was the owner of the rig, and indeed other companies, including Halliburton (a controversial company in its own right after its scandal in Nigeria the previous year) were also directly implicated as operator of the rig. It was almost certainly the communications snafu, not the disaster itself, that cost Tony Hayward his job as Chief Executive Officer (CEO). But Hayward is now flying high with his new – apparently very lucrative – venture. Would Lord Browne (Hayward's famous predecessor) have been more sure-footed in the firing line? Quite probably he would have been, given his 12 years as CEO, and vast media experience. It is perhaps BP we should blame for not giving Hayward more support and preparation for the Waterloo moment.

I worked as a consultant to Royal Dutch Shell in the aftermath of its *annus horribilis*, 1995. This was the year Shell ran into worldwide opprobrium due to dumping the huge but redundant Brent Spar platform into the sea, and its alleged complicity in the Nigerian Government's persecution of the Ogoni people in the Niger Delta, which culminated in the execution of rebel leader Ken Saro-Wiwa. Mark Moody-Stuart became Chairman of Shell in 1998, and was determined to take action to reduce the unpopularity of Shell with opinion formers and pressure groups and non-governmental organization (NGO) activists around the world. The bad feeling towards Shell was particularly strong, for instance, in Germany and Australia. The board of Shell were attracted to the idea of a global TV campaign promoting the consumer benefits provided by the company and its products. As I recall, the cost would have been somewhere between £200 million and £250 million. It would also almost certainly have been a dreadful decision. The advertising could well have been counterproductive, and provided even more ammunition for the company's enemies. In the event, the team that I was part of won the day. I had been hired by Tom Henderson, an ex-journalist, who arrived at Shell to work on a project and stayed for seven years. Intelligence showed that the people we really needed to influence amounted to little more than 1,500 globally, all told. We ran a pitch for teams of advertising and PR agencies, and unusually appointed the PR agency from one consortium (Fishburn Hedges), and the ad agency JWT from another (a brave and interesting decision). The campaign that ensued (colloquially known as 'Shell are nice people') was purely a corporate affairs initiative for the first year, apart from a few editorial-style ads in publications such as *The Economist* and *Der Spiegel*. TV and print advertising did not start till the second year, by which time the research feedback was starting to look encouraging. The campaign was an acknowledged success with consumers and the public, did wonders for internal morale, aided recruitment, and ran for several years.

What further is there to be said about News International? The Leveson Inquiry will eventually wind up in a report, which is almost bound to be severely critical of the culture of intrusiveness and illegal espionage that was the modus operandi of the journalists and their masters who put stories on the front page of the red tops. Inevitably Members of Parliament (MPs) have been prominent scourges of the company. We can only speculate as to how much of this has been as dutiful tribunes of the people, and how much to extract a degree of revenge for Fleet Street's hammering of them during the expenses scandal, originally exposed by the *Daily Telegraph*. Here are two blog posts that I wrote at the height of the *News of the World* drama. I even correctly predicted the launch of the *Sun on Sunday*!

Blog extract

Closing down the top-selling English language newspaper in the world – that's a Big Decision

I climbed the stairs to JWT's Centre Court yesterday evening with as much of a spring in my step as I can manage these days. The Marketing Society's Summer Party was in full swing, lots of old friends to catch up with, and my blog for today in the can.

Then someone told me that the *News of the World* was to close. The latest at the time I left the office was that Sunday's edition would run without any ads, which seemed a bit extreme. But for the NotW to disappear completely... that is big news.

And what must have taken place yesterday in the News Corp bunker? A very big decision indeed! Let me be frank. I wasn't present. Nor did either Rupert or James ring me personally.

So what follows is a speculative attempt to relate a momentous event to my decision theory, and to analyse what must have been going on. At least I'm in good company. There is a battalion of journalists who have already voiced and written about the closure – and they weren't there either.

News Corp's goal? Unless I and all those journalists are much mistaken, there were two:

● to try to head off the hacking storm at the pass;

● to avoid collateral damage to other News Corp assets round the world, and in particular to the proposed purchase of the 61 per cent of BSkyB shares it doesn't own.

Options: note that the three possible routes below all provide for generous doses of breast beating, and expressions of horror and revulsion at what has been done in the name of the paper:

1 Do nothing much, talk about the police and public inquiries, and tough it out.

2 Offer up Rebekah Brooks as a sacrifice, and bring in a new, squeaky clean management structure for their United Kingdom (UK) newspaper business.

3 Close the damn thing down.

On any normal upside–downside analysis, closing down the paper would look to be quite the most serious downside. After all public and governmental opprobrium is going to be an ongoing problem, whatever the scenario. But closing down a legendary (and still very profitable) institution means News International taking, perceptually and actually, a huge hit – quite apart from the publicity and financial cost of throwing a complete workforce onto the street.

So, why did they do it?

Wouldn't it have been in character to go route #1? Yes, because they are ruthless.

Would it have been inconceivable to dump Ms Brooks? No, because they are ruthless.

I believe they chose to close down the NotW for the following reasons:

- In the context of News Corp's chess game in the UK, it was a sacrifice of no more than one bishop. In the global context – a pawn.

- It was the strategy with by far the biggest chance of deflecting criticism of the company's role in the ongoing and potentially extended hacking scandal, and in terms of an upside, the one most likely to keep the bid for BSkyB on the table.

- It doesn't preclude using the NotW workforce, presses and distribution for the launch of the *Sun on Sunday* – or whatever.

The irony is that the biggest risk News Corp are running is that the appalling publicity does not go away. The Murdochs, *pere et fils*, are gambling heavily on their ability – as a news organization – to manage bad news.

Blog extract

Closing the *News of the World* was not a 'commercial decision'. Rupert Murdoch, 19 July 2011

Wow! Call me sceptical, or what?

That was quite a statement for a newspaper proprietor to make, in front of the Culture, Media and Sport Select Committee. Mr Murdoch, as we all know, went on to say that the title was closed 'because it had broken the trust with its readers'.

So the closure was not a *commercial* decision, and the newspaper – presumably in the shape of its journalists and editors – had let its readers down. 'Stranger, ever stranger', thinks the aspiring decision scientist.

If you are News International, and your largest circulation newspaper is facing a category five hurricane, your business, your share price and your reputation are all under threat. If you respond by taking the extreme step of terminating the existence of the paper and making the staff redundant, it's hard to see the decision as anything other than a commercial one. Murdoch presumably shut down the *News of the World* to lance the boil, and to head off even more trouble.

Analysing that decision on the evidence so far, it looks as if he overestimated the upside, and underestimated the downside.

If the motivation was to restore the readers' trust, one has to say that depriving them of their Sunday scandal sheet was an odd way to do it. In any case, how many News of the World readers walked out of their local CTN every weekend uplifted by their trust in what they were about to read?

It isn't wrong to be wrong

Many of us beat ourselves up about being wrong. Maybe you do. You would think that someone who is committed to spreading the word about a better way of making better decisions would reject wrongness and attack it in all its forms. Not me. I find it hard to imagine how you can get things right, simply by being consistently right. We all know that making mistakes is the way we learn.

There is a terrific book called *Being Wrong* (2011). It was written by a US journalist called Kathryn Schulz. She claims that it isn't a self-help book, but I believe it is. About the only thing in it that I really disagree with is her contention that 'Decision Studies' should be renamed 'Error Studies', because most of the books in the field are about bad decisions, and the lessons you can learn from them. That you can learn much from bad decisions is undeniable. But I am completely convinced that good decision-making practice can be taught – and more importantly put to excellent use by virtually the whole of mankind. But this aside, I heartily recommend the Schulz book. It is helpful, interesting and extremely well written.

I particularly liked this one-liner: 'The difference between being wrong about your car keys and being wrong about weapons of mass destruction is the difference between "oops" and a "global military crisis".'

What's the ROD (Return on Decision)?

In Chapter 4 I talk about the inputs to a decision – and how important it is to be rigorous:

- Clarity on your goal.
- Best data and intelligence – and keep looking for more.
- Frame – and if necessary keep on framing till the problem is well and truly defined.
- Structure the most viable options for solving the problem.
- Identify upsides and downsides in each option.
- Reward–risk analysis, ensuring that you are not swayed too much by the attractiveness of an option if it has a dangerous downside.
- Carefully weigh reward and risk, and then make the decision.

That's what a better way to make a better decision is all about.

People talk less about measuring the quality of a decision *after* it has been made. If our aim is to make a better decision, how do we measure that? I have come up with a rule of thumb currency of 'betterness', as far as decisions are concerned. It's very simple, and works on a percentage basis.

The answer is ROD (*aka* Return on Decision). If your decision meets your expectations, you score a 100. If you only achieve 50 per cent of what you aimed for that's a 50.

Clearly to judge this, you first have to have defined your goal – what success would be. Measurement is obviously progressive:

- The first test is how the decision goes down internally – and if it's just you on your own, how you feel about the decision having made it. So let's say 'so far so good'. That's 100.

- Then as you get into implementation, you will be able to judge degrees of apparent success at various stages. Real progress: 100, or possibly 115–120. Hit a snag: might, at least temporarily be down to 70 or even 50. Corrective action should then lift the score back up to, say, 80.

A rough and ready reckoner it might be, but does that matter? At least it provides a measurement discipline and emphasizes that any decision is a journey, not a single step.

But don't be wrong too often

No one is always right. It simply is not possible to make good decisions all the time. Nor would it help the learning process. By the very nature of things, we learn from our mistakes. The wisdom that comes from our errors is just as useful as the dividend from a couple of excellent decisions.

But that is not to say that it doesn't matter whether your decisions are right or wrong. It does. Very much. The Return on Decision (ROD) metric is a vital element in the accountability for our decision making.

Just as every considered decision is a journey, so our medium- and long-term decision-making record is iterative. But to make sense of that record, there needs to be some kind of hierarchy of seriousness. In making that evaluation, the ROD (consequence) of the decision needs to be taken into account along with the difficulty or otherwise of being able to put the learning to use in terms of being able to rectify the problem. Here are some examples of wrong calls that are capable of being turned round:

- Pick a team that loses a match, and you can make a more effective selection next week. You have lost a battle, not the war.

- Make an unwise investment or lay a losing bet, and you should still be able to recoup the loss in due course.

- Running an ad campaign that underperforms is not necessarily a terminal problem for a Chief Marketing Officer (CMO). There are always other ideas – and if necessary, other agencies.

However, the time dimension is important:

- Hire a loser, and it can cost you three ways: poor performance by the individual, severance payment, opportunity cost.

- Book a holiday in the wrong resort, and that is the family's precious two-week break ruined for that year at least.

- Intervene in Iraq, Afghanistan or Libya, and you have an open-ended commitment of lives, cost and potentially reputation, with no measurable limit to the downside.

Where in the decision process can we make one of these expensive errors? The answer is in any one of the input elements – or most of them. You cannot afford to compromise on:

- clarity on your goal;
- best possible information;
- problem definition and solution;

- constructing the best set of options;
- being honest about downsides as well as upsides;
- reward–risk assessment.

If I had to pick one critical point in avoiding major errors (ones that are difficult to rectify) it would be looking squarely at the potential downsides of any plan that you are keen on. In the first set of three errors above, the downside is one that you can live with in the short term. In the second set, the downsides are serious.

Sometimes people make really bad decisions

Most books on decision making feature a catalogue of nightmares that belong in the Chamber of Horrors. Obvious examples might include:

- Barbarossa – Hitler's invasion of Russia that cost him the war. Main Decision Trap – condemned to repeat the experiences (failure to learn from history, in this case Napoleon's equally catastrophic campaign).

- The Bay of Pigs – Kennedy's fiasco in Cuba. Decision Trap – group failure (refusal to accept that a group of seriously bright people can all be wrong).

- The collapse of Enron. Decision Trap – delusion (Lay and Skilling convincing themselves they wouldn't be found out).

- The Brown Government's management of the UK's finances. I have only room for a few Decision Traps in this case:

  - Undue optimism – optimistic about outcomes and blind to potential disaster.

  - Downside delusion – underestimating risks, and assuming too much control over future events.

- 'What if' wearout – not being rigorous enough in looking at possible scenarios.
- Outcome blindness – failure to accept bad news when it is staring you in the face.
- Policy pride – sticking to a policy when it had obviously failed.

These were celebrated BAD decisions.

I also worry about questionable decisions that can make bad situations worse. Take when Chris Huhne had to resign from the Government, and John Terry was stripped of the England football captaincy. I am not writing about any bad decisions Huhne or Terry might or might not have made.

What links these two high-profile characters – apart from the awkward fact that neither is particularly popular or loved? Both were charged with a criminal offence, and there existed and overriding sense that both were guilty before the cases ever came to court.

We used to have the presumption of innocence until found guilty. When did we lose that principle? And why? And why do apparently bad decisions imply guilt in the eyes of the masses?

How do we explain seriously bad decisions?

Early 2012 was a time for dire decisions. To name just two:

- Caving in to the letter of our misbegotten extradition treaty with the United States (US) in the case of Christopher Tappin conveys absolutely no credit on the Home Secretary, the Government as a whole, British judges or the wretched European Court of Human Rights.

- Did the Syrian regime have a shred of legitimacy left before the decision to shell the temporary press centre in Homs where Marie Colvin met her untimely end? Probably not.

But they are now well and truly damned, with President
Assad facing at least as grim a future as his oppressed
people.

How are we supposed to react to decisions like these? Is rational
analysis possible? Or are we better to rely on gut feel to condemn
them out of hand?

Using a slightly broader perspective...

Mr Tappin is alleged to have been involved in selling batteries for
missiles to Iran. Whether he has a case to answer is still a mystery.
The extradition treaty does not require evidence to be presented
in the UK. So Mr Tappin is presumed guilty, flown under guard
to the US and remanded in a high-security jail. Not a great decision
by David Blunkett who was Home Secretary at the time the treaty
was 'negotiated'. Not a great decision by this Government to submit meekly to the US demand. For my money the decision traps
involved are:

- Lack of frame control by the Labour Government when
  they gave in to the United States. They failed to define the
  problem properly, and were unduly influenced by the frame
  of the US government. Also lack of foresight. They surely
  wouldn't have agreed to the legislation if they had envisaged
  the kind of cases that would arise.

- This Government and the judges? Overconfidence in their
  own judgement.

As for the Syrian regime, it is not really worth arguing about which
decision traps they have fallen into. Plunging in? Sunk cost? Failing
to learn?

All we need is gut feel for this one. We are looking at what happens
when the veneer of civilization is removed. Assad and company
were beyond the pale before they decided to shell the messengers.
Now? Surely it is just a question of time before deliverance for the
suffering country and retribution for the butchers.

Why do things that aren't a good idea?

Behavioural Economics tells us that we can often be motivated by some 'nudge' or other to act in a way that doesn't fit with the stereotype of economic self-interest. In other words, we can be tempted by alternative upsides.

But to do things when we know there is a very obvious downside – that's something else entirely. Let's say we are talking about unwise or apparently illogical actions in our non-work life. Some of these wayward deeds will not even be the result of considered decisions: not so much mistakes, more instinctive errors.

But in other cases there will have been a decision to ignore a fairly obvious downside, and go ahead anyway with a course of action that doesn't seem to make a lot of sense.

Now, if we can do that when we are not at work, are we also capable of poor decision making and unwise actions in working hours? The answer has to be 'yes'. Illogicality and poor decision-making process is unlikely to be compartmentalized in a pigeonhole marked 'evenings and weekends only'.

We have also to add poor performance to bad judgement. Every day, it seems, the transmission system between brain and body fails us to lesser or greater degree. We can fail to do the right or logical thing through a failure of dexterity or memory, just as easily as through lack of will or good decision making.

Neither the great philosophers, nor you, should be even remotely surprised by the above. After all, we are talking about human beings, where genius and frailty are equally distributed – often to the same person.

Nor would it faze religious people. Christians, for instance, are well aware that in the Ten Commandments there are only two positive injunctions (keep the Sabbath day holy, and honour your father and mother), while the other eight are all 'Don'ts', suggesting that God had no illusions about our likely behaviour.

My message, I suppose, is that there are so many possible ways in which we can take poor decisions or make mistakes, that if we do seriously want to be successful, it is imperative to take decision making seriously.

We only need rules when something is difficult, and when there is a big difference between doing it well and doing it badly. To try to make sure we make the best possible decision, we need rules, and should you doubt it, the justification is above!

I think there's a big issue here. You see it clearly in spheres where leaders tend to come from people who have excelled on the way up. The military, medicine and particularly politics are hierarchical professions, where decision making at the top is hard to challenge. Clever subordinates are inhibited by both status rules, and the reputation of the top man or woman as a performer – an expert.

In his 2009 book *59 Seconds* Richard Wiseman said: 'Irrational thinking occurs when people try to make decisions in groups, and this can lead to a polarization of opinions and a highly biased assessment of a situation'.

Norman Dixon said something similar in the quotation at the head of Chapter 8 from his entertaining 1994 book *On the Psychology of Military Incompetence* (see Chapter 8). They were both alluding to a well-known decision trap, group failure. There is an assumption that with smart people involved, good choices will follow automatically. But it is well documented that too many talented people working together can frequently fail to manage the group decision-making process.

I interviewed Ellis Downes, a Harley Street gynaecological surgeon and obstetrician, who told me how concerned he and his colleagues had been at an unacceptable level of mistakes in theatre. It turned out that most of these mistakes had been made by the senior team member – the surgeon – and no one else dared say anything. Someone had the bright idea of talking to other mission-critical teams, in search of a solution. The best analogue, it turned out, was the BA flight crew. BA had decided that decision making – and particularly the problem-solving aspect of it – was too important to be the sole prerogative of the Captain. So the First Officer, Navigator and Engineer are all entitled to be heard as equals. So now when the top gynae is operating, the most junior nurse is allowed to speak up if he or she feels that something is not quite right.

Why do the mighty fall so often?

Jonah Lehrer's 'Frontal Cortex' blog for 18 May 2011 was inspired by the fall from grace of Dominique Strauss-Kahn. Lehrer's question was why successful people behave differently when in power, and why sometimes they seem to abandon the admirable characteristics that contributed to their elevation. He believes that power does corrupt by making leaders less sympathetic and caring. Here is a telling example. Lehrer writes:

> Consider a recent experiment led by Adam Galinsky, a psychologist at Northwestern University. Galinsky and colleagues began by asking subjects to either describe an experience in which they had lots of power or a time when they felt utterly powerless. Then the psychologists asked the subjects to draw the letter E on their foreheads. Those primed with feelings of power were much more likely to draw the letter backwards, at least when seen by another person. Galinsky argues that this effect is triggered by the myopia of power, which makes it much harder to imagine the world from the perspective of someone else. We draw the letter backwards because we don't care about the viewpoint of others.

Lehrer's piece is mainly about behaviour, but he includes a really interesting example of how the malign influence of power can affect decision making:

> One of my favorite studies of power corrupting comes from Deborah Gruenfeld, a psychologist at the Stanford Business School. She was interested in how positions of power altered our reasoning process. After analysing more than 1,000 decisions handed down by the United States Supreme Court between 1953 and 1993, Gruenfeld found that, as justices gained power on the court, or became part of a majority coalition, their written opinions tended to become less complex and nuanced. They considered fewer perspectives and possible

outcomes. The bad news, of course, is that the opinions written from the majority position are what actually becomes the law of the land.

Two aspects of this case fascinate me:

1 If we accept Gruenfeld's analysis of what senior judges did on the Supreme Court, it looks as if powerful people simplify their decision-making process. This is in contrast to the phenomenon we looked at in this blog for 10 June 2011, of people seeking to make problems look more complicated than they need be. Maybe that's the difference between decision makers who are already leaders, and aspirational people on the way up.

2 If the senior judges are looking at fewer outcomes and less options, is that because they care less what other people think? It looks as if they are chess players with a plan, but with little inclination to look into the mind of their opponent.

Overoptimism has a lot to answer for. Why do so many books and papers concentrate on disasters, and not on the recipe for success? It is easier to criticize and analyse disasters than decisions that turned out well. But it is hard to ignore the sheer scale of famous disasters stemming from poor decision making. For instance there have been several books, as well as a play, written about Enron – one of the most spectacular corporate failures of all time. Military history is full of nightmare outcomes, and millions of words have been written about famous British disasters in the Crimea, Afghanistan, Africa and Flanders. Even 'Lucky Generals' come unstuck one day.

Napoleon famously said, 'Nothing is more difficult, and therefore more precious, than to be able to decide.' Avenues and Metro stations in Paris celebrate his great victories, most of which came about because he was an adept problem solver and decision maker. But he will always be remembered for the retreat from Moscow and having come second to one of history's rare examples of Anglo-German cooperation at Waterloo, which naturally became the name of a railway station in South London, rather than in South Paris. Humans are naturally optimistic, and success makes you even more confident. If you have won famous victories at Montenotte, Mondavi, Lodi, Castiglione, Arcole, Rivoli, Mantua, The Pyramids, Aboukir, Marengo, Ulm, Austerlitz, Friedland, Eckmühl, Essling, Wagram, Lutzen, Batzen, Hanau, Champaubert, Montmirail, Montereau, Rheims and Ligny, you could possibly be forgiven for getting the weather forecast wrong in Russia, or failing to anticipate the arrival of the Prussians in Belgium.

Schadenfreude is another factor. When Napoleon said, 'Why should a man such as I be concerned about the fate of a million people?' he was asking for retribution. Not everyone saw the humiliation he suffered on St Helena as tragic. There are of course bad decisions as well as wrong decisions. You cannot control outcomes, so what must have looked like a good decision can turn out badly. Equally, poor process is always likely to result in a wrong decision. You cannot tell people what to decide. But you can encourage them how to decide. That is what this book is about. It is a 'How to' book, as well as a 'Why it happens' book.

Politicians are often the classic 'decision makers who haven't solved the problem first'. When parties prepare for elections and manifestos they tend to start from the premise of 'What needs changing?' They then pursue headline-grabbing policies. No attempt is made to think the decision through – in terms of problem solving or feasibility. All that matters is attracting voter support.

I wrote the following in the immediate aftermath of the urban riots of August 2011.

Have you ever wondered why so many decisions fail?

In the UK, and as we try to stare down financial turmoil and riots on our streets, the country is crying out for some great decisions. Yet our expectations are not high. We have been disappointed in our leaders before. Why do decisions – even those made by the great and good – so often fail to work out?

Decision making is a journey, not button pressing. It is more like chess than a high board dive. Many people – especially powerful people – do not understand that, and they often tend to make a mess of it.

I believe we are prisoners of powerful educational and business cultures. Most of our education has been about aggregated learning – taking on board as much knowledge as possible. We are encouraged to operate solo. We are tested on what we know, not what we do with the knowledge. No one gets the benefit of any teaching about decision making.

In business the emphasis is on teamwork. Solus operating and thinking are frowned upon. Our diaries are filled with endless meetings. We have little thinking time. The meetings are not designed as forums for making decisions.

In both education and business there is little encouragement to make decisions... unless you are very important!

There is no magic about decisions. We make them all the time. What matters is making them in the right way, and then managing it through.

Let's kill some myths. A policy isn't a decision. A goal isn't a decision. An idea isn't a decision. Doing something of itself isn't a decision. Just wanting something to happen (setting out a policy, or agreeing a goal) won't make it happen. Ideas – however powerful – need to be torture-tested and implemented. Actions may speak louder than words, but don't constitute a decision unless that decision has been properly made.

And there are two more myths to be addressed. Being decisive isn't necessarily good. Sitting on the fence isn't always a bad thing – or a sign of weakness. There is a value judgement in seeing decisiveness as a positive attribute of leaders, managers or whatever. Do the means justify the end? How decisive has someone been if it turns out that the decision they made was wrong?

It may sound tedious and boring, but there is no substitute for good decision-making process.

Language matters

We saw above the influence of a word like 'decisive'. Decisions themselves are often controversial – and that is before the outcome is known. Once we know what actually happened as a result of a decision, we tend to be even more judgemental.

You can see what a subjective area it is from the adjectives used by commentators (often armchair critics) of other people's decisions. Let's divide them into four categories:

1 Approving of positive decision making

2 Disapproving of positive decision making

3 Approving of caution

4 Disapproving of caution.

Here goes:

1 Positive – yeah!
   - brave;
   - courageous;
   - decisive;
   - strong;
   - daring;
   - bold;
   - fearless.

2 Positive – whoa there!
   - gung ho;
   - risky;
   - reckless;
   - aggressive;
   - irresponsible;
   - ill-advised;
   - hasty.

3 Cautious – well done!
   - responsible;
   - wise;

- astute;
- prudent;
- sensible;
- rational;
- considered.

4 Cautious – get down off the fence

- conservative;
- indecisive;
- nervous;
- risk averse;
- weak;
- timid;
- irresolute.

See what I mean? The moment we comment on a decision or some-one's decision-making ability we tend to go straight into a value judgement. This is particularly true of polarized groups:

- Old vs young.
- Men vs women.
- People on our side vs the enemy (eg in politics).
- Players/fans vs referees and umpires.
- Them and us (all categories).

I think we need to develop a more neutral vocabulary to allow us to recognize good problem solving and decision-making process. It's not necessarily brave to accentuate the upside and ignore the down-side. Equally it's not a sign of weakness to consider the downside of an option before lurching into action. It's balanced thinking to look before you leap, and to take a view on factors, both positive and negative.

Sounds boring, I know. But isn't that another value judgement?

Why are all of us susceptible to doing 'stupid things'? Decisions are made for both rational and emotional reasons, but most of the academic material assumes relentless rationality. So if so much effort goes into deciding correctly, why do we sometimes act irrationally, in a strange manner, or sometimes in a way that is against our best interests?

Stanovich's theory

I read an interesting paper on this subject by Kurt Kleiner from the University of Toronto in the University of Toronto Magazine (Summer 2009). He was reviewing a colleague's book, *What Intelligence Tests Miss: The Psychology of Rational Thought*, Professor Keith Stanovich (2009). Stanovich's speciality is the study of intelligence and rationality. He says:

> The reason smart people can sometimes be stupid is that intelligence and rationality are different. There is a narrow set of cognitive skills that we track and that we call intelligence. But that's not the same as intelligent behaviour in the real world.

He's even coined a term to describe the failure to act rationally despite adequate intelligence (as defined by performing well in IQ tests): 'dysrationalia'.

Summing up Stanovich's thesis, Kleiner writes:

> We are all 'cognitive misers' who try to avoid thinking too much. This makes sense from an evolutionary point of view. Thinking is time-consuming, resource intensive and sometimes counterproductive. If the problem at hand is avoiding the charging sabre-toothed tiger, you don't want to spend more than a split second deciding whether to jump into the river or climb a tree. So we've developed a whole set of heuristics and biases to limit the amount of brainpower we bear on a problem. These techniques provide rough and ready answers that are right a lot of the time – but not always.

Stanovich has another fascinating theory. Kleiner writes:

> To understand where the rationality differences between people come from, Stanovich suggests thinking of the mind as having

three parts. First is the 'autonomous mind' that engages in problematic cognitive shortcuts. Stanovich calls this 'Type 1 processing'. It happens quickly, automatically and without conscious control.

The second part is the algorithmic mind. It engages in 'Type 2 processing', the slow, laborious, logical thinking that intelligence tests measure. The third part is the reflective mind. It decides when to make do with the judgments of the autonomous mind, and when to call in the heavy machinery of the algorithmic mind. The reflective mind seems to determine how rational you are. Your algorithmic mind can be ready to fire on all cylinders, but it can't help you if you never engage it.

When and how your reflective mind springs into action is related to a number of personality traits, including whether you are dogmatic, flexible, open-minded, able to tolerate ambiguity or conscientious. 'The inflexible person, for instance, has trouble assimilating new knowledge, Stanovich says. 'People with a high need for closure shut down at the first adequate solution. Coming to a better solution would require more cognitive effort.'

Fortunately, rational thinking can be taught, and Stanovich thinks the school system should expend more effort on it. Teaching basic statistical and scientific thinking helps. And so does teaching more general thinking strategies. Studies show that a good way to improve critical thinking is to think of the opposite. Once this habit becomes ingrained, it helps you to not only consider alternative hypotheses, but to avoid traps such as anchoring, confirmation and 'myside bias'.

If Stanovich and Kleiner are right, it could explain quite a lot. It would support the Norman Dixon theory about the military, and the group failure Decision Trap hypothesis, by suggesting that not only do groups of otherwise bright people combine to make bad decisions – individual bright people can act irrationally on their own without help.

There is also an echo of the Tim Gallwey Inner Game of Tennis theory (see Chapters 6 and 9), where he talks about two selves (Self 1 is the thinker and teller, and Self 2 is the listener and doer).

Self 2 is instinctive and competent, but tends to be bossed around by Self 1 who is always rationalizing and giving unwanted advice. And we have all met the clever, but inflexible, colleague who is not interested in accommodating any new ideas. Overall I am attracted to the Stanovich view of the world. It could be the explanation for crazy decisions, the mighty falling – and a lot else besides.

Decision Traps

I acknowledge the contribution of two seminal books in the naming of Decision Traps: Russo and Schoemaker, *Decision Traps* (1989), and Paul Nutt, *Why Decisions Fail* (2002). Most of the best chronicled traps were covered in either or both books. *The Harvard Business Review* compendium publication *Making Smarter Decisions* (2007) unearthed some more as well as confirming the importance of the best known. A very few of the ones below I defined and coined myself. We have already come across some of the destructive traps:

- Analysis bypass – too much information or not enough time to analyse it properly.
- Anchoring – being overinfluenced by the first information or view we receive.
- Cold SWOT (strengths, weaknesses, opportunities and threats) – misreading a SWOT analysis.
- Confirming evidence – we believe in and agree with people who think like we do.
- Ethical bypass – missing ethical issues and angles.
- Group failure – dysfunctional group that makes bad decisions, despite having the right people in the room.
- Information overload – more data and information than you can deal with.
- Information underload – believing you have enough knowledge to proceed, when you actually need more intelligence and research.

- Lack of frame control – trying to solve the wrong problem.
- Outcome blindness – failure to accept bad news.
- Plunging in or gung ho – recklessness; rushing the decision and skimping on implementation.
- Policy pride – sticking to a course when it has obviously failed.
- Pressure paralysis – getting the frame of reference wrong under pressure.
- Shortsighted shortcuts – too reliant on information that is at hand or well known.
- Sunk cost – overinfluenced by schemes or routes that have already cost us money.
- Undue optimism – optimistic about outcomes, and blind to potential disaster.
- 'What if' wear-out – not being rigorous enough in looking at possible scenarios.

It is time to look at some more of the Decision Traps that lead us astray.

Condemned to repeat the experience

Once you start taking decision making seriously, it becomes second nature to follow a sensible process:

1 Clarity on your goal.
2 Best data and intelligence – and keep looking for more.
3 Frame – and if necessary keep on framing till the problem is well and truly defined.
4 Structure the most viable decision-making options.
5 Identify upsides and downsides in each option.
6 Reward–risk analysis, ensuring that you are not swayed too much by the attractiveness of an option if it has a dangerous downside.

7 Make the decision, having carefully balanced upside reward and downside risk.

8 Communicate.

9 Implement.

But nature abhors vacuums and also nine-point plans. What's missing? Learning and feedback. Being painstaking and systematic about making a decision and executing it can take time and sap your energy. It is easy to forget to track what happens next. It is equally easy to fail to take the learning on board and give feedback to stakeholders, team members, bosses etcetera.

It follows that one of the most common decision traps is what we call 'condemned to repeat the experience'. Refusing to learn from mistakes. Not tracking success and failure or doing it less than honestly. Our name for this trap is itself a corruption of the famous quote from US philosopher George Santayana: 'Those who cannot remember the past are condemned to repeat it'.

Good examples of this decision trap:

1 Evenings out when we overindulge. These can have lasting consequences as well as the inevitable short-term hangover.

2 Taking decisions under the influence of stimulants and stimuli other than alcohol – drugs, libido, anger, despair.

3 All punters – except the most experienced and systematic.

4 Agencies who lose too many pitches while underservicing their clients.

And while we are talking about advertising, Santayana had a quote for that too: 'Advertising is the modern substitute for argument; its function is to make the worse appear the better.'

Surely not, George.

Try to avoid the biggest decision trap of all: downside delusion

Downside delusion is when the decision maker underestimates the possible downside. When I say 'downside', I'm also talking about collateral damage, negative publicity, splits in the home team and so on.

It is probably the commonest mistake in the land of decisions, given man's innately positive inclinations. Never mind *Homo sapiens*. I sometimes think *Homo optimisticus* would have been a better name for the species.

When you are taking time to mull over a decision, it is natural to become enthusiastic about the upside. The keener you are on the outcome you have nominated, the more likely it is that you will pay less attention to worries, problems and other negatives.

Suppose you are looking to move up the housing ladder. You might have reduced the choice architecture to three of the criteria with which you set out:

- a better area;
- more space;
- superior design and finish – say in bathrooms and kitchen;
- fast forwarding, you have found a promising property in each category, but...;
- the house in the better area has only a postage-stamp garden;
- the bigger house is a bit tatty, and needs doing up;
- the smartest house is no bigger than the one you already have.

Staying within this decision frame, it's not difficult to prioritize and work out the trade-offs. You might, for instance, come down to a choice between the best address (nice street, good investment potential and there is a park nearby) and the biggest house (gives us more room, and we can always do the decoration and upgrade ourselves). But in this kind of situation, it is easy to forget the potential downsides you have already discussed, discounted and moved on from:

- Can we really afford the move? To any of these houses?
- Will we lose touch with the neighbours who have been most of our social life?
- How will the kids cope with new schools?

No easy answers here – especially if the competing positives have become more influential than the possible downsides. The best way to avoid downside delusion is to face each of the potential downsides head on. Keep asking the difficult questions, while you are weighing up the relative brightness of the blue sky in each option. Only choose the new house if you are satisfied you can live with the worst downside you have identified.

And this is without factoring in the respective chains. No wonder people often decide to stay put!

Loss aversion

There's a Behavioural Economics principle called loss aversion. This is the phenomenon whereby people are more motivated by hanging on to something, than by the chance of getting something new. It is a facet of possessiveness. I believe it can also turn into a Decision Trap.

Loss aversion in marketers is a driver for a lot of pitches. Marketers hate the ideas of their brand being in decline. And let's face it, brands do lose consumer love. Followed by sales volume and share. The Marketing Director feels the need to resuscitate their troubled brand. He or she frequently decides that only an agency review will solve the problem.

I can't count the number of optimistic pitch briefs I have seen that basically assert that the brand is going to grow/gain share/be a roaring success again. But there won't be a great deal in the brief about the how and why. The goal might be clearly expressed. But it is rare that there is any hard evidence that recovery is likely. There will seldom be any new behavioural insights. Whatever series of problems that have contributed to the brand's decline will probably not have been addressed.

So the pitch is announced, and of course agencies respond enthusiastically – despite the brief not being very convincing. Why? Because this is an incredibly competitive marketplace, and winning new accounts is really important.

Decision traps in this scenario? For the client: I call it upside optimism (gambling on a favourable outcome). For the agencies: frame blindness (setting out to solve the wrong problem), or downside delusion (so taken up with the chance of winning the account, that they don't think too closely about the brand's slender chance of hitting its goal).

What are the chances of a pitch like this leading to a brilliant outcome in the marketplace? Not high. In my opinion the chances would be a great deal higher if the pitching agencies were to be asked to contribute to the problem solving and brief writing – rather than being restricted to finding creative answers to the wrong questions.

Being too busy

Is busy the opposite of idle? Or the opposite of effective?

When a decision has not gone well, people give a variety of excuses. They talk about competitive action or external events, disasters, mishaps or sheer bad luck. Short of mildly suggesting that maybe some of these eventualities could have been predicted, there is not a great deal you can say.

Other excuses tend to relate to the decision making process itself:

- We didn't have enough information to go on.

- We had too much information. It was really confusing.

- So and so wasn't able to make the crucial meeting.

- He/she came to that meeting on 26 July, and overruled us.

- The boss said it would be OK, but maybe...

- We hired those consultants, and we felt we had to listen to them, but...

- Perhaps we didn't look at enough options.

- We looked at too many options, it was difficult to keep focus.

- We were so enthusiastic about the upside of that option, we must have underestimated the potential for disaster.

- We were so worried about downsides, that we were probably too negative.

However, the commonest excuse of all is (and there are some familiar variants):

- I was too busy.
- He was too busy.
- She was too busy.
- They were all too busy.
- We were all too busy.

It is a funny thing, 'busyness'. Busy is a word we use for various reasons:

- out of pride (I'm so busy, I'm indispensable);
- as an excuse for not doing something;
- as a putdown to someone we believe is not half as busy as us.

I am more convinced than ever that being busy, while it undoubtedly gives you more status than being idle, is no substitute for being efficient or effective. Nowhere is that more true than in the taxing world of decision making. Decisions – considered decisions – are by their very nature important. All the key stages in the process deserve maximum input and concentration. It's difficult to see how any member of a decision-making team could be too busy to give each of the important steps their undivided attention. If anyone was too busy, that's not an excuse. It's an admission. It is also a Decision Trap.

Keep watching out for the early decision

We've looked before at the early decision. It isn't a classic Decision Trap, but it is just as negative. The more deeply I study decision science, the more sure I am that the early decision is insidious, and capable of giving decision making a bad name, and making people cynical.

This is a polite way of describing a familiar restriction on options: the open or covert (often covert) determination by one of the leaders in a decision-making process to go one way rather than another. I am talking about early stages – before any balancing of upsides and downsides. To count as an early decision it has to take place before the reward–risk analysis.

This is a pretty simple thought – but as important in its way as the concept of limiters that I explain elsewhere. A limiter is a factor that restricts or excludes a decision maker's options. When the decision involves making a purchase, for instance, lack of funds could be a significant limiter. Time (in the sense of not having time or availability) is another factor that restricts options at the outset. The early decision is by definition not a balanced decision at all. Here are three examples:

Political policy

The government of the day decides on a policy, and it is floated by a Minister or the Prime Minister in a speech somewhere, or typically in an interview with a Sunday newspaper. A Green Paper is published. 'Consultations' and 'soundings' follow – but these will, at most, change the details. The policy decision is already made. Then to a White Paper and the legislative process follows. No weighing of the upsides and downsides in a number of options. There are no other options on the table. It is an early decision.

Picking a sports team

Sports selection involves multivariate analysis. In a cricket team you can only have a finite number of batsmen or bowlers, and one wicketkeeper is normally enough. For rugby or football squads, you again have to balance the ticket between backs and forwards or keepers, defenders, midfield and strikers. An early decision by a chairman of selectors to include or exclude either a 'problem child' or a particularly versatile performer can significantly reduce the room for manoeuvre, and weaken the final selection. It is an early decision.

Choosing an agency (to move into familiar territory for me)

If a marketing director insists on short listing an incumbent who stands no realistic chance of winning, it serves no useful purpose as far as the pitch is concerned, and also takes a possible place away that could have been occupied by a dynamic contender. We have also seen pitches where good agencies have been put off by the presence of an incumbent on a list. Anyone is entitled to bring a preconceived view into a process. But it is essential that the prejudice is openly declared in a way that the early decision is not made binding on everyone else.

Common sense really. If there is one universal truth in decision making, it is that common sense is never wrong.

Here's another way of looking at an early decision

Joseph Hallinan in his book *Errornomics* (2009) has a wonderful quote from Frank Bascombe, the hero of the Richard Ford novel *The Lay of the Land* and the other two books in the trilogy:

> At the exact moment any decision seems to be being made, it's usually long after the real decision was actually made – like light we see emitted from stars. Which means we usually make up our minds about important things far too soon and usually with poor information. But we then convince ourselves we haven't done that because a) we know it's boneheaded, and no one wants to be accused of boneheaded-ness; b) we've ignored our vital needs and don't like to think about them; c) deciding, but believing we haven't decided, gives us a secret from ourselves that's too delicious not to keep. In other words, it makes us happy to bullshit ourselves.

I suspect the Bascombe analogy to stars could be taken further. When we try to interrogate the process that produced a less than successful decision, our view of the time and place in the heavens when the decision actually took place is often obscured by heavy cloud!

Was the financial crisis caused by Decision Traps?

I am the first to say that many disastrous decisions stem from poor process, inadequate intelligence, and less than gifted decision makers. But how are we to assess the high-level decision making that appears to have led directly to the new financial crisis? Stock markets are falling sharply all over the world, as doubts multiply about Italy and Spain, and maybe other members of the eurozone.

How can the leaders of so many countries have been so wrong? What was going on at the International Monetary Fund (IMF) and European Central Bank? I believe we are looking at the disastrous dividend of five distinct, but well-known, Decision Traps:

- Frame blindness – solving the wrong problem. Were the leaders concentrating on the Greek bailout, without realizing there were other potential catastrophes waiting to happen?

- History bias – history tends to repeat itself. Were they fooling themselves that the measures that had worked before, would do so again?

- Information overload – the belief that more data is always better, and it's worth delaying a decision till you have even more information. We shall never know, but is it possible that the armies of civil servants and bank executives provided too much data? Busy people know from their own lives that there are only so many facts and figures that you can take on board.

- Group failure – the refusal to accept that a football team of powerful experts (plus more on the subs bench) can be spectacularly wrong. Writers on decision science always use the Bay of Pigs fiasco as the *cause celebre* in this category. Maybe the June 2011 European Summit will turn out to have been equally misguided.

- Strength in numbers – the illusion that larger political and economic communities are safer. How much protection does the European Union (EU) and devolved legislation now offer to an island kingdom of 60 million souls, which is powerless to deviate from rulings issued in Brussels on behalf of Latvia, Malta, Slovenia and 24 other formerly independent nations?

Whether my analysis is right or not scarcely matters. Far greater experts than me were cheerfully predicting that a crisis had been averted, and life would carry on as predicted. Yet in four short days, the FTSE is down £125 billion, institutions and individual investors are fleeing from equities. Our currency is losing ground, because interest rates are too low to attract inbound funds. Investors and savers alike are in panic.

This nightmare is being replicated in capital markets everywhere. Hedge funds and holders of gold are cleaning up. Ordinary people are frightened. The unemployed and marginalized are in desperate trouble. Big-deal decision makers have got it wrong – again. If this analysis is basically correct, they have shown themselves to be inept. When will everyone learn that making better decisions – and making them better – is the greatest single skill?

Blog extract

Don't believe your own publicity

I had a sobering experience this morning. I was invited to attend a demonstration workshop on leadership skills devised and run by a clever company called ProfitAbility, who specialize in business simulations. I have been a fan of the company since I went to one of their courses for Guinness in Kenya in the late 1990s.

The simulation today (and it was effectively a simulation of a simulation) is called Magnetic Leadership. It is extremely sophisticated – and very hard work, because no one sleeps at a ProfitAbility event. I am a big believer in learning by doing. For some time I have been eager to explore how decision-making skills could be enhanced in a simulation.

Why am I telling you all this? Because I was seriously embarrassed by how ineptly I performed. There were only two of us in our team who really didn't understand how the game worked. And my fellow struggler was an infinitely superior poker player. He used some good questions and an inscrutable expression to get by, to the extent that he actually became a practical contributor.

I was reduced to observer status, not least by the realization that if I persisted in wanting everything explained, I would slow down the whole team and jeopardizing their chances of winning. So... I admitted failure, having been hugely impressed by how quick on the uptake the rest of my team was, and what cooperative team workers they turned out to be. The lesson for me? Learn some humility!

It only took one session on an open course to reduce me to a gibbering dysfunctional wreck. The day was gorgeous, the venue splendid, and my fellow delegates delightful. But I was as much use as an ice lolly on a barbecue. I couldn't contribute to group decision making because I didn't understand enough about the task. Even all those years taking briefs, a decent understanding of decision making and the gift of the gab were to no avail. Never believe you can take any challenge in your stride. We are all as good as we were yesterday – or not.

We all have to learn that lesson. However great our publicity, it means little if you lose. I'm determined to be back on form the next time I have to grasp a tough brief in very little time, and in a pressured situation.

What makes a decision bad? (a checklist you can add to)

Is it all about outcomes? Most books on decision making are full of stories about decisions that didn't work out:

- battles, wars and lives lost;
- patients dying;
- mistakes by referees and umpires;
- mistakes by selectors;
- takeovers that failed;
- miscarriages of justice.

Authors often write about issues closer to home:

- invested in shares that lost value;
- sold a house at the bottom of the market, or bought at the top.

And of course decisions where the risk was very high:

- driving after drinking;
- driving when the roads were dangerous;
- gambling with the housekeeping money;
- being sent off early in a match;
- ending up in the wrong bed.

We need to understand whether these bad decisions were bad judgement, or bad luck:

- Do we always know the difference?
- Should we be equally judgemental if a badly taken decision works out well?

Bad judgement. Was failure due to...?

- poor process – including not managing decisions through the journey;
- poor goal setting or motivation;
- problem(s) not solved;
- mistakes in data and/or analysis;
- poor benchmarking (we assumed this situation was just like one we dealt with well in the past – but the parallel was wrong);
- wrong criteria;
- wrong options;
- poor risk assessment;
- poor anticipation of external factors, competitive initiatives or reaction;
- poor execution or management of the journey.

... or more fundamentally to not being in the right condition to make a good decision?

- angry;
- stressed;
- desperate – through for instance hunger, thirst, cold, heat, pain;
- mental – balance of mind disturbed, whether permanently, clinically or temporarily;
- duress – threats, beating, torture;
- alcohol;
- drugs;
- arousal (see Dan Ariely's book *Predictably Irrational* (2008) for some interesting experiments).

Bad luck?

- Was the process OK?
- Why was the outcome disappointing?
- Competitive or enemy reaction or initiative.
- Weather.
- Force majeure.

More questions to be asked after a failed decision

1 Did the decision takers have enough information or evidence? (Or not the right information? Or too much to analyse?)

2 Did they take enough time over the decision? (Or too much?)

3 Were the right people involved? (and were the team members in the most appropriate roles?)

4 How much time and effort was dedicated to analysing the profiles (personality and thinking) of decision makers?

5 How was the decision taken?

6 Was this a secret situation, where the real criteria and motives might have been concealed?

7 Was the decision influenced by hierarchy?

8 Did the end justifying the means?

9 Or was everyone more concerned about goals and motivation?

10 Was emphasis given to idea generation in creating options, and in managing the process through?

11 And how were those ideas validated?

Chapter Three
Opportunities and problems

Before making a decision it's critical to define opportunities and deal with problems

This is amazing. You're going to help people find love, but it's complex. It's going to require a lot of thinking. Also, from a career point of view, I knew that I wanted to move from a marketing role into an MD role.

(KARL GREGORY, NOW MD OF MATCH.COM, TALKING ABOUT HOW HE SAW THE OPPORTUNITY WHEN HE JOINED THE COMPANY)

Opportunities are just as important as problems as a spur to decision making, and here we should extend the normal definition of opportunity to embrace inspiration – which is a sort of higher level opportunity. Examples of opportunities that require decision making to respond are legion. The list could include:

- a new job (as in Karl's case above);
- a new house;

- a new relationship;
- a business proposition;
- an invitation.

Problem solving is bridging the gap between the way things are and the way they ought to be. (Steve Kneeland, *Effective Problem-Solving*, 1999)

Before embarking on a big decision you have to define the opportunity or solve the problem

This is going to require the best information, intelligence and data you can find. Problem solving and decision making are two different things. You can read numerous books and papers that confuse the two. It's an easy confusion to make. Many of the decisions people have to make stem directly from a problem, which has to be solved. The problem could be of our making, it could be the result of action by a competitor or enemy, or from a third party source. Whatever the cause of the problem, it still ideally needs to be solved before we move into serious decision making mode.

Defining opportunities and solving problems are essentially the first stage of the Smart Decision Making System, as described in Chapter 4:

1 Am I sure what the opportunity is? Or am I sure what the problem is?

2 If it's an opportunity, have I identified it correctly, and do I know how I am going to take advantage of it?

3 If it's a problem, do I know precisely what it is, and how I am going to solve it?

Opportunities and problems are similar in that they are both stimuli for decision making, but there is an important distinction. An opportunity, by its very nature, welcomes us with open arms ('good time or set of circumstances for doing something', *Little Oxford*

Dictionary), whereas a problem scowls at us ('a thing that is difficult to deal with or understand', same source).

Without being unduly semantic about it, an opportunity is an opportunity, if it is an opportunity. The 'opportunity' word is an essential ingredient in the decision story. It does double duty. An opportunity can be the trigger for the start of a crucial decision process ('now that x has happened, we need to move fast to make the most of our chance'). Or it can be the word we use to describe what we can achieve if we get it right.

In both cases, the opportunity needs to be carefully defined – and evaluated. Not all opportunities are of equal worth. Not all are worth pursuing. The new Business Director of an agency might see a terrific opportunity to win a famous brand. Their boss knows that the pitch carries the certainty of heavy cost and timeburn, with long odds against winning, and every chance of poor short-term profitability, even if the agency were to be successful.

'Missing an opportunity' is a phrase that carries a value judgement. Some opportunities should be resisted, at least until you have fully evaluated the balance of upsides and downsides. An opportunity may not be as attractive or accessible as it first looks. But that is why we need to be sure about what it is. Unless we have defined it precisely, we cannot know how best to take advantage of it. We will almost certainly need information to do that: facts and figures, details. These might be readily available, or we may need to ask for the information, or have one or more face to face meetings or telephone calls. We may also need intelligence – the inside track, an objective view, some more forensic information. After all that effort we might discover that the opportunity might have been a prima facie opportunity, but that it was less of a good idea the closer we looked. That's why we still have a decision to make: to go after the opportunity, or not; and if so, on what basis? If we do not exploit the opportunity, that is not, to coin a phrase, a problem. It is merely an opportunity we chose not to pursue. There were others before, and hopefully others will come along.

It is different with problems. The problem equally needs defining. What sort of a problem is it? How serious? Do I need to act, or can I live with it? Will it go away? If it won't, how should I set out to solve it? Unlike the unexploited opportunity, the unsolved problem is at least potentially still a problem, and might get a lot worse. If the opportunity goes away because you chose not to take advantage of it – or you were too late – it is quite likely another one will come along, or the original one might come back. Even if neither happens, you are no worse off.

Capitalizing on opportunities

Ellen MacArthur's big opportunity was one she envisaged and seized herself:

> I studied at that sailing school into the night; I worked on my boat because I had a plan to take her on a voyage. I worked on my little boat which I'd managed to get up there and the mariner let me park her for free in the shed. I slept underneath her in the boatyard in November. Absolutely every second I was putting into it. I was loving learning. I was asking more questions than you could imagine to everyone at the sailing school – all the guys on the barges. I wanted to understand how this whole world worked.
>
> You needed to be able to understand how an engine was taken apart. You needed to understand what the weather did. You needed to understand what happened with the shifting sands and the mud on the River Humber. This world of understanding was out there and I just wanted to learn it all. It amazed me, it fascinated me, and it challenged me, and, yes, it still does, and it always will because I love learning.
>
> I sailed around Britain when I was 18. I then managed to get a sponsor. I mean, this is abbreviating three years into two sentences and actually it's one of the hardest parts of the whole sailing business. That was a whole journey in itself. Finding a sponsor when nobody has a clue who you are is one of the hardest things you'll ever do. There were a few things that helped significantly on the journey. The sailing school I worked for put me in for Young Sailor of the Year Award before I sailed around Britain, unbeknown to me – I had no idea. And I won.

I ended up winning it aged 18. I'd never experienced anything like it before.

Colin Moynihan's big opportunity in politics is an interesting story. His Oxford career was stellar for someone who had had to work so hard to get in to the university from Monmouth. He ended up with a good enough degree in Philosophy, Politics and Economics (PPE) to be offered a postgraduate research scholarship at University College. He won blues at rowing (coxed the winning crew of 1977) and boxing. He also defeated Benazir Bhutto to become President of the Oxford Union. His rowing career went from strength to strength and he won a Silver Medal in the Moscow Olympics of 1980, coxing the British eight. But by this time he had been involved in controversy that threatened to end his political prospects under Prime Minister Margaret Thatcher, almost before he had started out. Thatcher was keen to persuade Great British athletes to boycott the Moscow Games in protest against the Soviet invasion of Afghanistan. Colin disagreed. He told me:

> The central issue was this, that however much all of us, and I think all of us in rowing and in other sports felt strongly that the Soviet invasion of Afghanistan was unwarranted and reprehensible, it was nevertheless my view that governments should not demonstrate their opposition to a move of such magnitude by focusing exclusively on the athletes and urging them not to compete in the Olympic Games. It was wrong because *our* Government continued to foster diplomatic and trade relations, and allowed – for example – the public to go down Piccadilly, buy a ticket on Aeroflot and have a weekend in Leningrad to see the Bolshoi. And the only thing the government was prepared to do *was* to say to the athletes, who'd given their lives to train and compete, you alone will be our method of demonstrating our opposition to this invasion. That was fundamentally wrong. The political battle should be fought firstly and principally in a political arena, and of course if we had a trade embargo, we'd withdraw our Ambassador. If we'd taken all these steps then the athletes would have responded accordingly, I'm sure.

I believed very strongly that we should go, and this was widely reported in the press. I still felt that we should take a different approach to the Games that we would normally have done. So we didn't go in British kit, and when the flag went up for getting a medal, it wasn't a Union Jack it was an Olympic flag. We didn't go to the opening or closing ceremonies; we went to compete and then came home.

Despite offending the Prime Minister (as Douglas Hurd made clear to him when he was summoned to the foreign office as a leader of the athletes' campaign), he nonetheless fought and won Lewisham East in 1983 at the age of 27. He was re-elected four years later at the 1987 General Election.

Colin takes up the story:

"I was pleasantly surprised and I took myself off to Dorset. It was Monday afternoon after the results had been announced. The phone goes from some extremely chirpy, happy young lady saying the Prime Minister would like to see you. This is No. 10, can you be here in an hour? I said I'm in Dorset so, no, I can't. I thought one of my rowing friends had set me up. Ken Clarke had by then become a really close friend in politics, and I'd been his PPS in a number of departments. So I phoned Ken and said I've just been set up, can you tell me the telephone number of number 10? So he gave me the number and I rang that number and the same girl answered, hello this is No. 10.

I said I'm really sorry, I thought I had been set up as a practical joke. She said, don't worry, they all say that. So I then got in the car and drove to London in my little MG 1100. I went to my small flat and put on a suit and walked down. First of all the policeman at the end of Downing Street wouldn't let me in until he'd got clearance.

Understandably he didn't recognize me, and wasn't quite sure that this young man had got an appointment, so I finally was let in, went upstairs and to the sitting room at the end. There was a very large sofa in there and I spent 10 minutes listening to Mrs Thatcher talk about the disappointment of losing a handful of seats. I was nervous about whether I should sit forward with my feet on the ground on this large sofa, or sit back with my feet only just touching the ground. I was shifting to and fro absolutely confident in the knowledge that I wasn't going to get Sport because of 1980, and I thought I knew Margaret regarded me as a member of the left of the party, a wet, and I was still very young [31]. I mean, I knew I wasn't being fired because I hadn't got a job, and was somewhat surprised to be there at all, and I thought I'd get Northern Ireland because I was single and the PM was very conscious about not sending young married ministers to Northern Ireland in the days of the troubles.

So I had my little thank you speech prepared for being appointed as a junior minister in Northern Ireland office and she said I'd like you to be Minister of Sport and take on the responsibilities of the Department of the Environment as well. I was very surprised, and she said, 'I want you to work exceptionally hard and listen to the *Today* programme every day, and if you hear anything on the *Today* programme that is wrong ring them up and tell them it's wrong.'

She said, 'Colin, I don't want you to say anything to the Press until six o'clock because the press have an uncanny knack of focusing on who is going to be the Minister of Sport. And it will be the lead story on the news.' She said, 'I have been appointing all these ministers all day but this is the story that will lead, and so please don't say anything at all.' I walked out of Number 10 to go back to my flat, and the Press are all lined up behind the barriers on the other side. Oh, so it's Sport then Col? So I just smiled and didn't say anything, went back to the flat and was so nervous that I didn't phone anybody. It was about half past five and I didn't phone a soul. I was just waiting for six o'clock. Lo and behold she was absolutely right, the six o'clock news was full of new Minister of Sport Colin Moynihan.

Simon Calver started his marketing career as a Unilever graduate trainee. It went well, but he was impatient. He told me:

"At Unilever I did my finance qualifications, my CIMA stages one and two, because I wanted to learn about finance and I thought to myself, if ever I want to run a business, I've really got to know how the finances work.

So on the back of that and other things I joined Deloitte's in their strategy and marketing group, and took a lot of the numerical, statistical, computer-based learning that I had and built a product which was about helping people understand how well their marketing mix works, and helping the decision-making process. It's important, how you enable decision making as a consultant, versus how do you enable decision making as a person, as a manager on the ground? It's actually incredibly different. It's easy as a consultant to do the, 'I'll borrow your watch and tell you the time', scenario. But actually, a good part of consultancy is being an enabler and stimulating both discussion and decision making.

After a time enjoying consulting, the firm merged with Coopers, and we all became small cogs in a very big machine as they were more public sector focused. So we worked on large jobs, for example a £5 million job for a leading insurance company, and a big government department. It gave me the desire to complete my CV and get out of there and try something else, which turned out to be Pepsi. I ended up in charge of Pepsi marketing, and had a stellar few years there.

My first job was to launch Pepsi Max, which was the first variant that had ever been launched outside the US, and that was my brand. Why did we launch Pepsi Max? The decision making was to produce a win–win–win for all parties involved in the proposition. There has to be a win in it for the consumer. I am a huge believer in having a consumer insight that differentiates you in terms of the market proposition. The consumer insight in the drinks market was that diet consumers drunk more, but didn't like drinking diet because of two reasons: one is because they didn't like the taste, and secondly because it had too many female, feminine, and swimsuit, you know, sort of connotations.

So our strategic aim was to produce a drink that was very masculine in everything it did, and that had all the flavour of full sugar, but without any sugar. So there was no barrier to consumption for people. We would give consumers what they want. We'd grow the total market, so we gave the trade what they wanted – our second win. Because of our structure and how we were able to charge for concentrates, we were also able to give a benefit to our business as well. So net–net, it was a win for all parties.

The Pepsi Max launch also was a win for Simon. It led to him becoming the head of marketing for Pepsi in the UK at just 27. Two years later, having been General Manager in Ireland, he was appointed Vice-President of Pepsi in the UK.

David Jones's break into advertising came through his ability to speak the German he was learning at Business School. He told me:

> I had always wanted to go and live and work in Paris. But my first job was in the North of England in a placement at an agency called BDH, which later became TBWA Manchester. At that time (1989), nobody in UK advertising really cared about anything to do with Europe. I was very passionate about Europe, and the agency had an opportunity on this big pan-European pitch for Henkel. Through a twist of fate, what happened was that the Board Account Director on the business ended up being seconded to be Silentnight's Marketing Director for six months. The account manager very sadly was ill, so I ended up working directly with Bryn Butler, who was the MD and Arnold Single, who was the CEO.
>
> I was responsible for supervising research groups in Germany, getting all the creative work translated, and had to present it all in German to Henkel's worldwide board. We won the business. I was 21 and supposed to be going back to business school at the end of my internship. The company basically said, look, we understand you're not going to want to start full time work until you've finished your degree, but can we get you in two or three days a week, working for us, because Henkel don't know you're a spotty student. They think you're part of the core team!
>
> I ended up spending my final year at business school with a quite amazing sort of life: flying to Germany in business class,

staying in a hotel that was three times as big as my student flat, and often presenting alone to the worldwide Head of Advertising at Henkel. I thought this was the most amazing business, and joined them after graduating. I worked on Henkel and some other big accounts. But I really wanted to work on more global and international business, and they only had Henkel. That was when I was hired by J. Walter Thompson in Paris. I'd always wanted to work overseas. And so I moved over to Paris, and it worked out very well.

Turning a big problem into an opportunity

Paddy Eckersley had to travel across Africa and beyond to find his opportunity. We last met him in Zambia, just having obtained his private pilot's licence.

I did some freelance charter work for various charter companies, but again met up with the usual problems. Passengers wouldn't fly with me, because most of the people who used these charter airplanes were the management of the big companies in Zambia, and the prejudices were always there, and the people had had them for so many years. I suppose it was very difficult for them to accept something that was not an everyday occurrence. So I had a lot of problems in that nobody would employ me, so I couldn't get a job. They said we can't employ you, because nobody will fly with you.

I was still teaching, but I wanted to get out. Then I got lucky, because I met one of the Zambian politicians, who later became a Minister, a man by the name of Valentine Musakanya. During the colonial days they had been grooming him for higher positions in the Northern Rhodesia government. He had been brought over to the UK, and even became a magistrate in London. He then went back to Zambia and just before the break up of federation, became secretary to the cabinet in Zambia. As Minister of Technical Education, he took interest in my case and said to me, could you stop teaching and help me set up a flying school in Lusaka? It was a real break for me, and I said great. So we set up the flying school to train Zambians as pilots and so on, and when we got it all running, he said to me, well, what can I do for you, seeing that you've helped me set this up? And I said, well, I'd like to join Zambia Airways, and he said, no problem, I'll get you into that lot, which he did.

The government had got Alitalia in to run Zambia Airways, and they weren't keen on hiring anybody else except Italians. But thanks to this guy. I became a First Officer flying turbo props, and then after a couple of years I progressed to become a Captain, and later a Training Captain on 737s. I'd applied for Zambian citizenship and was turned down, which probably did me a favour, in a way. I thought, well, there's no future for me in Zambia, there's no need to stay, and so I saw an advert in the papers for Saudi Arabian Airlines. And my wife and I decided, well, it's best to leave, if Zambia's got nothing for us.

I wrote to the Saudis, and they asked me to come for an interview in London. I sort of played it two ways, because I had to come up to do my medicals with a doctor in London for Zambia Airways. We're in the bar at the Penta at Heathrow, and the Saudi crowd were sitting opposite us in the bar, all having a drink and so on. One of them saw me and he said, we have a letter for you, you'd applied to join us. I was sitting next to my boss in Zambia Airways. It was a bit embarrassing, actually. Anyhow, I went to join Saudi Airlines, based in Jeddah, and started off on 737s and then flew Tristars, and then went on to fly jumbos, and instructed on all of them.

Wasting opportunities

Here's what the CEOs decided

In June 2011, *The Times* recruited more than 100 Chief Executive Officers (CEOs) and Chairmen of our biggest companies to take part in a two-day summit called 'Ambitious for Britain'. Their communiqué was published in the newspaper in the form of a letter to the Chancellor of the Exchequer. The letter concentrated on five ways to 'pull Britain out of its anaemic recovery'. (Hopefully in a positive direction towards a more full-blooded recovery, rather than out of a recovery altogether!)

In today's blog I will concentrate on what they decided: the five action areas. Tomorrow I will talk about how they [probably] decided, and whether there are any learnings there.

The five Action Areas:

1 Human capital: we must galvanize long-term investment in Britain's skills and science base.

2 The tax system must be used to champion wealth creation.

3 Get behind big infrastructure projects.

4 It is time for a step-change for investment in small and medium-sized enterprises.

5 Deal with the obstacles to investment: regulators, planning and local government.

Speaking personally, my first reaction was disappointment. Couldn't the great and good have come up with a more dynamic and motivating package?

- What about innovation and invention?

- What about marketing and the creative industries?

- What about measures to increase consumer confidence?

- What about encouraging exports?

- What about kick-starting growth in the value of equities by increasing shareholder value and the value of investments generally?

- What about incentivizing growth outside strangled, troubled London?

Then if you look at the 'Big Five Recovery Boosters', it all looks a bit thin.

1   The Human Capital goal starts with talk about encouraging young people to go for maths, science, engineering and technology. But that is not going to impact short term, so the emphasis suddenly shifts to encouraging skilled immigration!

2   The Tax System point was obviously not intended to come across as self-interest. But doesn't stress on reducing the 50p tax rate and corporation tax rather give the game away? You don't have to be unduly sceptical to ask just how many people believe that the tax system in this era of cuts is about wealth creation. Surely it is about increasing government revenue to match the reductions in government spending?

3   Big infrastructure projects? In principle fine. But they all have to be largely or completely in the private sector to make sense economically. Building a motorway between Oxford and Cambridge to form a 'high-tech corridor' has to be the most eccentric idea of all! We already have much of the centre of London in chaos to speed the building of that much needed rail link between Maidenhead and Stratford E. Imagine the joy and consumer take up when that is opened...

4   'Government should work with banks to identify the 3,000 SMEs that have the scope to create the largest number of jobs'. Honestly! Can you imagine the challenge of that as a project. Two years minimum to agree which SMEs. Probably another two years to achieve 10 extra jobs each out of them.

5   Reducing obstacles arising from regulation, planning and local government? Won't happen overnight, will it? And where do you start? Perhaps by regulating some changes? Don't go there!

It looks to me like an opportunity lost. It would be hard to find a more obvious example of the difficulty of making great decisions in a hurry.

I counted just six women, and there was only one female CEO photographed in the supplement. Why might 100 alpha males find it hard to deliver an efficient decision-making process? Was there a decision process? I have no inside track. So what follows is supposition and (hopefully informed) guesswork.

Let's start by looking at what decision traps await a big group of powerful business leaders, temporarily obliged to make common cause with each other? Are there particular problems when you take these 'big beasts' out of the packs they normally dominate?

There are several possible decision traps, all mentioned in Chapter 2, which might have hampered the group's work:

- Group failure: refusing to accept that a team of bright people can make bad decisions.

- Pressure paralysis: getting the frame of reference wrong under pressure.

- Analysis bypass: too much information or not enough time to analyse it properly.

- Information underload: believing you have enough knowledge to proceed, when you actually need more intelligence and research.

- 'What if' wear-out: not being rigorous in looking at possible scenarios.

But I think the greatest problem was not learning from Meredith Belbin. Belbin is the management theorist who, while lecturing at the Administrative Staff College (later to become Henley Management College) in the 1960s, discovered that well-balanced teams would always outperform teams more or less exclusively composed of 'stars'. His 1981 book *Management Teams* defined the key membership roles in most business teams. I write more about Belbin in Chapter 6.

Another problem for the Summit delegates must have been an imbalance of personality profiles: too many drivers and expressives, too few analysts and amiables. More about that also in Chapter 6.

Overall there is a big lesson to be drawn from the Summit, I believe: a big team comprised of dominant leaders is very unlikely to be functional! In this instance, it is not a criticism of the leaders themselves, but of the idea that the Summit could ever achieve its goals.

Solving problems

In 1999 a business psychologist called Steve Kneeland wrote a slim and straightforward book called *Effective Problem-Solving: How to Understand the Process and Practice It Successfully*. It is sad that so few people appear to have read the book, or made much of it. Why? Because I believe Kneeland crystallized one of the major issues in decision science: where problem-solving ends and decision making begins. Interpreting Kneeland, it goes like this: problem solving is bridging the gap between the way things are and the way they ought to be. It is basically an analytical challenge. The focus is on the past, in terms of what went wrong, and why we are in this situation. Normally problem solving is a delegated task, not – at least initially – involving senior people. Before we start looking for a solution, we need to ask some questions:

- What exactly is the problem?
- How urgent is it?
- How important is it?
- Whose responsibility is it?

Kneeland said that decision making is a broader activity. It is focused on the future, and will involve making a choice between two or more options. In a company or organization it is very much a high-level responsibility. It usually needs a creative approach. It requires that the main problem needs to have been solved first. Kneeland counsels not to ignore the 'do nothing' option, but warns that deciding not to decide has the full force of a decision. He also is wary about what I have called the 'early decision' – making a decision before it's needed (see the previous chapter). He wisely wrote that it is never too late to change a decision, and agrees with those who believe that changing your mind is not necessarily a sign of weakness.

Simple stuff, yes. But faced with endless problems, as we are, it is helpful to have some linkage between problem solving and the grown up task of making decisions. Thank you, Steve.

Keeping problems simple – and why we find it so difficult. Does education make us complexity snobs, or are we born that way?

Aspiring authors need to understand that the path of true research does not always have a smooth surface. Indeed I'm now particularly wary of that well-worn and clichéd adjective: seminal (as in seminal work, seminal article etcetera). The dictionary tells us that the word means 'highly influential in an original way; constituting or providing a basis for further development'. I'm convinced it sometimes means 'pertaining to semen – not much use unless it's fertilised'.

Here's what I mean. My friend Serge Nicholls drew my attention to a really interesting piece by Oliver Burkeman on the Guardian website: **http://www.guardian.co.uk/lifeandstyle/2011/may/21/ decision-quicksand-burkeman**. His piece was about our tendency to assume that the more complex a problem is, the more important it must be. And therefore that hard decisions are more important than easy ones.

Oliver was writing about a research paper written by Aner Sela and Jonah Berger. So I looked up the original paper on the internet. Was it impenetrable, or was it really impenetrable! Then I realized that Oliver had picked up not the original paper, but a highly readable summary of it in Jonah Lehrer's fascinating neuroscience blog at **http://www.wired.com/wiredscience/frontal-cortex/**.

Lehrer wrote the excellent *The Decisive Moment*, 2009, and to judge from that and his blog, he has the priceless quality of simplifying the complex – rather than the opposite 'skill'. This is a rambling way of telling you that I'm with the Sela and Berger thesis all the way. Even if I needed Lehrer and Burkeman to explain it. I'm not questioning the findings. All of us have observed friends, colleagues, partners, clients, agencies, those famous 'experts', and even ourselves adding complexity rather than taking it away. What intrigues me is why we are 'complexity snobs', and indeed (as other researchers have discovered) why we seem deliberately to want to complicate a problem, even if someone can show how simple it really is.

Possible explanations:

- Does it go back to our education where the tasks and exams we were set got harder as we got older?
- Is it plumbed into us from birth?
- Is it a jobs-worth thing? A yearning for some kind of status badge?
- Is it basically mercenary? (The more difficult the problem, the more I can earn – in salary or fee – by solving it.) Good old behavioural economics again!

Is there such a big difference between opportunities and problems?

Let's look at the world I have always worked in: marketing. It is supposed to be all about opportunities:

- sales and share growth;
- launches and relaunches;
- new product development;
- new markets.

Next only to CVs and car brochures, marketing plans have to be some of the most positive documents in this or any other language. So why is it that legions of agencies, advisers and consultants around the marketing world are employed by clients as problem solvers? Are they incapable of recognizing an opportunity when they see one?

Equally even the most severe problems seem to present opportunities for brand owners and their internal and external teams tasked with solving them. How can this be? Should we abandon the perpetual epithets, and start talking about difficult opportunities and simple problems?

I don't think so. For me, it is more that problems and opportunities are not as different as we have always thought. An opportunity is an unrealized opportunity until it has been fully grasped and exploited. A problem ceases to be a problem once the solution has been identified and implemented.

There's a clear learning from decision theory here. Skilled decision makers know that coming to a decision is an achievement – but only half the battle. For a decision to be effective it has to be executed. Just the same with identifying opportunities and defining solutions. Success requires not just accurate diagnosis and an agreement on the way forward. Whether it is marketing, politics, sport or war, you still have to score the goals and emerge a winner.

So maybe we should change the way we look at what we might call rare opportunities and well done problems. The rare opportunity is just another sort of problem, while the well done problem has actually created an opportunity.

Which came first – the decision or the problem?

Why do you suppose people think they can make decisions without first solving a problem? Even worse, why do 'policy makers' (eg politicians and leaders of companies and other organizations) think they can make their policy statements, when there is no evidence whatever that what they are advocating will work – in the sense of exploiting an opportunity, averting a threat or solving a problem? Spotting what I call good examples of 'early decisions' is easy. Every day, every newspaper and every news bulletin obliges. As I am writing these words the Lib Dems are at their Spring Conference in Gateshead. Party leader Nick Clegg made a speech yesterday advocating a 'Tycoon Tax'. For weeks the Labour Party and some Lib Dem activists have been calling for a 'Mansion Tax' on houses worth £2 million or more. Taxes on property in the UK have always been contentious since the infamous Window Tax (1696–1851). Conservative MPs would definitely not vote for this one after Mrs Thatcher's nemesis, the Community Charge (*aka* Poll Tax). So now Mr Clegg wants a new tax to ensure that wealthy Britons would have to pay a minimum 20 per cent on their total annual earnings. You don't have to be the son of a Tax Inspector (but I am) to know that armies of accountants, financial advisers and tax lawyers would weigh in – slowly but inexorably – to make sure that this doesn't happen! Mr Clegg assuredly knows this too, but it is incumbent on him to make belligerent statements at party conferences, and it gave him a Saturday headline.

But it is not as if this kind of policy making on the hoof is confined to politicians – of whatever hue. The pressure to be 'decisive' can make fence-rushers of us all. Sometimes it is worth being criticized for sitting on that fence. Identifying the goal you are aiming at should always be the first step. Then you have to look at whatever problem, or problems, might stop you getting there. Big tasks? Solving the problems and coming up with decision options.

Problem solving will often take a great deal more time than it takes to come up with a headline-gathering policy. Looking at the options and doing a reward–risk analysis on upsides and downsides also needs time and very careful consideration. Then you are in a position to make a decision. And announce it. And implement it. Sounds more scientific doesn't it?

Be really careful with those spontaneous decisions

Study decision science long enough, and you start believing that all decisions are stimulated by one of three prompts: an opportunity, a problem that needs to be solved, setting one or more goals.

Then, the theory goes, you drop into the practised routine of:

- best data and intelligence;
- frame – and if necessary keep on framing;
- structure the most viable options;
- identify upsides and downsides in each option;
- reward–risk analysis;
- make your decision.

Sadly or otherwise, this does not always happen! Most of the decisions you make are on the spur of the moment, or not fully thought through. With short-order decision making (armed forces, emergency services, driving, flying, sport etcetera) there is no alternative. There's almost no time to think or react, and training and technique will hopefully carry you through. It's the decision you make spontaneously when there was time to think about it, that often gets you into trouble. In companies a spending decision that involves commissioning work from an outside supplier requires a purchase order (PO). It's the PO that triggers the procurement process.

Maybe we should all mentally issue ourselves with a decision order (DO) every time we feel a spontaneous decision coming on. First, it would ensure that we look hard at opportunities and problems. At the very least the DO might make us think twice about the possible downsides as well as the more obvious upsides. As ever it's the way you make a decision that is as important as the decision itself. If you feel you have to DO something, think first. DO could become a useful mnemonic.

There's a place for dumb questions

There was a famous article by Geoffrey Colvin in *Fortune* (June 2005), called 'The Wisdom of Dumb Questions'. Colvin had been inspired by an aspect of the Enron Scandal, the revelation that the first line in accountant Sherron Watkins's famous memo to Ken Lay in August 2001 had been: 'Has Enron become a risky place to work?' It clearly had, and it was therefore an excellent question, however naive she was made to feel in asking it. Colvin went on to quote Peter Drucker's perennial consultant's question to his heavy-hitting clients: 'What business are you in?' Dumb, maybe. Productive, often. Lucrative (from Drucker's point of view), almost always.

This chapter is about avoiding the nightmares that can result from bad decisions. If a dumb question or two from a team member can avert disaster, it's worth sounding dumb. Colvin made up his own fictitious example: 'What makes us think the Cuban people will rise up?' (to President Kennedy before the Bay of Pigs fiasco). We can try our own. And should do the next time we seriously question the wisdom of a plan we are involved in.

I started to develop my own theory of what has now emerged as Smart Decision Making, derived from what I have learned from experts and gurus, but rooted in my own experience and observations.

Crucial to this theory is to be wary of natural optimism (yours or anyone else's). Marketing (the world where I have spent all my working life) is full of optimists. Every time you write a marketing plan, you have to make yourself believe it is achievable – even if you accept deep down that not all the brands in a sector can gain share. Every time you make a pitch you psych yourself up to win.

But optimism is dangerous. When you start looking at options and scenarios, it's very tempting to look to the one with the biggest upside, rather than steering clear of the one with the worst downside. The best option is often the one with the second best upside and the least damaging downside. What matters is making the important decisions in the right way – then managing it through.

There are three main tests: accountability (we have to be responsible for our decisions to everyone whom they are going to affect); process (was it taken rationally, logically and in a way that provides a good guide for the future?); and performance (did the decision have a successful outcome?).

We can make excuses for the 'mistaken mini-decisions' that can happen during a sequence of events, but without the whole project ending in disaster. It is harder to forgive real howlers. Hopefully we will always leave space for the 'dumb question' moment.

Sherron Watkins' question may have significantly reduced the employment opportunity at Enron, but it absolutely clarified the problem. So did the one to President Kennedy. Drucker's question on the other hand – and his normal follow-up: 'Do you know who your customers are?' – both point to potential opportunities.

Two problems are better than one

It sounds counterintuitive. Surely if you have a serious problem to solve or a big decision to make, you need to give it your full attention?

I am not sure. Studying decisions and decision makers, I have come to the conclusion that 100 per cent focus on any one issue is not necessarily a guarantee of a successful outcome. For most of us, the more taxing a problem is, the tendency is to analyse it from every angle, and to bring more and more data and information to bear, up to the point where you can easily go round in circles. Before long you are going over aspects for the second and third time. Almost inevitably you end up with two or more options that are more or less equally attractive – and equally dangerous.

My suggestion is *not* to give it your full attention *all* the time. Why not simultaneously address another problem? Hopefully it will be a less demanding one. Maybe it is one you have subconsciously moved down your 'to do' list, because you know it is one you can unravel, given some time. Put it up there – right at the top of your list. Swing into problem-solving mode on problem #2, and within a day or so, you will have an option on the table that is a clear winner. Make the decision, and work out an optimum implementation plan.

Refreshed and motivated by your winning performance, return to problem #1. Almost inevitably you will find it less intractable. One of the possible options will start looking the most attractive, with a less worrying downside. What were you worrying about? You are a talented problem solver. You proved that with a stylish performance on problem #2. Make the big decision with confidence. It is yet another example of that well-known maxim: 'If you want a job done, give it to a busy person'.

Problem-solving techniques

Agreeing on the core question, and differentiating between givens and variables guides every decision. There is a big contrast between trained decision-making specialists and experienced professionals on the one hand, and clever people who have not been trained to make decisions. Success has to be judged on both input measures (was the process good?), and outcome measures (has the problem been solved, and have goals been achieved?). Problem solving starts with distinguishing between 'fix it' (something needs fixing: make the problem go away), and 'do it' (move us in the right direction) problems. It also helps to break down big problems into small ones – so that you can start solving at least some of them. It is also essential to extract the maximum information and significance from data and facts.

There is a wealth of accredited problem-solving techniques, and it is not practical to recommend just two or three of them. Every organization has its favourites, and some techniques are a better fit with company culture than others. Some are useful across a raft of problem areas, while others are very specific. Some can easily be adopted by a team with no previous training. Other more sophisticated techniques require programming skills, and inevitably more time.

We can group the methods though, and the ever useful internet can give you an outline indication of each one, because they are all in the public domain. This list is not exhaustive, but covers the most familiar options:

1 Financially based:
   - cost–benefit analysis;
   - cash flow forecasting;
   - risk analysis (a way of quantifying threats and downsides);
   - Monte Carlo method (exotically named simulation system originally developed by nuclear scientists – but now used to compute degrees of uncertainty).

2 Values (appropriate for individuals, entrepreneurs, explorers, adventurers):
   - value analysis (basically a simple listing approach – what are my values?);
   - spiral dynamics (measures changes or likely changes in your value system).

3 Gathering and organizing information and data:
   - Kepner-Tregoe (severely rational and sequential approach designed to eliminate bias);
   - blindspot analysis (we all have blindspots, this is an organized way of computing, aggregating and analysing everyone's blindspots).

4 'Pros and cons:
   - SWOT (most basic way of looking at a balance of now and future);

- forcefield analysis (how to optimize opportunities and minimize or neutralize threats);

- paired comparison analysis (prioritization technique – which is the most important problem to solve);

- PMI (short for plus, minus, interesting; plus and minus are going to be objective assessments; the 'I' gives you the chance to introduce subjective factors to the mix);

- grid analysis (more sophisticated way of looking at pros and cons);

- Pareto (scoring problems on the 80/20 principle of estimating the balance between effort and return).

5 Making the team function better as it looks at problems and options:

- De Bono's Six Hats;

- avoiding groupthink (applying one or more of the techniques below to deter dictatorship and coerced consensus);

- ladder of inference (clever way of challenging people – or groups – when they jump to conclusions);

- decision trees (projecting outcomes);

- futures wheel (brainstorming ways of looking at future consequences of change);

- nominal group technique (each group member is treated equally at evaluation stage);

- stepladder technique (each group member is introduced to the group one-by-one having been pre-briefed);

- Delphi technique (the same result achieved by a facilitator analysing individual – and sometimes anonymous – written submissions).

Chapter Four
Smart decision making

We are all looking for a system that works. It has to be a mixture of good thinking and harnessing the power of the subconscious brain

I am a big team player. I love making decisions, and I feel very confident about making decisions. But I absolutely believe in involving and engaging and deriving the benefit from my team and their wisdom and advice, and that strength that comes from a consensus about the way forward. I'm happy to make the decision, and make the call if necessary, but much prefer to do it as a team.

(SIR NICK YOUNG, CEO BRITISH RED CROSS)

The Holy Grail – better decisions

Decision science is a casserole of business theory, psychology and neurology. Decision making is about making the best call from the best possible set of options. Unless you have planned a number of compelling scenarios – each with its upside and downside – it is impossible to know whether you have made the right decision and that you have employed the most rigorous process. It has been a pleasure not a chore to read the experts. A great recommendation was the Russo and Schoemaker classic *Decision Traps* (1989). When I started to take decisions seriously, I read this book voraciously and realized that there is such a thing as decision science. People can be taught to become more expert. Maybe it is going too far to say there is a right way and a wrong way. But we can safely say there is a better way, and one that is less good.

Decisions need to be based on a balance of upside reward and downside risk, not on a ranking of attractive upsides. We are educated to fly solo. We are tested on what we know, not what we do with the knowledge. No one teaches us how to make decisions.

Business emphasizes the importance of teamwork. Solus operating and thinking are frowned upon. There is little time to think. The calendar is filled with endless meetings – many of which are to rubber-stamp or question 'plans', which are usually undeliverable. Meetings are mostly not designed as forums for making decisions. Language often doesn't help. Being decisive isn't necessarily good. If you make decisions all the time – and half of them are wrong – are you 'decisive'? Equally, sitting on the fence isn't always a bad thing, or a sign of weakness. Just wanting something to happen (setting out a policy, agreeing a goal) won't make it happen. Just because you have done something does not prove you have made a decision.

I then wanted to look much more widely than clients and agencies. The year 2002, when I first took an interest in decision science, was peak time for corporate disasters like Enron and Arthur Andersen. Academics and journalists were drilling down to find explanations. I started to develop my own theories – derived from the experts and gurus, but rooted in my own experience and observations.

I realized how important it is to be wary of natural optimism (ours or anyone else's). Marketing is full of optimists. Every time you write a marketing plan, you have to make yourself believe it is achievable – even if you accept deep down that not all the brands in a sector can gain share. It's a world that isn't determined by multivariate analysis. If you have a really big idea, and can turn it into clever advertising, the brand can be outstandingly successful.

And measuring the success will also be straightforward (sales up 50 per cent, brand share doubled – whatever).

Optimism is dangerous, because when you start looking at options and scenarios, it's very tempting to look to the one with the biggest upside, rather than steering clear of the one with the worst downside. I worked out that the best option is often the one with the second-best upside and the least-damaging downside (a bit like a wine list, when you want to balance hospitality with frugality!).

What matters is making the important decision in the right way – then managing it through. There are six rules:

1 Every important decision is a journey, not a single step – and you need to establish a goal, a route and a team before you set out.

2 You must ask the right questions at the outset to make sure you are operating within the correct frame.

3 Plotting scenarios is how you come to the right decision, and for that you need the best possible intelligence.

4 No decision means much without buy-in. The likelihood of gaining acceptance and buy-in is inevitably going to be a factor in deciding which way to go.

5 Execution is critical. A great decision badly executed will fail.

6 Learning and feedback are fundamental, because decision making is a constant activity – every decision you take will inform every other decision you have to make in the future.

It is like the world of medicine, in that you have to do the tests and diagnosis before deciding on the treatment and starting it.

All the time I have been looking for...

A smart way to make decisions better

Great decisions are far more likely to come from a good decision-making process. I believe that setting up in a rigorous way shortens the odds on making a good decision. To judge by comments posted on my blog, and conversations with experts and seasoned decision makers, I am on the right lines.

So much in decision making is connected with change management, where the key question tends to be: what is the ultimate goal? Until everyone has agreed on the goal, it is unsafe to move on to the decision process.

Part 1 of the Smart Decisions Approach is the 10 steps up to, but not including, taking the decision itself:

1 Am I sure what the opportunity is? Or am I sure what the problem is?

2 If it's an opportunity, have I identified it correctly, and do I know how I am going to take advantage of it?

3 If it's a problem, do I know precisely what it is, and how I am going to solve it?

4 So what is my goal? This must be exactly what I am looking to my decision to achieve. Unless everyone concerned with a decision knows what the desired outcome is, you cannot assess the wisdom of a decision or particular course of action. A politician can choose between different goals: winning the election, reducing taxes, becoming Prime Minister. The decision might be what to put in the election manifesto. A general might have decided in his own mind to try to recapture a town lost last week. But what's the goal?

5 Is pursuing this goal one for me to tackle on my own, or is it a team task – in which case have we got the right team on the case?

6 Having agreed on the opportunity or problem, and set a goal, it is then time to look at options: how many possible answers are there? What are these options? Are we sure we have explored all the meaningful ones?

7 Is there enough data and information to analyse each of the options, and can we get more if needs be? We need to leave reasonable time here (if available) for gathering and analysing information and intelligence. Control what we can, and we must do our best to predict what we can't.

8 Have we looked at the upsides and downsides of each option? For each option we need to write down the best upside (highest reward) and the worst potential downside (biggest risk).

9 If it isn't immediately obvious which is the most compelling route, first look at the worst downside, and eliminate that route, unless the upside is particularly alluring. Then look at the upsides in order of attractiveness. We are looking for the best balance.

10 What looks to be the best decision?

This sounds cumbersome and complicated. But I don't believe it is.

Steps 1–3: should have been taken care of, as indicated in Chapter 3.

Step 4: having been rigorous in interrogating the opportunity or problem, we should be in shape to define the goal, in pursuit of which we have to make a decision. Committing to a goal is absolutely essential. Neither capitalizing on an opportunity nor solving a problem is of itself going to be the goal. We have to know what we're aiming at.

Steps 5–10: the essence of the rational side of the Smart Decision process. Every step is important for all decisions except the ones that have to be made instantly, or very quickly (see Chapter 5).

Steps 1–10: this is as far as you can take a purely rational approach. We still need to:

- Get buy-in to the decision. This may involve selling it up – to your boss, a director, the Chief Executive Officer (CEO), the board. It may mean obtaining the agreement of colleagues, peers, opposite numbers. Until a decision is jointly agreed, it hasn't passed an essential test: to be a mutual decision.

- Think about how best to communicate the decision, because a decision only becomes real when it goes public.

- And crucially how to implement it – initially and ongoing, which will inevitably involve feedback, more intelligence, and more decisions.

But vitally we must also provide for gut feel before making the decision. How do we do this? Well, obviously we will already have had a lot of less than purely logical thoughts as we evaluated the options. One of the options will almost certainly have been more attractive, as opposed to be more logical. Even when we are being at our most rigorous, it is difficult to be completely cold and analytical. Just as steps 1–10 will have given us a winner in the mind, we will almost certainly also have a winner in the heart. Hopefully – but by no means always – the same one.

The more I thought about this rational–gut feel conundrum, the more it reminded me of what I have been doing in my day job for 24 years. On behalf of clients, I have overseen hundreds of agency pitches – using a structured system that still had plenty of room for right brain thinking and reaction.

The Agency Assessments method – rigour, but also room for chemistry and gut feel

The Agency Assessments International (AAI) search and selection process is both logical and rigorous. The search sequence goes like this (see Figure 4.1).

FIGURE 4.1   Search roadmap

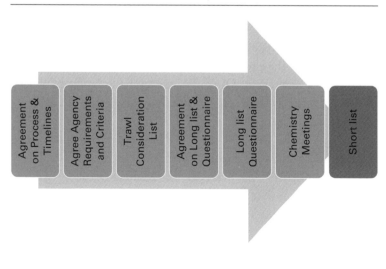

FIGURE 4.2   Selection roadmap

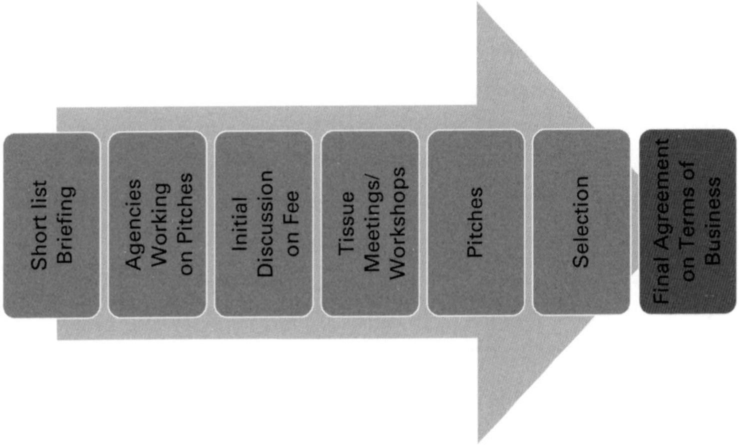

Short list Briefing · Agencies Working on Pitches · Initial Discussion on Fee · Tissue Meetings/Workshops · Pitches · Selection · Final Agreement on Terms of Business

The client has no face-to-face encounters with the agencies until phase 6 – Chemistry meetings. The written responses to phase 5 (Long list questionnaire) may well have pre-conditioned the client team. But the Chemistry sessions are important inputs into the next phase – agreeing the short list. And selection follows with a further seven phases (see Figure 4.2).

The client team now sees plenty of the three or four individual agencies left in the pitch – at phases 1, 3, 4 and 5, and probably offline from the process chart as well. That is plenty of time to start building emotional attachments.

But equally the client's decision to appoint the winning agency is only one part of the equation. The other is for the agency to decide to take on a new client. Of course agency body language during the pitch process is largely, if not wholly, enthusiastic. But agreeing to work with a new client is like agreeing to accept a job offer, or buying a house you have set your heart upon: you still have to agree terms and sign the papers.

Rebranding AAI's pitch service as 'Mutual Decision' was an acknowledgement that the agency's decision is as important as the client's in establishing a new and potentially productive commercial partnership.

Allowing for gut feel in the Smart Decisions Approach

Part 2, Steps 11–15, works like this:

11 If there is one route that is obviously the best, sleep on it. How do you feel about it the next morning? Don't be too rational. Now's the time to trust gut feel, having set up the process in a logical way.

12 Or if there are two possible decisions, spend a day thinking about the first, and sleep on it. Then the next day, think about the second option, and sleep on that. How do you feel about the one against the other? Again, trust gut feel.

13 Decide. Then communicate the decision to everyone involved – which includes selling up, and gaining the buy-in and approval needed to make the decision mutual. Naturally in a confrontational situation, you won't want your enemy or adversary or the other side to know what you have in mind. In many situations the decision only becomes real when you communicate it.

14 Put as much energy into implementing the decision as you did into coming up with it.

15 Keep tabs on how the decision works out. Try to at least make notes, so you can learn for next time.

Decisions need to be based on a balance of upside reward and downside risk, not just on a ranking of attractive upsides.

Another reason we need to accommodate gut feel

I was very taken with Errol Wirasinghe's book *The Art Of Making Decisions* (2003). Without Errol I would never have known about a helpful paper dating back to 1956. It was written by George A Miller, a cognitive psychologist from Princeton. Miller coined the phrase 'the Magic Number Seven, plus or minus two' to describe one of the key limitations of the brain's capacity. Apparently the conscious mind can only hold seven (plus or minus two) pieces of information at any one time, either things we have thought of ourselves, or those that we have imported from outside. Somewhere between five and nine units of information is not a great deal, when you think about it, to coin a phrase, especially in something complex like the decision-making process. It goes a long way to explain why choice (see Chapter 7) differs from other kinds of decision making. When we choose, we have to eliminate less promising candidates (often one at a time) to give ourselves a do-able task, with only a limited number of binary comparisons to make. In decision making the Miller '5–9' rule makes it essential to allow gut feel to play its part – albeit in a process that was structured to begin with.

The emotional side of decision making

Despite what we have learned about gut feel (and the '5–9 pieces of information' rule), most books and learned papers on decision making work on the assumption that rationality and logic are the main drivers. The theory of evaluating upsides and downsides by applying reward–risk analysis is based on individuals and teams going about their deliberations in a cool and detached fashion.

We have already worked out that this assumption is not safe. Another famous paper written in 1979 by a Japanese academic, Masanao Toda from Hokkaido University, challenges it. In 'Emotion and Decision Making', a Hokkaido University Behavioral Science Report, Toda asserts that emotional decision making was the norm in the earlier period of man's evolution, when man was living on the edge, and was frequently stressed (*Homo iratus?*).

Toda believes that the wild and primitive environment in which our forebears lived required an emotional approach, because so many decisions were related to life and death. His theory is that a non-emotional, more analytical decision system was the product of a much later period in evolution. But interestingly he felt that this cognitive approach was designed not so much to replace the emotional approach, as to supplement it.

If he is right, rationality is not meant to be the only organizing principle. Rationality and emotion might be often in conflict, but it may be that the cognitive decision system cannot operate without some help from the emotion system.

Taking this viewpoint into practical application in 2012, I question whether we should automatically elevate the logical approach, and dismiss earthy motivators like love, hate and revenge. Certainly there is massive empirical evidence that 'ordinary people' (that is, us) make many decisions driven by affection or dislike, and by the desire to avenge wrongs, insults and what we see as unfairness.

I would argue that when we are in positions of authority, on committees or wearing a uniform, we are quite likely to take illogicality and prejudice with us into our deliberations. Add self-interest to the list of emotions, and there is absolutely no doubt about it.

It could be that an acceptance that decision making has an emotional content exposes a major difference between decision making and problem solving – which is likely to be more or less totally rational.

In this book I am taking a particularly close look at areas outside business to see whether we might have underestimated the influence of emotion. We already know from the psychology we use in marketing and advertising that making personal choices of partners, careers, houses, cars etcetera is just as much guided by emotion as logic. Maybe behavioural economics looms large in a wider area of decision making than we had believed. A good question is whether the emotional influence comes from the conscious or subconscious mind. Prejudice, almost by definition, comes in by autopilot from the subconscious. But we can all relate to situations where we have been consciously emotional in our judgement or decision making. Emotional doesn't imply that we are out of control – just that we are not being wholly rational.

How do we rationalize gut feel?

The theory goes that some decisions are made only after careful consideration, while others are on the basis of gut feelings. Generally speaking, the longer we have to decide, the more we are going to at least weigh the options – based on making a list and assessing pros and cons (as Benjamin Franklin advised his nephew on how to choose between two potential wives more than 200 years ago). If there is little or no time available, we usually rely on experience, instinct and/or training. Look at pilots, soldiers, firefighters, referees, triage nurses and so on.

So far, so true. Two books, Malcolm Gladwell's *Blink* (2005) and Gerd Gigerenzer's *Gut Feelings* (2007), are good for taking us through the ins and outs of short order decision making. I found the Gigerenzer book useful, because it explains how our instincts work – and makes us feel better about trusting them, for example:

- It is the Recognition Heuristic that explains brand loyalty, even in the face of a cheaper own label.

- I love his Beneficial Degree of Ignorance, which enables intelligent quiz show contestants to work out the right answer from how a question is put, even when it is out of their knowledge comfort zone (and he has probably never watched Chris Tarrant).

- I find Unconscious Intelligence a really good way of explaining how we often manage to use rules of thumb to solve problems and make decisions as accurately, and often quicker and better, than we can using logic and method.

Gigerenzer uses another phrase that rings true for me: the Evolved Brain. Most of us are so conditioned by our education, that we want to make learning a totally logical and linear process – with a predictable ratio linking inputs and outputs. In *Gut Feelings* we read about numerous examples of the brain working out things for itself:

- The intuition of detectives (which also I suspect extends to other 'outwitters' like referees, umpires, teachers, suspicious partners).

- The determination of pioneering scientists.

- Love matches (and Gigerenzer tells us sternly that intuition is as much a male skill as a female one – despite the urban myth!).

- Even an instinctive moral code.

In *Blink*, Gladwell's central theme is that intuition is not some vague ability we are born with, but a raw skill (he calls it 'thin-slicing', as in simplifying by getting quickly under the surface of a situation) that we can consciously develop and sharpen, to make us better decision makers. He also cautions that instinct can let us down as well as help us. For instance, the way people look (sex, colour, shape, size) can influence the way we think about them and react to them. Herein lies prejudice, and a closed mind, rather than the open one we need for unbiased decisions. It is interesting to read online reviews of *Blink*. Gladwell has been criticized for giving more and more examples of where unconscious bias has hampered decision making, without providing a convincing case for thin-slicing as a reliable tool. I think this is harsh. Thin-slicing would probably have joined 'Tipping Point' in entering the language if the term had been as instantly understandable.

Both books reassure that a gut feel decision can turn out to be just as right and just as successful as one painstakingly arrived at. Once we have crossed that credibility barrier, we can cheerfully embrace instinct and intuition and accept that they are useful (and indeed reliable) tools in our toolkit. In this way we rationalize gut feel and give it the same respect as logical process and thinking. Neither method of making decisions is infallible. Equally it would be wrong to regard logic and rationality as the obvious route for men as opposed to women, or when you have more time.

The realization that emotions, gut feelings and Benjamin Franklin's algebra all have their place, and are complementary skills, makes it a lot easier to get through life! Instead of looking at rational decisions and decisions influenced by emotion and gut, we should probably accept that most decisions need to have a liberal sprinkling of both reason, emotion and gut. The conscious and subconscious minds might be fighting for supremacy, but often they work together, whether we realize it (consciously) or not.

Fast and frugal

In a paper he wrote with Daniel Goldstein in 2004, 'Reasoning the Fast and Frugal Way: Models of Bounded Rationality', Gigerenzer praised simple heuristics that do not require vast amounts of data collection and analysis. But there is a problem:

> Simplicity creates not only robustness, but also transparency. One danger is that the complex methods so often used by managers in areas such as finance, economics, marketing and strategic planning can become an end in themselves, a ritual to impress others yet one that may not offer even an iota of additional marketplace punch. Besides wanting to impress others, leaders sometimes choose to advertise complexity instead of transparency because they believe it has a calming effect on stakeholders, letting them know that state-of-the-art machinery is hard at work on the important problems.

As the authors point out, we are back to that familiar misquotation from Albert Einstein, 'Make things as simple as possible, but not simpler.'

Lessons from modern neurology

Conscious mind vs subconscious

Kia Nobre is Professor of Cognitive Neuroscience at Oxford University. Her book *Attention and Time* (with Jennifer Coull, 2010) fully bears out the Miller theory. Although we can notice literally hundreds of things (including information and data) in a short period of time, the conscious mind can only deal with a tiny fraction of them. Apparently we blink five times a second and thus take a 'snapshot' every 200 milliseconds. We know from digital cameras that it doesn't take long to acquire far too many images, so that we have to delete regularly. The subconscious does the same thing. Not surprisingly it skews what we take on board according to our interest level, as in 'Time flies when you're having fun', and 'A watched pot never boils'.

Automatic and unconscious control

Julien Doyon is Director of the Functional Neuroimaging unit at Montreal University. His research is into how we painstakingly learn skills that require dexterity, and then store the skill set in the cerebellum, so that we can subconsciously call it up when we need it. The brain has the ability to reorganize itself by forming new connections between brain cells (neurons). The way the brain adapts itself to any number of the skills we learn and use is known as neuroplasticity, or plasticity for short. It may take us a long time to become really proficient at, say, knitting (an activity on which Dr Doyon conducted experiments), golf, fretwork, cooking, anything... but whenever we have learned something new, it is memorized by plasticity. It's ours to use, and we don't even have to press a button, click a mouse, or issue a command to retrieve the learned skill. Scientists have described the state we are in when we are subconsciously using one of these skills as autopilot or cruise control. Like the 'watched pot' above, we have plenty of phrases to describe the results of plasticity, often using familiar examples like learning to swim or riding a bicycle. I looked on the internet at random and found the following reassuring words on a site called about.com: 'Bike riding is easily learned, and not easily forgotten'. Exactly. At the beginning of Chapter 9 there is a memorable description of the same phenomenon by Nigel Jones, who was a chess professional before becoming an advertising executive.

Can the subconscious misfire?

Indeed it can, like every part of our body. Unsurprisingly much neurological learning came about as a result of the search for knowledge and potential therapies in geriatric care. Older people forget more, and this can become a serious problem. There is also fascinating research into dexterity problems. Both Professor Charles Adler of the Mayo Clinic in Arizona and Dr Mark Edwards of the UCL Institute of Neurology have gone public with treatment case histories on a golf professional and a guitarist, respectively. Both suffered from a condition called dystonia – involuntary muscle contractions. For the golf pro this showed in a putting malfunction all golfers call 'the yips'; for the guitarist it was quite simply preventing him earning a living, because his playing was not fault-free. The treatment involved sending direct electric current to the cerebellum.

The learning from neurology

I deduce:

- The subconscious plays a vital part in all learned activities.
- Learning any activity is achieved by consciously following rational instructions or guidelines, and then committing it to memory (thanks to plasticity).
- Decision making – and the constituents of decision making – constitute a high-grade learned activity.
- All decision making (even when it is not perfectly executed) must be using plasticity as well as logic.
- We must use a lot of autopilot.
- We can learn to make ourselves better at decision making – and retain that knowledge. This improvement, like the initial learning, is bound to involve both the conscious and unconscious mind.
- Descartes' theory (that only the mind thinks) was not so much wrong as incomplete.

Rear Admiral David Snelson talks about the effect of 'autopilot'

"The Navy talk about ship handling ability. It's a lot to do with spatial awareness. Spatial awareness is something that you've got or you haven't got, but you can enhance it. Perhaps the most clear cut case of where you really need spatial awareness is the traditional fighter pilot. If you talk to somebody who's flown a fast jet in aerial combat, they can keep their brain gimballed in space with north pointing north, while the vehicle that they're in is doing something quite different. Yet the brain still knows where everything is around them. That is an extraordinary ability, and fighter pilots have it. Interestingly mariners have it too, especially submarine captains, because they pop briefly up towards the surface, have a look around at what the ships are doing on the surface and go down again and turn their submarine and go around in a different direction. Meanwhile they're thinking about that ship which they last saw. He was over there, he was heading that way, I'm now heading this way. So there's a very complex spatial awareness thing going on in the brain. Putting a ship alongside is a minor version of that, because you can still see everything that's going on around you. For the fighter pilot and the submariner you can't.

Decision making is best played as a team game

One aspect of our educational inheritance is our built-in tendency to try to tackle challenges and solve problems on our own. Square that with a basic example of behavioural economics – the role of the personal computer in making us self-reliant loners – and we have a prescription for underperforming decision makers.

If it wasn't already obvious that teamwork is an essential ingredient to successful decision making, the framing aspect is the clincher. The better way to make decisions is significantly dependant on the frames we use to focus our thinking. The process sequence starts like this:

1 What's the problem forcing us to make a decision?

2 *What thinking frame are we using?*

3 *Can we think of other possible frames?*

4 Have we all the information, experience and feedback needed to make a decision? Or do we need more intelligence?

One of the great benefits of teamwork is that we are likely to have almost as many frames as participants. On this the day of the electoral referendum, I had a stab at the different frames used by the main political protagonists in the proportional representation alternative vote (AV) debate. Of course the objective in a team is not to maximize the number of frames, but to learn from the relevant ones that each team member is bringing to the party.

But before we fix meetings to seal a cosy consensus, let's be a bit radical. Consensus (in the sense of willing adherence to one point of view, line of thinking or course of action) is very difficult to achieve in conventional meetings. Meeting culture, hierarchy, personality profiles and shortage of time mean that getting together in a conference room is a really inefficient way of sharing different approaches, like thinking frames. There's an excellent article about this phenomenon by Ram Charan ('Conquering a Culture of Indecision') published in *Harvard Business Review* on making smarter decisions (2007). Charan talks about 'false decisions' emerging from such meetings. They are false because the buy-in is not sincere, and the meeting participants who don't agree (but won't say so) will do their level best subsequently to undermine the decision and overturn it.

The answer? Charan advocates candour and honest dialogue – so that all key members of the decision-making group buy in to the agreed way forward, but acknowledge individual (and often highly informed) dissenting views. My own view is that without artificial consensus, the implementation of an important decision is far more likely to be flexible (and therefore probably more successful), because team members can apply expertise to crucial aspects of the execution of the decision.

Teams need to work together synergistically, not agree on everything. But one thing they do need to agree on is the key question.

The key question

You must ask the right questions at the outset to make sure you are operating within the correct decision frame. Frame and carry on reframing for as long as necessary to ensure that you are asking the crucial question. It might seem counterintuitive to be asking questions when others are looking for answers – but it is key to decision science. Of all the common Decision Traps, frame blindness (trying to solve the wrong problem) is probably the most destructive. Ensure that you are asking – and answering – the right questions. What are the problems? The opportunities? What pressure are we under, and is that stopping us thinking straight? Most disastrous decisions are made under pressure, and based on incorrect assumptions about problems and opportunities. Identification of the key question is crucial.

The journey – not the single step: mapping a decision process, and managing it over the life of a project

When we evaluate options, we are looking at four aspects: understanding what the risks are; identifying threats and potential threats; predicting possible outcomes; and assessing feasibility: can we execute it? The winning formula demands critical thinking – rigorous use of information, experience, observation and reasoning. Also impact analysis – identifying all the consequences of change, and contingency planning.

You cannot be an effective decision maker unless you have mastered a range of problem-solving and decision-making techniques. Essential also to:

- be able to master processes for dealing with data and information;

- know how to ask the right questions;
- understand the common decision traps, and how to avoid them;
- be prepared to deal with what can go wrong in implementation;
- be dedicated to feedback and learning (otherwise you may be 'condemned to repeat the experience');
- be prepared to do enough proactive and systematic thinking to balance the reactive pressures of recency – from smartphones, e-mail, and wall to wall news.

There are relative degrees of stress in play here. To have to make a decision at the end of a controlled process, triggered by your own ideas or those of colleagues, is materially less stressful than having to decide reactively. In his book *What They Don't Teach You At Harvard Law School* (1987) Mark McCormack says that he would never take a business call in the office. He'd have it answered, and call back fast, having checked files or talked to the relevant colleague. Interestingly, Nigel Jones of Publicis told me something similar: 'Don't try and take a big decision or reply to a crucial e-mail without sleeping on it.' It is important as well to understand that implementation is as important as deciding. It requires just as much planning, and impact and risk analysis.

'Morethanism'

This brings us to prioritization – a major element of decision making. Both as individuals and as teams in organizations we constantly need to take decisions not in a vacuum, but in relation to other goals and other decisions.

We prioritize in all sorts of situations by ranking one goal ahead of another, or by judging that 'x' is more important than 'y'. I call it 'Morethanism'. Some examples:

- India's cricketers clearly value playing in the IPL more than Test cricket.

- The recent Defence Review judged that maintaining capability on land was more important than naval power, hence dispensing with carriers, Sea Harriers and the Nimrod replacement.

- Within the Coalition Government spending on the National Health Service (NHS) is more important than spending in any other department. The Government has also made the call that spending cuts are more important than defending jobs.

Morethanism works like any other decision matrix, except that you need data and intelligence to help rank the relative importance of different goals before coming up with a number of options. So the process looks like this:

1 Best data and intelligence – and keep looking for more.

2 Clarity on which goal(s) is/are more important than others.

3 Frame – and if necessary keep on framing till the central question (and any others) have been well and truly defined and agreed upon.

4 Structure the most viable options for achieving the goals (in order) and solving problems.

5 Identify upsides and downsides in each option.

6 Reward–risk analysis, ensuring that you are not swayed too much by the attractiveness of an option if it has a dangerous downside.

7 Carefully weigh reward and risk, and then make the 'Morethan' decision.

What we always have to remember is that prioritizing is not an end in itself – all it achieves is the ranking of goals. We still have to frame questions, solve problems and make decisions.

Prioritization – like any multidimensional mental challenge – is what makes champion decision makers stand out from the rest. It is also really difficult to do by yourself. Even corporate despots, maverick generals, and you and I as individuals are well advised to ask around, before setting out to try Morethanism in a single scull. I am not a fan of most meetings, but to prioritize in a tough situation, or in one where there are conflicting opportunities, you are going to need meetings – and productive ones at that!

Identify the limiters, and you will make decisions better

So far we've concentrated mainly on the need to evaluate the upside and downside of various options before taking a decision. Indeed reward and risk assessment is fundamental to any choice situation.

But it is unrealistic to exclude the role of 'limiters' (factors that restrict or exclude options). Money is an obvious example. Whether it is a young couple looking at washing machines or a Russian oligarch window-shopping ocean-going yachts, there are always going to be budgets and price points. But Behavioural Economics has taught us that choice architecture is not purely shaped by financial considerations. Money is not the only limiter. Examples from a bizarrely wide spectrum could include:

- career choice: inadequate qualifications, lack of experience, shortage of attractive jobs;
- selecting an agency: lack of capacity, account conflict;
- choosing a holiday: no crèche facilities, no organized water sports;
- providing air cover: no aircraft carriers, or no planes to fly from the carriers you do have;
- enforcing the follow-on at cricket: strike bowlers unfit, fielders exhausted.

Downsides and limiters are different things. In golf a water hazard in front of a green is a downside (you might land in the water if you don't hit the perfect shot). A tree obstructing your shot to the green is a limiter (you have to take evasive action). Failure to recognize the difference can be expensive. The same forecast for continuous rain could be a downside for a F1 team (the forecast might not be accurate for the whole race time), a limiter for a cricket team (even if the rain stops, a wet ground will prevent an early resumption), or an upside for gardeners (no need to water). Factoring in limiters makes decision making more realistic. It prevents time being wasted on considering hypothetical options.

Why is it that marketing planning so often fails to make allowance for limiters? Probably the toxic mixture of natural optimism and fear of being fired for not being optimistic enough that bedevils much of marketing. If generals made the same mistake, they might win the odd battle – but a war? Unlikely!

Luck

We have talked about limiters – the factors that restrict or exclude options. Money – or rather affordability – is an obvious example for most of us. But the limiter is only one of the factors in decision theory that is neither an upside nor a downside on any option you might be looking at. Another massively important consideration is luck. My blog site is called 'Making Better Decisions, Better'. The first 'better' refers to how the decision turns out. The second to the quality of the decision-making process. The process can only really be judged by reason and logic. It was either a sound, well-thought-through way to arrive at a decision or it wasn't. But a decision can turn out to have been inspired, brilliant, farsighted etcetera, when in reality there was a large slice of luck in how things transpired. 'The best decision I ever made!' is frequently a thing of beauty only in retrospect. Equally a team of the talents working in perfect synergy can weigh up all the options, decide on the path that strikes the optimum balance between reward and risk, and come up with what turns out to have been a lemon.

Luck is often the decisive factor. Ask gamblers big and small – the ones who only place three or four bets a week, having factored in untold amounts of data and evidence, and the ones who have a consistent record of backing slow horses. Professional punters can see their 'certainties' lose, just as the little guy can win the Tote Trifecta. Luck will play a huge part.

You can be in the right place at the right time, and have your life turned round. But if you're in the wrong place, you might stop a bullet, or meet the drunken driver on the wrong side of the road.

You can be clever, calculating, organized and weigh the odds. But without luck, you can still lose out. If anyone knows how to be lucky, buy their book!

Go back if you have to

One weekend I was driving from my home in Reading to play in a golf match nearly 40 miles away in Surrey. As I sped down the M4 I realized I had left behind my sports bag, containing a change of clothing. I thought quickly, 'Hot day like this, I will really need a shower and a clean shirt for the prizegiving.' So I decided to turn tail at the next junction, and go back home. The false start cost me 20 minutes or so. But it was worth it. I still arrived on time, and, boy, did that shower feel good after four hours in the baking sun.

'Sitting on the fence' doesn't get a good press in traditional decision theory. Neither does going back. But why? We all take decisions (complicated ones, simple ones) on the basis of having worked out a series of options, and gone for the best balance between positive upside and negative downside. When I left home on that golf trip, I hadn't factored in the downside that I might have forgotten my bag. But once it was in the equation... time to recalibrate.

So often things change between making a decision and implementing it. If the new set of circumstances is not so favourable, by all means go back on the decision. Widely differing groups, like businessmen, football managers and politicians recognize the truth of this.

In business, strategists and marketers frequently make assumptions about competitive action (or lack of it). But if the competition launch a new product or slash prices, there's no point relentlessly sticking to a plan, when to change tack would be more advantageous.

A starting line up at the 3pm kick-off may have looked the strongest available, but an injury to a key player or two early goals by the opposition may completely change the scenario. Go back, and try something different.

'The situation has moved on'

Decision makers do not have the luxury of just standing behind the oche and aiming their darts. The situation moves on after you have made your decision, and you always have a moving target.

The best illustrations of this come from fast-moving encounters like sport and war. However cunning a cricket team's game plan, it all hangs on weather, the toss, what the opposition decide to do and how they perform. Cricket captains have to accept that none of those four factors are within their control – although they do have the resource to influence or mitigate #4.

Equally, generals cannot rely on forward planning. There are so many things that can change or go wrong – from unreliable allies to unfamiliar weaponry, and from our old friend the weather to enemy strategy and tactics. That is why chess is such a good analogy to the decision making journey. Look at the move by move reconstructions of the great encounters of history (for example Fischer vs Spassky in 1972 or Karpov vs Kasparov in 1985), and after almost every pair of moves, you can correctly say 'the situation has moved on'.

It is not enough for decision makers to adhere to the rules:

- set goals;
- best data and intelligence;
- frame – and if necessary keep on framing;
- structure the most viable options;
- identify upsides and downsides in each option;
- reward–risk analysis;
- make your decision.

You also have to implement the decision, and be prepared to navigate through all the ups, downs, ins and outs.

Students of decision making continue to watch avidly as the Coalition Government makes a whole series of strategic and tactical, long- and short-term decisions to deal with both the aftermath of the riots, and the challenges ahead.

If one cliché is 'the situation has moved on', another is 'knee-jerk reaction'. It is a little hard, I feel, to use this phrase to label all the Government's short-term responses. After the shock and brutality of burning high streets and looting gangs, it would be a poor Prime Minister who confined himself to wise words and medium-term plans.

Business emphasizes the importance of teamwork. Solus operating and thinking are frowned upon. There is little time to think. The calendar is filled with endless meetings – many of which are to rubber-stamp or question 'plans', which are usually undeliverable. Meetings are mostly not designed as forums for making decisions. Language often doesn't help. Being decisive isn't necessarily good. If you make decisions all the time – and half of them are wrong – are you 'decisive'?

Blog extract

Plan B: the semantics of a cliche. You do need a backup

It is now a commonplace to hear critics of the Coalition's economic policies saying, 'they never had a Plan B'. Presumably they mean that the new Government decided on an immediate debt reduction programme without considering other options.

Personally I doubt that. After so many years out of power (14 years for the Conservatives, 96 for the Liberal Democrats) it wasn't exactly the obvious decision to risk alienating virtually the whole population with cuts in their standard of living.

The policies announced by Cameron, Osborne and Clegg were pretty much the only sensible solution to the economic disaster which confronted them. The Coalition must have calculated that the unpopularity that lay ahead was more than compensated for by the rightness of the decision, and the hope that drastic pruning would eventually produce a healthier tree.

But no one back in early summer 2010 was predicting meltdown in the eurozone. The Bank of England's forecast for the UK economy was very modest growth. Over and above the disastrous situation faced by our biggest trading partners in continental Europe, we have seen a serious rise in inflation, spurred not least by an explosion in fuel prices.

So now what will the Government do? Surely they are now working on, and will shortly unveil, Plan B. Not the alternative Plan B, but the sequential Plan B. Everyone who makes a big decision realizes that it is a journey, not a single step. Generals, transitional governments, CEOs, even football and rugby managers, and cricket captains need a follow-up plan if the big decision doesn't work out quite as planned.

Cameron is talking about easing credit restrictions and stimulating housing starts. Osborne admitted yesterday that debt reduction is running a year behind schedule. Lack of growth will cause further economic problems, unless action is taken. Soaring unemployment has major political and social, as well as economic, consequences. Youth unemployment threatens the validity of the country's educational strategy as school and college leavers join their predecessors on benefits.

The Plan B designed to put things right – or at least setting them on a more positive course – must be on the stocks now. When announced, will it be an admission of failure, or a demonstration of sensible decision making? We all know how important it is to weigh up pros, cons, and all available data and factors before coming to a serious decision. What is sometimes forgotten is that the making of a decision is just the first step. It then has to be implemented and managed. Plan B is part of that management.

Difficult decisions

'It's going to be a difficult decision' is one of those phrases that both betrays the speaker's anguish, and communicates what might well be bad news to the recipient. I asked Sir Nick Young of the Red Cross about the most difficult decision he'd had to make:

"Making 500 people redundant. I absolutely hated that, because they were just people who had given everything to the organization, who believed in the organization, were passionate about the organization, had done nothing wrong, but they just had to go; we just had to save £14 million. And that was a ghastly, ghastly, ghastly time.

I asked Colin Moynihan of the BOA the same question:

"To decide to seek a settlement to the dispute with LOCOG over a lasting sports legacy fund rather than pursue it through the Courts; that was a tough decision. Seeking a settlement was right at that time to enable us to focus on the athletes, but I knew we were right on the dispute and I knew we should have seen it through in the interests of sport.

We actually use the phrase 'difficult decision' in two different ways:

- It's a tough decision; ie I or someone else is going to get hurt or lose out.
- It's difficult to make this decision; ie the problems are hard to solve, the reward–risk analysis is not easy to do, or it's tricky to choose between two courses of action.

Should we be looking to make decisions less difficult – in both senses? Or is the tough decision and the taxing decision process par for the course if we start to take decision making seriously? I honestly believe the latter is true. As HL Mencken said, 'For every complex problem there is an answer that is clear, simple, and wrong.'

For instance, you don't need abnormal acuity or great powers of deduction to do any of the following:

- score an open goal (literally or figuratively);
- accept a job offer to work in congenial conditions for less hours and more money;
- return a smile from an attractive person;
- accept a free lunch;
- agree to take on an assignment or contract without a pitch or competitive tender.

On the other hand:

- If the goal is that open, could it be a trap or lure?
- Might the 'dream' job have strings attached?
- Is he or she smiling at you out of sheer joie de vivre, or could it be a calculated move? See 'open goal' above.
- Now come on, you know about free lunches!
- Might have been a good idea to be more cautious about taking on that contract. Why didn't they go through the normal competitive process?

So the quick 'not a difficult decision' can easily become: 'it's quite a difficult decision really', as soon as you start looking at possible downsides along with the obvious upside. Furthermore all good decision-making process was designed to be rigorous – therefore taxing and difficult. Weighing up combinations of upsides and downsides is never going to be easy. You are not just looking at calculating reward and risk. You also have to aim off for the difference between more and less reliable data. It is not enough to predict the respective winning potential of your side versus the enemy, or your horse versus the favourite... you also have to second-guess the weather!

Blog extract

Resignation is one of the biggest decisions

Sir Paul Stephenson hit the headlines when he resigned as Commissioner of the Met after only two years in the job. It was then the turn of Assistant Commissioner John Yates – another very prominent policeman. Added to the top-level resignations from News International and News Corp, the fall-out from the phone-hacking scandal has been spectacular already.

It is a commonplace in British politics for the opposition to call for highly placed individuals to 'consider their position'. But however shrill the call, it is relatively unusual for people to tender their resignation this quickly.

As far as I know, there's not a lot to guide the aspiring resigner, apart from tailor-made and inevitably expensive legal advice. I did however come across a practical website, called **www.i-resign.com**, which has some practical advice, for example: 'If you're leaving in strained or bad circumstances, resist the temptation to badmouth and let off steam.'

In decision science terms, the big question (and I am talking generally, and not addressing any particular case) has to be: what are you trying to achieve by resigning?

- Is it expiation – making amends for presumed errors by sacrificing your job?
- Is it throwing in the towel – putting distance between yourself and a mess?
- Is it a quest for sympathy?
- Is it clearing the decks for taking on something more congenial, better paid, less stressful or nearer home?

In many elevated circles it is also potentially career-limiting, not to say financially costly. The trouble with resignation is that it is always open to misrepresentation. Friendly people can say or write in one way. Enemies or critics can impute presumed motives:

- 'He did the honourable thing.'
- 'He threw himself on his sword.'
- 'He went before he was pushed.'
- 'There's more to it than meets the eye.'
- 'It's as good as admitting it.'

One thing is for sure: resignation is neither easy nor comfortable. Of all the categories of personal decision making, it is one of the most difficult. Sometimes the weighing up of upsides and downsides can leave the decision maker feeling the best upside is not that great, and all the options have potentially huge downsides.

Decisions and journeys

Every significant decision is a journey, not a single step. Without getting too metaphysical, a decision journey starts well before you know what decision you are going to take. It starts in the planning stage – usually with a problem. If we define 'problem' as the difference between where you are and where you want to be, that problem could actually be an opportunity.

Solving the problem – and considering the options – is the prelude to seeking the preferred way forward. That's when you are ready to take the decision itself. The journey doesn't end there. It continues into implementation, where changes of tack or more serious adjustments may be necessary to navigate towards your goal.

Talking of journeys and navigation, I remember a few years ago when I had a new woman in my life. We travelled together. She led. I followed. The whole experience gave me a new perspective on life – particularly on the vexed issue of communication between the sexes. You don't have to be a 'women from Venus, men from Mars' activist to believe that in business as in personal life, men and women talk to each other in fundamentally different ways.

Men: how many times have you alienated a female colleague by mistakenly using a male-to-male debating ploy, such as 'Which bit of "Do it my way" don't you understand?' Women: can you remember the look on the face of your male colleague when you told him that his breakthrough idea was clearly based on something you painstakingly explained to him six weeks ago?

My new girlfriend was different. She came up with one word that solved inter-sex communication. When a problem arose, she didn't go in for womantalk ('I can't concentrate if you're shouting at me'), or even mantalk ('Why didn't you tell me to turn right before we hit the dual carriageway?'). She simply used the word 'recalculating'. No blame attached. No rancour. No 'I told you so'. No 'It's your fault'. Just 'recalculating'. She didn't criticize my mistake. She made a positive attempt to find a solution. Pure behavioural economics.

It works in the car. Or at home. It would work in the office. Or seeing a decision through. Well done SatNav.

'All the emotional intelligence of a lamp post'

Let's fast forward from a perfectly executed decision process.

The fiendishly difficult problem has been solved.

The best possible option has been chosen after carefully weighing upsides and downsides, risks and rewards.

We have a decision, and the key team members are flat out working on the implementation plan.

All that remains today is for our dear leader to announce the decision within the organization and to the media. This isn't warfare, so it's perfectly all right to lift the security blanket we have all maintained for weeks.

And what does he do? He gets it completely wrong. Hence the unflattering description of his performance in the headline.

Why does this happen so often? Why do governments and organizations announce perfectly sound decisions in a way that alienates and grates? Three main reasons, I believe:

1 Decision making is tough and time-consuming.
   Tired and relieved can unfortunately give way to downbeat and underprepared when it comes to preparing and delivering the communication. This is a trap that people as diverse as politicians and those at the top of sporting organizations often fall into. The demeanour that carried the day in the smoked-filled room can look distinctly unimpressive at the press conference. Tony Blair understood it, and flourished. Gordon Brown was the exact opposite.

2 Many leaders quite simply overestimate their communications skills. What passes muster with colleagues, family and friends can come across poorly on TV and radio, or under pressure from a journalist. The unfortunate Tony Hayward was a recent example. It wasn't so much what he said about BP's response to the Gulf of Mexico oil spill, as how he said it that caused his downfall.

3 It is easy to forget how much damage can be done by non-powerful people if a decision that affects them is put across in an unsympathetic or alienating way. All that is needed to turn the non-powerful into effective opponents and protesters is a sense of injustice and the oxygen of publicity to fan the flames.

So, to all the cerebral, process and analytic expertise that make a great decision maker, we need to add the plausibility and communications skills of an accomplished spokesperson.

'Send three and fourpence, we're going to a dance'

The bizarre message above was the probably apocryphal corruption of a First World War signal that should have read: 'Send reinforcements. We're going to advance'.

Incidentally, how much was three and fourpence? Answer – 16p, about half what you'd now need to use the loo at Paddington on your way to the party! Only the over-forties in the United Kingdom (UK) remember the introduction of decimal currency (on 15 February 1971). The under-forties and the rest of the world's population struggle to understand how we could have ever bothered with 20 shillings to the pound, and 12 pence to the shilling.

Miscommunication is a major enemy of good decision making. Clarity is everything – and we all understand that. So how do wires get so crossed, so often? I think e-mail has a lot to answer for. We completely rely on it. But if you think about it, e-mail works differently from any kind of mass communication we used before:

- It is not basically designed for a conversation (like a meeting or telephone call).

- It is a convenient way for me to ask a question while at the same time giving the answer – or at least my spin on that answer.

- If you and I enter into a two-way e-mail dialogue, we will be as concerned to register our own point of view as to find out what the other thinks. So it's also a filing system.

- Pre-internet, we used to write letters to each other – often for the same reason. But the pace of mail delivery determined a much longer time frame – usually too slow to be described as a dialogue. We simply had to meet or talk on the phone if we wanted to move things forward in real time.

Texting is subtly different, because of the restriction on the number of characters you can use. It's also – even in a business context – more intimate. An exchange of SMS is like a version of a telephone call, with the contributions from either side staggered for convenience.

So why do I say that e-mail often leads to miscommunication? Mainly because it is a talking medium, not a listening medium. If I am more concerned to tell you what I think, than listen to what you think, that's a recipe for those crossed wires we looked at earlier.

Not a great outcome in a two-person dialogue. But it can be a disaster if participants in an important decision-making process are using e-mail to disseminate and compare views – which happens all the time.

Mistakes, misunderstanding and miscommunications arising from such situations will cost a lot more than three and fourpence to resolve.

Highlights on decision making from the interviews

Daniel Topolski is most famous for his remarkable record as Coach of the Oxford crew in the Boat Race. He led them to 12 wins out of the 15 races when he coached, including an unprecedented 10 wins in a row from 1976. He is also an author, broadcaster and traveller.

Topolski made an unusual admission:

"I'm not a good decision maker on the whole. I tend to leave things quite a lot. I tend to mull around something for quite a while. But I do and can make very fast decisions if I have to. So, for instance, where we are here – in this house – I walked in and I said, yes, we'll have this. It just seemed that we knew we had to do it quickly otherwise we'd lose it. We just had to make it happen. So a decision like that, you know, absolutely; go ahead, go for it.

A decision, for instance, to go to Africa, drop everything and spend a year travelling around Africa and maybe do a book, take photographs, that sort of thing – yes, that's what I'm going to do; I'll do that as well. I booked a ticket and a date and then thought about where I'd go. The rest of it was just going as I pleased and spending the time where I wanted to. But I decided I'd go.

Those sorts of decisions, decisions on a practical level, I'll make very easily. Am I going to go six o'clock tomorrow morning for that particular part of my journey or am I going to stay here? Decisions like do I start a family, do I get married, I put it off. I don't decide things like that. In terms of which route to take career-wise. Hopeless. Hopeless.

Fast, decisive people I'm a bit suspicious of because, it's 50 per cent you'll get it wrong, and I'd rather a doctor who took his time with a decision than a doctor who said, yes, that's what we're going to do. I'll put it in tomorrow and we'll get that all done. Same thing in business, same thing in the city. You know, these guys who are gambling with our money in the banks – fast decision making, high risk – do we respect them? I'm not sure we do. So that's highly prized – a decision maker at the top of business. I don't know that I'm all that moved by it. I would prefer to take my time.

For me, the Germans, the Japanese, these are all people who have a kind of flat hierarchy, and they take advice from the shop floor. So their decision making is really well informed and they base their whole business ethic on it whereas we have this

thing of I'm the boss and I've got to make this decision.
I think it's a little bit to do with class. It's officer class,
and we tend to move that into the business world.
The guy who's in charge is the guy who makes all the decisions.
The buck stops at me.

Nigel Jones CEO of London advertising agency Publicis told me something similar: 'Don't try and take a big decision or reply to a crucial e-mail without sleeping on it'. He said

'I've done exactly what I did in chess, which is, I want to move
fast, I want to be able to do 50 things a day, not just one.
You've got to find a way of thinking that allows you to do that,
which is robust, so I have this sort of gut-feel-aesthetic-step-in-
the-dark-and-then-backfill approach to life, and it gets me
where I've got to so far. I'm not saying it's perfect, and I'm sure
I make a lot of mistakes, but I think more times I'm right than
wrong.'!

My interview with Nigel was remarkable. Absolutely nobody else has described the decision process visually (see Chapter 9). Of all the people whose books I've read, and all the people I've spoken to, he is the only one.

The person who was nearest to it is Ellis Downes, the gynaecologist, who says he probably conducts 15 or 16 procedures a week. He told me that he instinctively knows there is going to be one case in every week – 'it's never more than that, really' – which isn't what he was expecting to see, or presents differently, as they say in medicine. In other words, he's done the scan, he's looked at the medical history, he may well have treated the woman before, and therefore he says, 'I have probably 98 per cent certainty that when I open somebody up I know what I'm going to find, and I can do something about it. But just occasionally something unexpected occurs'.

I shared this with Nigel. 'Well, that is actually how I feel,' he said. 'I feel that about briefs – if you gave me a brief now that you'd written last night, I would read it and I would have a gut feel. It would be an aesthetic gut feel: is that beautiful or ugly?'

Ellis Downes told me:

> Even experienced doctors make mistakes, and other team members will know enough to know when something isn't right. I always remember that although not every decision I make (and I probably make a hundred every working day) is difficult, it's of monumental importance to my patient and her family. Medicine is different to other fields in that doing nothing is not an option.

Ellis told me that decisions in medicine can have dramatic financial and geographical biases. The same gynaecological intervention has a frequency in Dallas/Fort Worth of 200 compared to 19 in Leeds/Bradford – with approximately the same population. Equally the resuscitation limit in the UK is two hours. It is very much less in Zambia.

Sir Jeremy Greenstock is a retired diplomat, who had a lengthy stint as Ambassador to the United Nations (UN). He told me:

> I didn't consciously get in front of the mirror and say, 'Am I a decision maker? What is decision making?' If you're doing what is needed in your career, and you're moving somewhere, you gradually realize that you're more capable of making decisions on the issues that hit your screen as you move along than people junior to you who have less experience, or than you were 10 years earlier or 20 years earlier. You look at your colleagues or your opposite numbers who have similar experience, and you make judgements about whether they can make decisions or whether they have to refer, because you're looking for competitive advantage the whole time. And my career was in a competitive profession, and therefore you make judgements about your opposite numbers as you would on the sports field as to whether you can get the ball past him or go in a different direction where he won't be able to follow. Or if you meet, as I did in Sergei Lavrov in the Security Council, a very formidable fullback who's capable of destroying your forward movement, you find some other way of outmanoeuvering him.

Bishop Urquhart told me:

> Theories of decision-making are, as that marvellous sociologist Zygmunt Bauman would say, 'to get from complicated to complex', because most organizations, and particularly ones like the Church of England, are overcomplicated. I think, actually, our legislature now in Parliament, is overcomplicated. We have too much legislation, making it too complicated. But what human beings are good at, and I would say as God made us, is working with complexity. So, variety, creativity, lateral thinking, all these sorts of things. So, I'm looking for effective decision making in a complex system, which is not complicated by unnecessary complication.

I asked General Sir Mike Jackson, former head of the British Army, whether he taught decision making as such when he lectured at Staff College.

> Not when you put it in capital letters like that. It's endemic in soldiering, but it's not looked at as a separate skill,competence, or whatever trendy word is in at the moment. The military way of approaching a problem is coldly analytical, but includes the decision, but it's not just the decision. It's the analysis of the situation, the emergence, unless you're very lucky, of more than one course of action, and they will have their advantages and their disadvantages, and it's weighing that in the balance, coming to the judgement, coming to the decision, and then implementing. Now, if all of that wraps into the two words 'decision making', as you wish to define it, that's fine. But much stress is placed on the analysis which leads to the best decision available, depending on time. Time, of course, is going to be very often at a great premium. Sometimes it won't be, but it is the whole piece and the plan that then emerges from the chosen course of action. The better intelligence we have, the better the decision we're all likely to make. It's one of the factors which you will consider as part of the analysis. You'll be looking at ground, you'll be looking at relative troop strengths, and that's partly intelligence; enemy intentions; the time you've got.

Again, time is a means if you use ends, ways or means as part of your analysis, which we do. What's the end? What's the objective? What means do I have? And then, of course, the art of leadership is the way in which you apply the means. And so intelligence, of course, plays into that.

Sir Tom Hughes-Hallett, CEO of Marie Curie told me about some of the most important decisions he has made:

> What I found was a remarkable organization with a large number of staff, 5,000, utterly committed to what we were doing. We weren't robust financially, and with quite a wide spread of activities – as well as our nursing service, the largest provider of hospital care, £1 billion on education and training, and running a scientific research institute – and not raising enough money.
>
> I couldn't work out why we employed quite as many nurses as we did. I then became slightly City-like. So I restructured fund raising, as a result of which a number of directors chose to leave, like, all of them, and I became director of fund raising as well as chief executive. And I've done that in every area of the organization except for one. So once I'd sorted fund raising out, our head of Care decided to leave, after he and I had talked about the way forwards, and I then ran Care for two years.
>
> So I really got my hands dirty and improved the organization from the strong position it was already in. And we now have 1,000 less staff than when I joined, we provide three times as much care, and we raise over twice as much money. So it is a dramatically different organization. In that way, it's much more efficient. It's also more focused. I got rid of education and training, and I closed down our scientific research institute, which actually was sold yesterday. So it's now a much more focused charity, true, and it just does one thing now, which is giving people the chance to die where they want to and looking after them. And we look after 55 per cent of all people who die at home, of cancer. And now of all terminal diseases, so we've stopped being cancer-only, because I thought it was

unethical. So I approached the trustees and said, will you lift the restriction in the articles, so that we can care for everyone? There was a time and a season.

Those decisions at the beginning were lonely, difficult. It's not easy to reduce numbers in a charity, because in the City you've got a cheque book. You can pay people off. You can't here. And, almost without exception, that has been painful. But after about year four, about 2004, I stopped making decisions on my own.

I made another decision that was very countercyclical in the charity world in terms of behaviour. I started promoting people. And charities have this weird habit of going outside to appoint their most senior people, like me, and then are surprised when their senior staff aren't very motivated. So if you look at our board now, they are all promoted from within the organization – with two or three exceptions. So the board's nine, and six are home-grown and pretty bloody passionate as a result.

And some one-liners.

Ellen MacArthur: 'Before the voyage we thought about all possible problems / disasters... You have to make hundreds of decisions a day at sea, but you do it by processing information.'

Colin Moynihan tells the story of an unusual decision made by his political mentor Earl Jellicoe:

> George Jellicoe was at the heart of the Conservative Party, he was a great sportsman in his youth, an extraordinary skier and was one of the founders of the SAS at Churchill's request. His decision at the end of a brave and well decorated war (the Second World War) was to throw his watch away. He never wore his watch again, and yet knew exactly what time it was. He felt the war years had been determined by precision timing, and his watch represented that, so he decided never to wear a watch, and yet knew exactly what time it was. He had a hugely full diary and a very busy life, and was never late.

Karl Gregory of Match.com:

> It's the most important decision you're ever going to make in your life. When you ask people, what are the big decisions you made in life? They all say, my house, my job, my car ... but actually, when you think about it, it's finding your soul mate and deciding to have kids with them and going through that whole experience. It beats everything else.

And of course this decision – almost more than any other – has to be mutual!

Chapter Five
It's a matter of time: the magic number 60
It's vital to know how long you have got

I hear a distant voice in my ear: 'Before we start this section, let's go through the minutes of the last meeting. And can I just make sure that you, David, are happy to do the minutes of today's session.'

Mr Chairman, I just wish it was minutes.

Our global obsession with meetings is not costing us minutes. It's taking hours out of our day, days out of our week and weeks out of our year. If we allow for weekends, public holidays, annual leave and days off sick, we probably have an effective working year of 220 days. Let's suppose that on average we are involved in one meeting lasting an hour, and one lasting an hour and a half every day. That is 550 hours in the year spent in meetings – more than four complete working months! From the department of invented, but plausible, statistics I believe that 50 per cent of all meetings take the participants no closer to a decision, and that more than 60 per cent of the people hours are wasted.

I blame a meeting culture that gives us all the illusion of 'moving things on', when so often meetings serve no useful purpose, and absorb billions of people hours that otherwise might have been productive.

For me a meeting is an intrinsically low-tech phenomenon, born out of the gregariousness of *Homo sapiens*. I see it as generated by social instincts, not commercial ones. We like getting together to chat!

Time is relative

Decision making is all about time. When we are confident, we have plenty of time to take a decision – any number of decisions in fact. Take driving a car. Or getting to work or school. Or walking along crowded pavements. Or cooking. Or playing a sport we are practised in. If the activity and the environment are familiar – no problem, and you don't need to build in time for endless micro-decisions. You are on auto-pilot.

This is equally true if you have been trained to make quick decisions – in 60 seconds, or much less – as part of your job.

We tend to assess options in terms of best upside consistent with least-worst downside. But sometimes there is little obvious upside, and you have to vote for the least unattractive downside. It is probably just as well that many examples of this kind of choice are faced by people with good training and long experience: soldiers, police, doctors, paramedics, lifeboat crews, the triage nurse in Accident and Emergency (A&E). There is often very little time to think, and absolutely no chance to intellectualize. But the fact that these sorts of decision have to be made quickly doesn't make them any less tough.

But if you are in a 60-minute meeting, you can plan in advance to make it as productive as possible. Advance planning is even more practical if the project time is 60 hours, 60 days or 60 weeks. These are bigger projects, but more room for failure. With longer time frames, there is time to plan. But it will not work unless there is a mix of linear and lateral thinking – and the process is managed through. It is also helpful to profile team members to make sure that the team is complementary and functional (see Chapter 6).

Kevin Murray, Chairman of Bell Pottinger, has written a book called *The Language of Leaders* (2011). He interviewed 60 Chief Executive Officers (CEOs) and Chairmen, and was pushing them on their communication style. He ended up with about 500,000 words of transcript, and he did frequency checks on the words they used, and the two commonest words were 'speed' and 'agility'.

These are people in the fortunate position of being able to call on armies of lieutenants. They have access to all the resource, data and intelligence money can buy. But they still feel that speed and agility are crucial. In decision making, as in the rest of their business lives, time is critical.

60 seconds or less

Fast decision making is a function of training and experience – whether it's a matter of life and death, or just routine. From soldiers to fire-fighters, from air traffic controllers to triage nurses, from the police to referees, time is a luxury that simply isn't there.

> I opened the cockpit door and I walked in the cockpit, and of course there was absolute chaos. There's a bell ringing, and red lights flashing, and, oh God, and he was pushing his seat out and saying, get in, get into the seat. And I thought, well, there's too much noise. First thing, cancel the noise from the bell.

Paddy Eckersley, then a Captain with Saudi Airlines. He was flying as a passenger from Jeddah to Casablanca, when one port engine blew up and the other caught fire. His boss was flying the aircraft, and called Paddy to the flight deck to take over. Paddy dealt brilliantly with the emergency because he has been meticulously trained. This is the same for everyone expected to decide in seconds or less. A soldier interviewed on radio about the actions that earned him a military cross said simply, 'all the training kicked in'.

60 minutes

The average time for a meeting. We can streamline business decision making by making meetings super-productive. The numerous 60 minutes slots we have in our daily and weekly schedules deserve to be given more attention and planning, and to have much more useful outcomes than is often the case.

Meetings, Bloody Meetings: title of Video Arts training film, starring John Cleese (1976). A memorable training programme ridiculing pointless, badly run meetings. It is still there on YouTube, and sadly just as relevant.

60 hours or more

The winning formula: the journey – not the single step. Mapping a decision process, and managing it over the life of a project. Often significant projects start their life as an issue to be looked at over the weekend, or when you are given an outline brief on Monday, and the boss says, 'let's talk about it on Thursday, when you have had a chance to think about it'. In all organizations there needs to be the capacity to assess quite big decisions, without having the time needed to do all the necessary consultations, with limited opportunity to analyse available data, and with no possibility of doing any new research. The 60 hours time span is usually long enough to take a view, but insufficient to make a firm decision.

Paddy Eckersley's emergency (which was both a 60 seconds and 60 minutes challenge)

So I went to sit in the back, in the upper deck. I didn't want to sit up in the front because I had to do the flight back, I might as well have a rest. The idea was that my boss, the most senior Captain, wanted to go to spend a couple of nights in Casablanca, so he didn't have to come back with the flight. That was his idea. As we're doing the take-off roll, there was this loud bang, and the airplane sort of shook, and I thought, oh, we have a tire burst, because we had a full load, very heavy, full fuel, full passenger load. Then he came on the tannoy, the intercom, and said, 'Paddy, come up to the cockpit', and I thought, what's going on? So I got up, of course this was my boss, all those things in your head.

The cockpit door is locked at take-off and landing, but I opened the door and I walked in the cockpit. There is a warning bell that sounds when you have a fire or something in the engine, so I leaned over, cancelled the bell, and I said to him,

'Why do you want to change the seat?' And he said, 'Get in, just get in', and he got out and just pushed past me. Oh God, this is a no-no. You don't change in an emergency, and I didn't know what was going on. So I got into the seat, strapped myself in. The First Officer, an American, was flying the aircraft at that stage, because my boss had just unstrapped himself and got out of his seat.

I noticed he was turning right. In Jeddah, we had three runways, and we were taking off on the left runway, they all face North–South, and facing North, of course, the sea is to your left. And he was turning right, and if you're turning right you're turning towards the hills ... We were still climbing, around 300 or 400 feet off the ground.

I said to him, 'I've got control, declare an emergency.' They hadn't even declared an emergency. I had a quick scan and saw that I had no indication from two engines on the left hand side, they appeared to be both dead, and the airplane was very difficult to control, because the flaps were down about 15 degrees. You could only get them that far, they wouldn't move any further. So I told the flight engineer, another American, to start dumping fuel. The next thing I knew, the senior Captain was back in the cockpit standing behind us, watching what's going on. He said, 'You can't dump fuel, you'll be dumping over the King's palace.' I said, 'Look, I don't care, dump. You know we're too heavy, we can't climb, we've only got two engines.'

Because they hadn't declared an emergency, the tower didn't know what the hell was going on. They were watching us turn right, and they had heard the bang, the people in the tower told us afterwards. They could see fumes, smoke, and so on coming out, so they knew there was a problem. So when I put the headphones on I heard the tower man say, 'Okay, do whatever you have to do, declare an emergency. What is your emergency?' I said 'We have two engines out' – we have our engines, one, two, three, four, starting from the left. Number two engine had more or less exploded. What had happened is the turbine, the main turbine, had expanded and touched the side walls of the engine casing, and that had caused it to disintegrate into three major parts. One part had gone into the fuselage just below the first class passengers, into the cargo hold. A second had gone into the loom of wires that run across the front edge of the wing, carrying all the information from the different engines to the cockpit, and bits had gone into the number one engine. The third piece had gone out through the top, just missed the fuel tank, and gone up into the sky and Boeing worked out how fast this piece was travelling from the weight of the piece of iron they recovered, and because it buried itself 11′ down in the soil. This was after going up into the sky, and then coming straight down through the roof of a little villa down by the seaside. It had penetrated a concrete roof and a concrete floor. Fortunately there was nobody in the building.

We went through the usual emergency drills and emergency check-up and so on, and managed to dump enough fuel to get us light enough for me to make a final approach. On the final stretch, I couldn't get the nose gear down, because there were not enough hydraulics, because the hydraulic system was damaged. I thought, we'll just have to land with no nose gear. That's not itself a serious problem, but we couldn't get all our flaps down, and we came in at a very high speed. Anyway we managed to isolate the two damaged engines and landed safely. The whole incident had taken 15 minutes or so.

No fire, no more problems, and then everybody out. We were grounded and told not to leave town and so on, with an enquiry coming up. I climbed up the stairs to see, and the hole was so big I could put my whole body through the wing hole and have a look around. For some reason it just missed the fuel tank, otherwise you'd just have a ball of fire, it would have just gone up.

Just shortly after that, an El Al plane, the same model of 747, also lost two engines on takeoff. The Captain lost power on one side, and had this symmetry problem. The live engine pushes the airplane around, and if you don't get it in control soon enough it's going to just flip over. This chap, unfortunately, went into a block of flats in Amsterdam, and blew up. Fortunately it was a cargo plane, otherwise it would have been a lot worse. I think there was something wrong with the flywheel on the engines, and they sorted it out after that.

It's funny, people asked me what was foremost in my mind during the emergency. I think there were two things. Number one, I don't want to die. Number two, I was worried about what my peers would say – all the pilots I worked with – if I screwed up. It's weird, just those two things. At that stage I didn't think about my family or anything. I wasn't thinking of the passengers. I had 400 passengers on board, but not once did they come into my mind or my thinking. It's something that's bothered me. I've never been able to explain why. But afterwards, then all these things bother you.

David Jones of Havas on fast decisions

He told me:

"Fast decisions are critical. Companies who make decisions faster do better, even if they've made the wrong decisions. Because they actually then make the right one subsequently, quicker than the companies who sit around. The speed of decision-making is absolutely critical.

The decision-making I thought was very good and got this completely, was around the Galliano scandal with Christian Dior. The President, Sidney Toledano acted the second the Galliano thing hit. He fired him immediately. He didn't sit there and go hey, he's a big, famous fashion designer, we may need him, let's see how this plays out. He just went straight ahead and said, we do not tolerate behaviour like that in our company, he is fired. He is gone, and it stopped. You have to respond instantly now, because it's really a real-time world.

I in decision-making, you should definitely use facts and data, but don't wait until you've got 100 per cent of the data.

Simon Calver of Lovefilm told me about fast decisions and how important they can be

"I had a meeting with Jeff Bezos (President and CEO of Amazon, who own Lovefilm) where he turned around and said, look, we've got two decisions now. We either get on with it or we go home. And he said, I'm just not a go home sort of guy, so let's just get on with it. Right? And that was it, bang, millions of dollars worth of investment quickly done, 45 minute meeting. This is what we're going to commit to, this is how we're going to make it happen because this is how I see the pieces fitting together.

I've also learned that the right decision at the wrong time actually is the wrong decision, if I'm not able to execute it. In 2005 we launched a digital download service which was a download, not a streaming service. A third of all people who downloaded it called customer services because they had a bad experience. That was a great idea at the wrong time. Broadband infrastructure wasn't there, technology wasn't there, people's PCs weren't there in terms of how that worked.

In any organization, you need to have a clear structure for understanding how decisions are made, and therefore what are the degrees of freedom for each manager, so that they can feel confident. If you don't provide that framework and it's a sort of political mish-mash of decision making, you will never have efficiency in an organization. Large successful American corporations tend to be run by one or two people that make the decisions. They then have a swathe of intelligent people who help make the decisions so they can be very swift, very decisive about what they do.

There is a certain set of American senior and middle management who are incredibly smart. Ivy League educated. MBA-type people. They have probably had one of the smartest educations in general business. They are comfortable at a middle and senior management level within large organizations, driving the data, and using it in a way that European managers don't. You know, the stereotypical European manager, who thinks, 'I've reached this level, I don't need to get in the data any more.'

In American companies the focus on metrics, the transparency around metrics and decision making is absolutely critical. The managers understand exactly what is happening, and have huge intellectual curiosity as to why. I have really good people around me, we can be egalitarian, and roll up our sleeves. We can look at the data together. We can make it happen. That is how decision making works in larger American companies that I've worked with, and it's the same in each of them. It all makes the Americans swift and effective decision makers, which is important overall – especially so in people decisions, where you have to move fast.

Daniel Topolski, the rowing coach, told me why he is suspicious of fast decisions

My role as a coach involves decision making based on evidence. Some of that evidence I have basically created (by setting tests, time trials and so on). Also I've created the theatre in which the evidence can be played out. All the time you're trying to build the confidence of your group and their own confidence in themselves to perform. You're giving them the arena in which their motivation can blossom, and how they can develop. But it's down to them to prove themselves. My decision-making process is from the experience that I have with those people and what I've had in the past. So the longer you're at it, the more informed your decision is by the end of it.

I shared two thoughts with Daniel – the 'Early Decision' trap, and the concept of a decision being a journey:

I agree. Big decisions, complex decisions, have to be journeys. They can't simply be one point in time. In a way I like the decisions to be almost taken out of my hands. I like the decisions to emerge from the experience we're going through, rather than me having to make a decision. I think people who make fast decisions very often make the wrong decision because it's a moment in time. And they don't give it time... they don't give it time to develop because you might make a different decision further down the line. But the point is when do you make the decision? I mean, you can go on saying it's still too early, it's still too early and in the end you don't make the decision.

I don't regret not being a fast decision maker, but I can make decisions quickly when I have that gut reaction. I don't make pro's and con's lists, but I do like to have a good hunch if something's right. So I will seek advice and I'm not ashamed or embarrassed to ask people's advice and get their thoughts and have a joint effort in making decisions. Because so much of the stuff that's been written about decision making ends with the decision having been made, whereas there isn't an important decision of which the acid test is not the implementation and what you learn from it.

A moment of indecision

It is a cliché: 'a moment of indecision cost him the chance of a lifetime / an evening with a beautiful girl / the winning goal / his life'.

If you are someone whose working life is judged by acting or reacting under pressure (in one of the armed or emergency services maybe, or driving or flying, or even as a referee or umpire), you are trained to avoid moments of indecision. If it's a matter of life or death (or if it just seems that way with 50,000 spectators baying at a referee), you simply cannot afford those moments. Even checking with technology, a fourth official or whatever counts as a decision. So does asking a fellow crew member for an opinion. But you cannot delay the decision any longer than it takes to check or ask. Indecision in those circumstances may be figuratively – or even literally – fatal.

But for the rest of us, in situations where there is time to consider and think things over, a moment or two (or even an hour or three, or a day or several), will do no harm. Don't make a decision until you're ready. There is the familiar checklist:

- Are we sure what the opportunity or problem is?
- Do we know how we are going to capitalize on it or solve it?
- Is this one for me to tackle on my own – or is it a team task?
- Have we got the right team on the case?
- Is there enough data and information?
- Can we get more if needs be?
- Have we explored all meaningful options?
- Have we looked at the upsides and downsides of each?
- Have we carried out an objective risk assessment?
- Have we also given weight to gut feel?
- Do we know how we are going to communicate the decision and implement it?

Taking time out to make the best possible decision in the best possible way is not indecision. It is sensible and logical. It is vital not to worry about being seen to be indecisive when you are fully geared up to spend what time you have in optimizing the decision. It might of course be prudent to keep team members, family, partner or whoever in the loop. As we saw in Chapter 4, we are almost certainly going to need buy-in to whatever big decision we make, so that it can become effectively a mutual decision.

Experience is a strange ally. Sometimes it tells you to get on with it, because you've seen a similar situation before, and you know what to do. On other occasions it tells you to take your time.

Experience also tells you that over-promising about the outcome of a decision can be as misguided as rushing it. The Chancellor and his advisers must have been tempted to sugar the pill in the 2011 Autumn Statement. The Labour leadership must have wanted to endorse the protest strikes that followed. It would have been easy for the surgeon who operated on my knee last winter to promise alleviation of all pain and problems.

I'm pleased that they all did what they did. Being realistic about outcomes is as important as making big decisions well.

Are there decisions we are happy to talk about – and others we would rather forget?

When you start taking the subject of decision making seriously, it's easy to look for logic and rationality, where none exists. That's because we are human and emotional. We know that emotion can sometimes lead to our judgement being impulsive and flawed. As with most things in life, we are keener to talk about the decisions that have worked out well. What about the decisions we regret? What about the involuntary decisions? What about the decisions that fail? There are numerous activities where we simply have to make one decision after another:

- driving a car;
- conducting a negotiation;
- playing any sport;
- gambling.

Not all the 'mini-decisions' we make are going to work out. On the law of averages, they simply can't. We just have to use our experience and instincts to be as sure as we can that the mistakes won't be disastrous.

Take the 'fork in the road' moment (whether it is literal or figurative). We have to go left or right – because standing still and staying put isn't a valid option. There is often little enough evidence to go on. We don't suddenly become a bad person by making what turns out to be the wrong choice.

Travelling is both a great analogue for life, and a source of excellent examples of the hazards of decision making. We have all been en route to a meeting when the flight has been delayed, the train is late or the motorway is blocked. At least we have mobile communications nowadays, which helps. But we still have to decide:

- Should the meeting go ahead without me/us?
- Should we ask for the meeting to be delayed till we get there – but when will that be?
- Or should we suggest refixing the meeting?

It is counter-culture (some remnant of the 'show must go on' mentality), but sometimes it is a better option. In these circumstances, NOT making a decision is not possible. Delay, procrastination or a short stay on the fence can work fine on a long-running project. But not in any kind of crisis.

Talk to professional short-order decision makers (pilots, fighting men and women, professionals in the emergency services). You have to make a decision. Even with very limited time, it is still best to do an instant reward/risk calculation. All skilled decision makers will instinctively avoid the temptation to max the upside, if the potential downside is really bad.

Nor is there always time to solve the problem before making a decision. Sometimes you will not yet know what the problem is – let alone have a ready solution. Remember that being a decision maker is a way of life. And that life isn't perfect. Sometimes the decision you make will not stand up. The important thing to remember is that you need to be able to stand up afterwards – and if necessary fight another day.

Surely technology has made it easier to make great decisions?

Just look at all the artificial aids we now take for granted:

- ubiquitous mobiles and other hand-held devices that ensure everyone is accessible 24/7;
- instant news on countless broadcast channels, on mobile, and in the street and at transport hubs and reception areas;

- text, e-mail and messaging services (as well as phone lines) to speed up conversation with colleagues and associates;
- video and tele-conferencing;
- Skype;
- social media;
- the vastness of the internet, which has massively speeded up research and made libraries and information departments redundant.

So why do so many people in organizations and in their non-work lives get it wrong so often and in so many different ways?

Regular readers know that I lay considerable blame at the door of our commitment to the meeting culture that gives us all the illusion of 'moving things on'. It is ironic that technology has now given us the automated invitation system that has institutionalized meetings to an even greater extent. But the meeting is not the only villain of the piece. Here are five other contenders:

- Conference calls (non-video). Catastrophically flawed whenever you have more than four participants, and/or when the people on the call don't know each other.

- E-mail language: limiting, prone to emotional and irrational overlays, and can easily provoke over-fast (and misguided) responses. It is also easy to give the impression of working by simply exchanging e-mails!

- Facebook and Twitter – potentially time-wasting and narcissistic, unless used judiciously. They take people's eye off the ball far more often than they incite others to riot.

- The tendency to phone and text people who are not with you, instead of engaging with the people who are.

- The unreliability of so much data that your researches can turn up. This can be, as Simon Hall of Savvy Friends (formerly founder of BHWG) says, because it is so easy to skew and bias it for commercial reasons. It can also be because of what journalist David Aaronovitch of *The Times* calls 'Bad Science'.

It wouldn't take you long to add to my list. We would be lost without our whizzy tools. But I am far from convinced that technology has overall advanced the cause of making better decisions, better.

Blackout

One day last week I turned on my Blackberry. It wouldn't let me call out – 'congestion'. Then the broadband connection in the hotel didn't work. We have been having power cuts recently. The drought situation raises the spectre of water restrictions.

Just suppose one day this – and worse – happens, and is permanent. No calls, no texts, no e-mails, no internet, no connectivity at all. London's new tall buildings would be useless without electricity. The much criticized public transport system would be even less impressive.

What would we do? How could we work? Would we get through the day? The next day? Have we become completely dependant on technology? Does it matter? Yes, I believe it does. It matters a great deal. We were brought up to be self-reliant, OK on our own, reading books, working in libraries, talking to the people there in the room with us, not the ones at the end of a phone.

Look at your fellow passengers as the aircraft lands, compulsively telling their colleagues and nearest and dearest what they know already: they have just landed in New York, Milan – or wherever. Now if they had been diverted to Monrovia, or were trying to get to Paris by lifeboat, tram and hitching lifts... well worth a call.

I was discussing this with my friend Fefa Romano, and she told me to read *The Last American Man* by Elizabeth Gilbert. I have, and it's extraordinary. It is the story of Eustace Conway, a real-life Davy Crockett, living in a tepee and eating only what he can kill and gather. Don't think I'd ever consciously wanted to nail a chipmunk to a tree or wipe my bottom with leaves. But it beats the hell out of being frustrated that you've lost all your contacts because you dropped your smartphone two feet from a bedside table onto a deep pile carpet in Istanbul. You wouldn't catch Eustace fretting at lack of connectivity.

I have also just read an excerpt from Lady Greenfield's new book: *ID: The Quest for Identity in the 21st Century*. She is convinced that computer games can affect brain function and increase the chances of contracting attention deficit hyperactivity disorder (ADHD). She writes about the dangers of pursuing 'pure pleasure'. She worries about young people:

> It's pretty clear that the screen-based two-dimensional world that so many teenagers – and a growing number of adults – choose to inhabit is producing changes in behaviour. Attention spans are shorter, personal communication skills are reduced, and there's a marked reduction in the ability to think abstractedly.

Susan Greenfield's core thesis is that our malleable brains can be adversely affected by electronic devices and pharmaceutical drugs. She is an authority on both Parkinson's and Alzheimer's, and very concerned about the alarmingly higher incidence of both.

Maybe there's a happy medium. We would certainly be better off not being quite so dependent on computers and communication devices. The potential problems are not just personal:

● Have you ever stopped to wonder at how much time we all take on e-mails?

● I am a Facebook rejecter, but can understand just how important a driver it has become in people's lives.

● I Tweet, I text, I spend more time looking at screens than faces.

The problems also affect business and careers. Is it any longer possible to hold down a professional, managerial or academic post without delivering solutions in Word, PowerPoint or Excel?

The problems are strategic as well. The West is obsessed with Iran's quest for a nuclear weapon capability. Whoever emerges from the current political struggle in Tehran – Ahmadinejad or Khamenei – could create far more problems for Israel by knocking out or jamming communications satellites. The apparently indestructible Mr Putin could paralyse Europe in the same way.

I am some way off learning to live off squirrel meat or cancelling the broadband and loo paper, but I am going to take our 'addiction' more seriously. The way we are going, it's not going to end well.

Maybe there is learning from marketing

Most governments and large organizations suffer from numerous of the Decision Traps listed in Chapter 2. But let us single out group failure and information overload. I worry about how many senior business people and officials fail to understand that the old command-and-control era has been conclusively ended by universal access to the internet.

This is where marketers can help. We have had to cope with a dramatic switch in power and influence from brand owners to consumers. We understand that people are now more powerful than companies. It is not a big stretch to say that people are now more powerful than all the apparatus of government.

But tragically many business leaders, politicians, ministers, senior civil servants, police and military chiefs simply have not got it. They believe that oratory, press releases and spin still work. My suggestion is remarkably easy to spell out, although I know it is going to take time to work. I think political and other leaders should make decisions the way marketers do. It is standard practice for marketers to conduct continuous dialogue with consumers – with thinking shared on both sides. This means that marketers can make their decisions using research and scenario planning. I also think political leaders in particular should be more like kids taking a maths test. It is not enough to come up with the answer (*aka* decision); they should also have to explain how they worked it out. This is also going to help with selling a decision upwards and securing buy-in.

Exchanging transparency for spin is not going to happen overnight, but what a refreshing change it would make.

Blog extract

So CEOs do give themselves time to think

There was some heartening news today. *The Times* reported on a study of the work habits of 94 CEOs working for British, European and US companies. The researchers were from the London School of Economics (LSE), the European University Institute and the Harvard Business School – so academically the findings should be unimpeachable.

And the sources were reliable: the Personal Assistants (PAs) of the CEOs. Arguably a PA has far more idea of what a CEO does than the man or woman in question.

So what did the survey reveal? Unsurprisingly that bosses spend 60 per cent of their time in meetings. They clearly haven't been reading this blog. Otherwise they would have worked out how futile some of these meetings are – particularly if anyone seriously believes that the meeting is going to lead to a decision.

Conference and other telephone calls and the events and appearances that go with being a CEO accounted for a further 25 per cent.

The remaining 15 per cent? 'Working alone'. What wonderful news. Our leadership elite actually carve out thinking time – as advocated on this URL (**www.makingbetterdecisionsbetter.com**, 26 May 2011). That will do far more to help them make better decisions, better than any number of meetings. When you think about it, 15 per cent of your week is quite a lot.

But before you all succumb to joy unconfined, there is a bit of information about this study that our friends at *The Times* underplayed, shall we say. All the CEOs were based in Italy!

Does this study mean *that all CEOs everywhere* also spend 15 per cent of their time in their offices? No evidence at all – until the researchers spread their wings and check out work patterns in London, Paris, Detroit etcetera.

A more interesting interpretation of the findings would be that this goes some way to explain why in recent years Italian corporations have done rather well, and indeed why so many companies have turned to Italians for the top jobs.

What we now need is comparative data from elsewhere. We could even postulate a formula: 15 per cent or more 'working alone' is highly positive, while less than 15 per cent is worrying and may lead to poorer performance.

Just one more thing in the piece worried me. Apparently consultants occupied nearly an hour a day of the 'meetings' time. Yet the CEOs regarded this activity as largely unproductive. I do hope this seditious thinking doesn't spread beyond Milan and Rome!

Why are meetings so frustrating?

The meeting looms large in decision science because it is supposed to be the forum for discussion and decision. But so often, the discussion is inconclusive, and no decision is taken. Was it ever thus? Or are we living through an era where the 'Meetings, bloody meetings' adage holds particularly true?

One of the advantages of having been around the business world for a while (OK, I admit it, since 1965), is that I can make some comparisons. My impression is definitely that things are much worse now. I'm going to put forward a couple of theories, and sketch in some background to each. Incidentally I have a feeling that both theories come straight out of the Behavioural Economics textbook (negative section). In each case the behaviour driver comes from people under 30. But sadly it is copied well up the age scale – although interestingly not in all countries and cultures.

Theory One: behaviour and manners have deteriorated to the point where many in the workplace have personal styles that are so acerbic and uncooperative that they are unsuited to any recognized form of constructive debate.

Without going overboard with generalizations, I don't believe you have to look much further than TV programmes like *The Apprentice*, *Come Dine with Me* or indeed *Question Time* to see evidence of what I am talking about. Confrontational broadcast journalism has made direct attacks and interruption the default setting. Glorification of naked ambition and abrasiveness on programmes like *The Apprentice* gives licence to young business people to behave rudely and egotistically. Put Sugar's babes and lads, or the round robin diners in one room, and the producers make sure the sparks fly.

A casting director looking for a latter day Genghis Khan would have a field day. I certainly don't believe Genghis spent a lot of time around an Arthurian Round Table. (I'm not convinced that Arthur did!)

Theory Two: and this is a more recent development – many people today seem to be happier talking on the phone, texting, e-mailing or social networking than actually meeting anyone in a live show.

The nearly universal ability to keyboard and publish one's own material has given the class of 2011 more confidence in their opinions and indeed their personal 'brands'. Remote one-to-one interface has become the preferred way of interacting with other people. Plenty of opportunity to chat and listen – basically 50 per cent share of airtime in fact. And you can choose compatible chat partners – in terms of personality and interests. By comparison a meeting of, say, 10 people in a conference room is a much less attractive prospect. There are all sorts of disadvantages, compared to the one to one mode:

- hierarchy;
- discipline;
- diversity (age, culture, education, style etcetera);
- no control over time (either the meeting is too long, or it's too short);
- above all the expectation that everyone is supposed to sublimate their opinions in the search for some form of consensus.

Is it surprising so many meetings don't work out? I am not saying that I started out in a halcyon era where corporate democracy and beautiful manners were always on display. But it was a lot easier to manage meetings then, and to bring groups to some form of (at least interim) conclusion.

Where do we start putting the meeting into rehab? By recognizing the problems above, I would suggest. Also by talking about the need to adjust some personal behaviour in the interests of making meetings more constructive.

What can go wrong with meetings

Why don't most meetings succeed? Here's just a short list of possible explanations:

- People attend so many meetings, it is difficult to create any sense of specialness or occasion.
- Most meetings are not set up with an agenda that drives decision making.
- Most meetings either have too many attendees or too few.
- The effect of having too many people at a meeting is either that some attendees try so hard to get in a word edgeways, that they are not listening to what others are saying, or that others are inhibited from making any contribution at all. My friend Mark Williams has been recently elected to the General Committee of the Marylebone Cricket Club (MCC), one of the most prestigious positions in cricket. I asked him how he was able to influence things. He explained to me that with up to 26 people in the room, it is extremely difficult to make any live contribution at all!
- When there are too few it is often because most individuals with decision-making power and ability are too busy to attend, or otherwise occupied.
- Too little time is spent setting agendas.
- Often too little attention is given to recording what action is required from whom after these meetings.

There's an excellent article in the June 2011 issue of *Harvard Business Review* by Nobel laureate Daniel Kahneman, supported by a McKinsey advisor (Professor Dan Lovallo), and a McKinsey executive (Olivier Sibony). It's entitled 'Before You Make that Big Decision...'. The authors provide a 12-point checklist for detecting bias in group decision making:

1 Is there any reason to suspect motivated errors, or errors driven by the self-interest of the recommending team?

2 Have the people making the recommendation fallen in love with it?

3 Were there dissenting opinions within the recommending team?

4 Could the diagnosis of the situation be overly influenced by salient analogies?

5 Have credible alternatives been considered?

6 If you had to make this decision again in a year, what information would you want, and can you get more of it now?

7 Do you know where the numbers came from?

8 Can you see a halo effect?

9 Are the people making the recommendation overly attached to past decisions?

10 Is the base case overly optimistic?

11 Is the worst case bad enough?

12 Is the recommending team overly cautious?

Bias is one thing. Poor decision-making process is another. As I have said before, the 'early decision' is a popular favourite – my polite way of describing the open or covert determination by one of the leaders in a decision-making process to go one way rather than another. I am talking about early stages – before any balancing of upsides and downsides. To count as an early decision it has to take place before the reward–risk analysis. Political parties do it all the time, and so increasingly do business leaders and other people prominent in public life.

60 minutes to an hour is enough time to bring a meeting to a decisive conclusion; but there need to be special rules

Theoretically 60 minutes should be enough time to make a decision or move it along its journey. But we have all suffered the frustration and limitation of one-hour meetings. They can appear as a curse. Is a meeting to facilitate decision making, or to delay it? Are meetings democratic? Are they for discussion or rubber stamping? Is a decision made in a meeting likely to be 'better quality'? Do meetings simply clog people's schedules to the extent that they have no time to think?

If you run meetings, here's a quick checklist of what might work better:

- Set a goal for the meeting – and publish it in advance.
- Make sure the right people are there. Only invite contributors, and as few of them as possible – the more attendees, the less will be achieved.
- Write a simple agenda. This agenda will be a subset of the goal – the less items on it, the more will be achieved.
- If a decision has to be made, clarify the options in advance (your job to have overseen this essential preparation).
- And use the meeting to help assess risks and rewards – maximum upside consistent with minimizing downside.
- Decide in principle.
- Agree how the decision is to be ratified: so that it becomes a mutual decision.
- Fix another meeting to agree implementation.
- Make sure you (or someone reliable) tells everyone who needs to know what they need to know.

If the meeting is not about coming to a decision, do you need the meeting?

Meetings – 10 suggested hygiene factors

1 Is this meeting absolutely necessary?

2 Does it have to take place tomorrow / this week / on the 31, or whenever?

3 Who HAS to be there?

4 What advantage is there in inviting the 'nice to haves'?

5 How long have you allocated? Is that long enough? (Or indeed too long?)

6 What's on the agenda? Can we get through all those items in the time given? Really? If we can't, which items shall we leave out?

7 Who's kicking off and managing the meeting?

8 Who's responsible for winding it up, summarizing what's been achieved, writing up the conclusions / decisions?

9 Who is in charge of deciding what to do next, eg:
  - Endorsing the decision?
  - Communicating the decision?
  - Implementing the decision?
  - Or – give me strength – setting the next meeting?

10 Who round here is responsible for working out the optimum balance between thinking, doing and meeting?

Delegate assemblies like the Roman Senate and most parliaments and legislatures are obvious examples of the need to have meetings. These gatherings generally have a purpose: to decide things.

Unfortunately in business we seem to have adopted the second type of meeting (let's get together for a chat). Is it any surprise they seldom lead to decision making? The 10 Hygiene Factors might be worth a try the next time you have that 'let's have a meeting' urge.

Listen if you want to be heard

My heading is a quotation from Kevin Murray's book *The Language of Leaders*. The entreaty to listen is as important as it is sometimes (for many of us at least) difficult to do. I am reminded of my own weakness in this area as I read through the transcripts of the interviews I carried out for this book. Several times I read 'DW interrupting', or 'DW overtalking'!

How embarrassing it is to have one's faults so graphically displayed. But that's not important. What matters is that in our need to communicate, we often put our desire to get our point across ahead of the need to understand where everyone else is coming from.

Let's return to that familiar Aunt Sally, the unproductive meeting. Think back to the last time you emerged from an hour's or hour and a half's worth of meeting frustrated that nothing was achieved, no decision taken. All that effort in juggling diaries to assemble the key stakeholders, and you and your colleagues are no further forward. I'll bet there was at least a trace of all of the following:

- somebody important either failing to make it, or having to leave early;
- the more dominant personalities doing the lion's share of the talking;
- 40 or 50 per cent of people in the meeting making very little contribution (not talking – maybe not really listening either);
- the agenda not completed;
- main problem still not solved;
- no decisions;
- time on the project running out.

All this is crucial in today's corporate environment where, as Kevin points out, leaders need to demonstrate speed and agility as well as consummate communication skills.

Is there an answer over and above persuading even the most loquacious and articulate to try to listen? That is certainly a big part of it. In his book Kevin Murray quotes David Nussbaum,

CEO of the WWF in the UK, as advocating listening with our eyes as well as our ears, to ensure we can read the body language of others.

This is very reminiscent to me of Professor Charles Spence's emphasis on synaesthesia (using two or more of the senses at the same time), in his analysis of consumer decision making in Chapter 7.

But behavioural change in adults (particularly corporate heavy hitters) is not easy to bring about. Equally important in redressing the balance between listening and being heard is ensuring that all decisions (including those determining how companies communicate in public) are made on the basis of the best data.

Best data has to include consideration of the views and recommendations of the quiet ones as well as the dominant 'over-talkers'. These views can just as easily be written down and read, as spoken and heard. Even metaphoric listening is far better than not listening at all.

David Jones of Havas was the creator of an ambitious 60-week (plus) project, One Young World

He and his colleague Kate Robertson (Global Chair of the Havas agency) had the vision for One Young World, a non-governmental organization (NGO) which is a worldwide forum for young people with leadership potential. It is one of the most innovative initiatives started by an ad agency. I asked him when he realized it was going to change his life:

> We didn't know in the first 12 months. It took that time to just get it to happen. We'd never done anything like it before. Everyone was kind of, yes this is a great idea, and please show us what it is. It was in the middle of a recession. Some of my colleagues who didn't necessarily like my rise within the company wanted this to be the thing that undid me. There were probably about 12 Sunday nights where I thought, I'm going to

have to call Kate and tell her we're going to have to stop. But once we did the first conference, we completely got it. We were going out to our clients and saying, you know, the business needs to be more socially responsible. That's what consumers want, so that's how we have to behave.

I think for me the moment was standing on stage and in London, with, you know, nearly 1,000 young people and alongside Desmond Tutu, Bob Geldof and the rest, and seeing the projects that they were coming up with and the ideas, and the energy, it was pretty incredible. It was unbelievable, and I knew what a great decision it had been.

David Jones has published a book called *Who Cares Wins* (2011) about socially responsible business.

Barbara Cassani was responsible for another 60-week project: the launch of a new airline – Go

She wrote a book about the experience, *Go: An Airline Adventure* (2003). She told me about some of the decisions she took – not all predictable – in a start-up:

> So, for example, I outlawed pilot jokes, which was very funny, because it was the pilots got really pissed off, because they like telling jokes about themselves. I said, no, you can't do it as a pilot story, you have to make that joke work with another person. It was funny, but I had made my point.
>
> I had to be demanding, I was unhappy with many of the things we were doing, and for good reason. At the beginning the financial results were horrible, but the product was good. It was always good, but it could have been better. I was very conscious that almost everybody in the team had never done really anything that important or on that scale, and so there was a lot of coaching to develop everybody within their own roles. There was nobody to do that for me for a while, which

was kind of hard, and then I eventually went and got
an external coach, which was really valuable later on.

He helped me manage my team better, and to prioritize. It
was great being able to talk to somebody who didn't work for
me or didn't provide my money. When you're a CEO it's a bit
dangerous to let your hair down with your team. Similarly you
don't want to share everything with the people who are holding
your purse strings.

I discovered that to be an effective CEO in a start-up
business, you need to be ahead of everyone else. So you had to
do an annual budget. But in a start-up, it's just a joke, because
as soon as you start trading the first day, the budget is toast,
because you have no understanding of what you're going to
be able to do. You have to put something down on paper, but it
evolves constantly. It's like doing reforecasting weekly, which is
just a nightmare, particularly when you're someone like me
who's used to having budgets that only moved by 2 per cent.
All of a sudden I was in this world, like, oh, we're 200 per cent
off on this one! You want to be accountable, but you have to
deal with huge variables.

But I found that we could set a course. For example, we
worked out that based on our calculations of average fares and
costs; we would need to get up to about nine planes to hit
break-even financially. Then, after only five or six months,
I realized that was wrong. Prices were lower than I had
anticipated, so you had to lower prices even more to fill up the
planes. The costs were lower, but not as low as the reduction
in the prices. So we decided we would need 11 planes before
we would break even financially, which was very tough.
I felt very pressured. I felt remorse that we'd gotten it wrong,
and I was very worried that we would not get support from our
parent to go out and secure the extra aircraft to do it. There
was tension, mostly me, because I didn't communicate it to
everyone.

But I found I had a gift for seeing that the path we were on
was okay for now, but we would need to make a change in
order to be on a better path in six months. The reason most

people who worked for me would say that I was impatient was that I was never happy with where we were.

I asked General Sir Mike Jackson a question about his judgement of time: did he think the second Iraq War would be a long-drawn-out affair?

Yes, but not in the way everybody did, including many commentators whose knowledge in matters military you could write on the proverbial postage stamp. Do you remember that, oh, Baghdad will be like Stalingrad? Street fighting for months, years. And I remember sitting next to a very august editor a few weeks before it started, and he said, something terrible is coming. It's going to go on forever. I said, no, it won't. The manoeuvre, the defeat of Saddam Hussein's forces in the field, I said, will last three weeks. It actually was three weeks and three days, I think. But I said, after that, it's going to be very messy, because you're into what Donald Rumsfeld called – though he loathed the phrase – nation building. It's what you then have to do after the military phase. It's what we did in Bosnia. It's what we did in Macedonia. It's what we did in Kosovo. It's what is going on in Afghanistan.

It's messy, it's awkward. Some people don't want you to do this. Others want you to do it in a different way, and it cannot be done by Monday morning. It's going to take a long time. It does. Because Northern Ireland was 38 years. Bosnia ... there's still a military international force in Bosnia, two decades on. Kosovo, the same, one decade later. Afghanistan, the War has been going on a decade already.

Chapter Six
The people factor

Personality profiling creates teams that work, and helps us all understand ourselves – and one another

De Bono – the Maltese Eagle

> A small tribute to a philosopher with a mighty wingspan
> I've embarked on a serious mission
> To raise the humble decision
> From just one of the things we can
> To a towering achievement for man
>
> The prophet who showed me the way
> Wore hats, but none of them grey
> He is the thinking man's thinker from Malta
> De Bono: the lateral exhorter
>
> Schoemaker gave us the rules
> And Belbin told us the roles
> But de Bono allowed us to learn
> By playing each role in turn

Wear the red hat for passion
And the black one for trashin'
Yellow hat says you are sunny
And green that you are creative and funny

But the cleverest hats are the blue and the white
White hat means you only say what's right
No editor's gloss on conversation
Just unvarnished truth and information

Blue is the smartest hat of all
You're the conductor in the hall
Fusing the sounds the hats are making
By thinking, solving, decision making.

(Wethey 2011)

I was fortunate enough to be invited to have Sunday lunch at de Bono's house near Cambridge, when I was up at Oxford in the early 1960s, and he was teaching at Cambridge University. As can be guessed from his rich harvest of academic distinctions and his prolific output of books, he was an extremely impressive person to meet. He obtained a medical degree at the University of Malta before studying Physiology and Psychology as a Rhodes Scholar at Oxford. He is rightly famed for his development of Lateral Thinking, which has passed into the language. But he has been responsible for a huge volume of academic and consulting work on the people factor in organizations, as well as a bewildering variety of inventions, ranging from new forms of poetry, to games, to an alternative to the penalty shoot-out at football. I singled out 'Six Hats' for my odd ode, because it seems to me that role-playing is a particularly useful way of helping people to understand how everyone is different, and what a strength that is.

In the study of decision making, it would be a serious weakness not to take people factors and profiling seriously. Lack of curiosity – in general – is a fault. Corporates are notorious for underestimating the importance of personality, nationality, culture, religion etcetera. Profiling is standard in recruitment, but tends to be left behind in active service, and when teams are being formed. Why people act the way they do, why they take the decisions they do, why some people do it this way, and others that – these are all endlessly fascinating questions, which we should look at now.

How I have always profiled client and advertising agency people

I have used for many years a version of a popular personality profiling model as a key diagnostic to help our clients find agencies that suited them. We have also used it extensively in our relationship management practice to provide people-based solutions in cases of malfunctioning client/agency situations. Surprisingly few agencies use profiling in either selling ('new business') or servicing to help create better chemistry with clients, through the right casting and right content, presented in the right way.

As with most models, we use four primary groupings, which can be combined in any combination of two for people who are not clearly one type.

The model (which I call the Headline system) was based on the classic DISC model, invented by William Moulton Marston. Marston was a US psychologist with three other claims to fame. His invention of the systolic blood pressure test contributed to the development of the polygraph or lie detector. He was also a feminine theorist who took his research seriously enough to set up a polyamorous household with his wife and another woman. Whether it was because of this, or coincidentally, he also became the creator of Wonder Woman!

The typologies in common use in the 1980s business world were Drivers, Expressives, Amiables and Analysts. This model was adapted for advertising agencies by Stuart Sanders, a consultant from Richmond Virginia, to help his agency clients understand better themselves and what made their clients and prospects tick. I first met Sanders in London in 1990, and worked with him on a number of projects thereafter, mainly in the United States. The version of Sanders' model illustrated here owes much to the development work of Mike Longhurst, Senior VP in McCann-Erickson EMEA, based in London. Sanders' clever contribution was to use advertising terms to bring the typologies to life, and also to devise a methodology by which trained agency new business specialists could profile their client opposite numbers using all sorts of observation tests, without asking them to fill in a questionnaire (impractical), and without the clients realizing what was going on. McCann developed and updated this for international use. Sanders' material was mainly US-focused. They also devised a straightforward non-technical self-profiling questionnaire. The four types (with descriptions tailored to client marketing executives) in the Headline model are as follows (with explanatory diagrams).

Headline – typical Chief Executive Officer (CEO) type. A driver who makes things happen. Good delegator, but makes the decisions himself/herself. Demanding, often intolerant and totally task-oriented. Makes well-informed, but ultimately intuitive decisions. Likes authority, leadership, drive, energy, compliance with their wishes.

Illustration – can be a global brand director type. Outgoing, mercurial, inspirational, entertaining and with good people skills.

FIGURE 6.1   Orientation

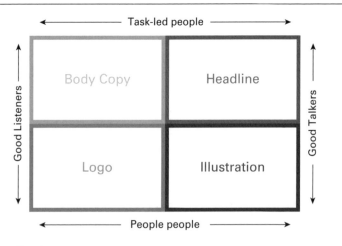

The Headline System

FIGURE 6.2   Personality

Analytical Detailed Precise Thorough Cautious	Short attention Straight to business Demanding Decisive Fairly formal
Very welcoming Likes to get to know Hospitable Appreciative Team-builder	Great fun Easy to get to know Very sociable Enthusiastic Inspirational

The Headline System – tier 2

FIGURE 6.3   How they get things done

Assemble the facts Analyse Write a recommendation Rational process Research	Take the lead Give clear instructions Delegate Set targets / dates / incentives / rewards
Form a team Hold frequent meetings Discuss openly Build consensus Share responsibility	Define the vision Blue sky solutions Sometimes impractical Change mind Have fun

The Headline System – tier 3

Likes to be part of the agency team and feels very creative. Must see big ideas, excitement, optimism, fun.

Logo – typical 'nice person'. Gains power and influence by getting on with people. Likeable, honest, fair and a great team worker or leader. Likes consensus, relaxed style, no controversy or risk. Wants to get to know people he/she works with personally.

FIGURE 6.4   What they like

Process / Methodologies Experience Case histories Strategic development Research / test results	Their person (who they call) Senior management Be brief / decisive Results Costs and timings
Meet "Their team" Get to know you Teamwork Human interest Meetings	The creatives Big names Awards Entertainment The big vision / idea

The Headline System – tier 4

Body Copy – typical Marketing Manager or Director type. A professional. High on knowledge but can be low on taking responsibility. Often with poor people skills, but gets by through being the one with the knowledge. Likes detail, info, strategy, keeping on top of complexity.

The guiding principle of the way we have used this profiling system is that people want to work with people like them. This is particularly true of Headlines and Illustrations. The strength of Logos is they can get on with anyone. Body Copies accept that many of the colleagues, bosses and people in other companies will be from other typologies, because that is the way of big organizations. (But they do enjoy working with other Body Copies!). The real human resources (HR) world is obviously more complex than four typologies can do justice to. There are more possible typologies than the basic four:

- Intensified characteristics: Headline/Headlines, Illustration/Illustrations and so forth.

- Headline/Body Copies, Body Copy/Headlines, Headline/Illustrations, Illustration/Logos, Logo/Illustrations, Logo/Body Copies and Body Copy/Logos. Personalities only very rarely stretch across the diagonals.

There are of course numerous other personality profiling methods in use – notably Myers Briggs (one of the very few inventions by a daughter and mother) and 16pf. My purpose in featuring the Headline system is based on close personal experience and the fact that it was fashioned around the ad industry. What is important in the context of this book is to underline what a major influence personality is on decision making.

This sample profiling report will bring the advantages of the process to life. It was used by an agency to analyse the make-up of members of the client team who were going to be the decision makers on a pitch.

Sample one – initial view on the team and its leader Shaun

- There is a complex mix of people in this meeting, but Shaun will probably set the tone. He has wrought changes in his division and is the change agent in the mix. Others however may have a veto, so there needs to be something for everyone.

- The dominant profile groups seem to be Illustration and Body Copy, which means ability to deliver outstanding creativity on a sound strategic platform will be essential. It is about big ideas accurately directed.

- We need to have enough people to cover the territory (which is broad) but no excess people to prevent bonds being established. We must not be a sea of faces.

- There will be a lot of agency experience in the room and most of it from creative hotshops, so we have to be lively. Our team must bond well before the meeting, not in it.

- It will be useful to read Shaun's interview at the end and to consider theme-linking our content around some of his highlighted principles.

There follows Shaun's photo, job description and potted CV, with education details, previous employment, achievements and honours.

Juror's biography (for an awards festival)

Shaun is Chief Marketing Officer (CMO) at Megacorp, where he is responsible for the efficiency and effectiveness of all Marcom materials globally. Over the last five years, he has led the radical transformation of the company's consumer communications. In that time, he has successfully rejuvenated the brand and demonstrated that creativity is actually a prerequisite for effectiveness.

A champion of big ideas, Shaun has a proven record of developing innovative, effective, and award-winning campaigns. He has won numerous creative, media and effectiveness awards (listed). He is a frequent speaker at industry events and has served on a number of other juries.

What he says about himself

- Unique combination of creative, strategic, and analytical skills acquired through marketing communications, brand strategy, and consulting experiences.
- A strong passion for understanding and influencing consumer behaviour.
- A champion of big ideas, coupled with the ability to bring them to life.
- A proven record of developing innovative, effective and award-winning campaigns.
- An inspiring team leader with broad experience working in international and multicultural environments.

Assessment

Is Canadian and a big fan of creativity. Hates committees on creativity. Big integration fan. Also tweets a lot and is a blogger.

Despite use of phrases like 'big ideas', he sounds basically Body Copy, but with a lot of personality and drive. He is no backroom bean-counting guy, but very up front. Likes awards too.

Could think of him as an Illustration, but with more detail and application than the norm. More of a very successful articulate Body Copy.

He is unlikely to see a wide difference between client and agency side and will probably respond to being treated as part of the agency team. See interview in Appendix.

Could guess he will have great influence over the others. This guy needs to be faced with real communications experts and might not respond to people with non-communications roles.

Account planners understand what makes people tick

Nigel Jones of Publicis London was originally an account planner at the BMP agency (now DDB London). He explained his background as a planner, and gave me some insights into his own character: 'I have always been a risk taker. At 50 I'm much less cautious than I used to be. Typical planners are risk averse, or only take risks without bad downsides.' I asked Nigel if he had ever in business came across an alter ego who thought and acted like he does. 'Not really. I don't think I have ever come across anyone like me in advertising,' he told me.

> I'm a very good listener; probably my biggest asset, I think. But actually that's what I think planning is. You can't really decide to become a planner, I think you either are, or you aren't, in my definition.
>
> If someone said to me a few years ago, well, how do you define a good planner, I'd have said, someone with the biggest ears in the world, and I don't just mean to hear, but to see and to feel and, you know, I think planning is all about empathy. So the really good planners are people who, by the time they've got here, will have had an idea that has been inspired by something that happened on the Tube. So, wow, I just noticed someone who only reads the first line of each page of a book

on the Tube. I wonder what that means? I wonder what they're getting out of that? I wonder what that tells us about modern life? Or, there are three people there with one iPad, and they're all listening to the same thing. With me it was how people talk to each other, or which bits of the newspaper they're talking to each other about, would go into my head. Probably unconsciously, I suspect. But I would just watch all the time, listen, take it in, and then apply it to the next problem that comes up in work. The really interesting bit of planning and the thing that I still enjoy doing is the jigsaw fit between those observations about people and the things that clients tell me about their brands.

You know, in a recent pitch which we just did, I think the insight that the client brought to the pitch meeting was like one I'd had about 30 years ago, and I had been thinking about and refining over the last 30 because it was an insight about my life. I was just waiting for a product that needed that insight to make the whole thing click.

I'll tell you the story. I have a view on life which has developed in my head over the years. There are things that happen to people in life which are quite small, but which are completely fundamentally life-changing. It might be a glance on the Tube, it might be meeting someone in a bar accidentally, it might be reading one line in a book and getting an inspiration. It usually involves other people, but not always. The problem is, most people don't see these things, so they go through life missing them. It's as if they have their hearing switched off, or their eyesight closed down. As a result they have less interesting, less fulfilled, and less dynamic lives.

But there are other people who are much more alert to those kinds of things. I feel I'm lucky enough to be one of those, and people always say to me, you've had a really interesting life. It isn't true! It's just that I've just spotted more of it than most people do.

All the things that happen to me I put into that little analysis: does it reinforce it, or does it knock it down? And then this coffee brand came along and said: 'We've got this product, and we're not quite sure what it does or exactly how it affects people and their lives, but we've done loads of consumer research, and it's something about making you a bit more alert, and something about little moments in life, but we can't quite work it all out.' And within a minute – I knew. I knew the answer to this. I've been living with this answer all my life: the role of coffee is to help you become more alert to those moments that you would miss if you didn't drink it. It works on two levels. One is on a chemical level because there's caffeine in coffee. The other one is the coffee moment – you have to take five minutes out of your day to make the stuff, sit down and drink it. And in those five minutes you see more, and you open yourself to more of these little moments than you would do if you didn't take those five minutes out. And the clients said, 'This is what we've been looking for.'

And that was the entire pitch on one piece of paper. There was no planning in the traditional sense. No groups. I didn't talk to any consumers. I am the consumer in that sense. I am representing the 5,000 consumers I have watched over the last 30 years. Now, you need to go and check it out. You'd be mad to just take my view of the world as gospel. So there's a lot of research going on now to justify it. But all the research we've done so far has come back ten out of ten, and I think it's going to work.

Blamers and Pacifiers

I had a long car journey last week with an old friend. We were talking about relationships, and he said, 'There are two kinds of people. I'm not talking about men and women. I mean Blamers and Pacifiers. Show me any relationship that has survived the test of time, and one partner is the Blamer, and the other the Pacifier.' I did think about it, and the more couples I thought about, the more I was convinced of my friend's theory.

It even occurred to me that when couples split up, and the partners start new relationships, they sometimes change roles. The former Blamer becomes a Pacifier and vice versa. So I started thinking beyond personal relationships and into partnerships in business, and within organizations.

Do business teams contain Blamers and Pacifiers as well as Men, Women, Drivers, Expressives, Amiables and Analysts? I am sure they do.

Maybe it explains lack of progress on certain projects. Change management zeal can easily be dissipated by spending too much time blaming the company, senior executives, people in other parts of the company, colleagues etcetera, for mistakes and sins of omission. Pacifying – essential as it is for diverting the blamer's attention back to the job in hand – also takes time that could be better spent on planning, analysing, driving, or indeed taking decisions.

Talking of which, we ought also to look at Supporters and Critics – as well as Deciders. Not everyone has either the opportunity or the aspiration actually to make the decision, and this can have a significant effect on the effectiveness of teams.

Meredith Belbin – the hero of team theory

We have looked at Blamers and Pacifiers – two clear typologies from the world of personal relationships, who undoubtedly also play a role in business problem solving and decision making.

But no analysis of the dynamics of successful teams would be complete without acknowledging the huge contribution of Cambridge academic Meredith Belbin. Now 86, Belbin carried out seminal research at what was then called the Administrative Staff College at Henley-on-Thames during the 1960s and 1970s into what contrasting and complementary skills are needed to form a successful team.

In the post-war period, with most leading business people, civil servants and academics being military veterans, command and control was the order of the day. Teams were either vertically integrated or formed on an organogram resembling the family tree of John of Gaunt. Hierarchy ruled (to coin a phrase). The boss basically issued instructions, and his (always a 'he' in those days) direct reports did the same to their minions, and so on.

Belbin's genius during a week-long class was to be able to pick a team with different abilities and styles, which could always defeat any assemblage of drivers and power figures selected by his fellow lecturers. It's choosing a playground football team all over again. You do need a goalkeeper, some defenders and playmakers as well as strikers.

In his 1981 book *Management Teams*, Belbin gave the world nine typologies (originally seven), each one constituting a key team role:

- Plant – the left-field problem-solver.

- Resource Investigator – networker who recruits outside expertise, so reducing the group's dependence on received wisdom.

- Monitor-Evaluator – the devil's advocate and objective stickler.

- Completer Finisher – detail zealot.

- Shaper – rigorous visionary who can guide the group under pressure.

- Co-ordinator – the one who insists on everyone being consulted and listened to.

- Team Worker – HR person.

- Implementer – tasked with finding workable solutions and implementation.

- Specialist – expert in whatever discipline is needed.

Critics have questioned whether nine is a magic number for a successful team, and whether or not certain roles couldn't be combined in the same individual. But Belbin's insight about the need for a balanced make-up has been crucial in the search for effective problem solving and decision making. We owe him a great deal.

Thinking time

Inevitably we apply a value system to the language we use in the business world. Let's try some basic categorization:

Good:

- busy;
- successful;
- important;
- decisive;
- ruthless.

Bad:

- not very busy;
- doing quite well;
- follower, not a leader;
- open-minded;
- easy-going.

But that's a view of the world through the eyes of alpha males and females, leaders, and those who aspire to lead. It also speaks volumes about the personality profiles of both the describer and the described.

None of this is radical. We all know how our psychological make-up affects behaviour, and how we are perceived. Belbin and others have used the insights tellingly to create balanced teams with a higher than average chance of success.

What worries me is what I believe to be the most obvious casualty of the ethic that is characterized by being (or being seen to be) mega-busy, multitasking, and rushing about: having no time to think.

You can draw simple pie charts for yourself, colleagues, bosses, direct reports, anybody; dividing each day into thinking and doing. Am I wrong, or is there a drastic doing-over-thinking imbalance in the executive workplace these days?

I see even in the best companies (especially in the best companies) two dangerous trends emerging. The first trend shows itself as an over-reliance on meetings. Here are some of the warning signs:

- Too many meetings...
- ... which rob everyone of thinking and analysis time.
- Too many people at the meetings...
- ... with the result that attendees are trying so hard to get in a word edgeways, that they are not listening to what others are saying.
- Too little time spent setting the agenda for these meetings.
- Too little attention to recording what action is required from whom after these meetings.
- Worrying about not being at a meeting. You can't think if you're always in meetings.

Trend #2 is about communication – and particularly about computers and mobile devices. Watch out for:

- Spending too much time sending e-mails and texts.
- Being over-reactive in terms of putting a priority on answering every e-mail and text you receive.
- Devoting potentially productive time to social networking sites.
- Times when you use e-mail and text to avoid speaking to someone and risking reaction and debate.
- Times when you're more concerned to engage with people remotely than with people around you.
- Worrying about being out of touch. Switch it off!

Thinking time is food. It's fuel. It's an investment in problem solving and decision making. It's priceless.

High confidence, low self-esteem

Simon Calver CEO of Lovefilm has a clear view of the ideal personality profile for success in a dynamic company. He told me:

"Everybody in this organization is on a quarterly performance plan, which means they are set goals every 13 weeks, they are measured against those goals, and they get an element of pay based on how well they perform against their goals on a quarterly basis. This is very unusual. I had a group of top dogs who came here, and we talked about it. They said, doesn't it put your people under stress? Don't they find it tough being appraised on a quarterly basis?

They actually think it's wonderful, because people understand what they're doing. Every quarter, I have a list of everybody in the organization's score where 100 is on target, and 110 is above target, and 90 is below target, and I look at the whole organization and I can see how well we're doing on a 13-week cycle. Actually a slight lacking in self-esteem means that you are driving, and pushing, and always want to achieve. You don't ever think you've got there because you really want to push and make it happen. You don't get complacent, you don't get arrogant, and when something doesn't work, you don't shoot yourself. When something doesn't work you have that feeling in the pit of your stomach which is ... it didn't work, what can I learn, what can I do differently, how can I do that? And that comes from wanting to achieve.

A lot of American middle senior management fit into that category. They've always been told to strive. They've been told there are always smarter people than yourself out there in the world. You know, and I try and hide them, people that are incredibly more smart than I am. You still need confidence, but the moment that your self-esteem is high and your confidence is high, you become arrogant, you alienate people and you lose them in the journey, and you can't bring them with you. You need high confidence, but not the high esteem that seems to go with it, in Europe particularly. High confidence and low self-esteem seems to work best in companies.

There are three components of competency that I think are really, really important, and every competency, I think, can fit into one of these three categories, which is: Can you make the right decision? Can you make it happen? And thirdly, can you bring others with you? In Pepsi we built a lot around those three types of competencies.

With the third component Simon puts his finger on the crucial mutual decision. 'Bringing others with you' is a good indicator that a decision is the right one, and that it can be implemented.

Blog extract

Larks rise at Candleford – and everywhere else

It is high time this blog was a bit more controversial.

And, talking of time, it is important you know that this column (like nearly all its predecessors) is being written at 7 am. I am a lark, not an owl. I'm also prepared to step aside from the cosy orthodoxy of saying that it doesn't matter which you are.

You see, I think the larks have it. Certainly as far as making decisions is concerned. It stands to reason. In most organizations there are more meetings in the morning than the afternoon. Often the first meeting of the day will be at 9.00, or even 8.30. Typically one meeting will then follow another.

When can you do your preparation for these meetings? The night before, you say? It is possible, but you have to be on line to access facts, data, reports and so on, and that is so much easier at the office. And even owls are more tired in the evening.

The lark on the other hand has that priceless two hours or so before corporate hostilities commence in earnest to do the preparation, to rehearse arguments, and generally to limber up for what is hopefully going to be a series of decision making (or 'decision-contributing') sessions.

The early start also allows you to reach the Californians before they go to bed, the Aussies before they go to bed the next day, people in Asia while they are still at the office, and Europeans before they rush into meetings.

In the morning the eyes are wider open and the brain is sharper. Additionally how comforting it was to read in the paper this morning that people from northern climes have bigger eyes and bigger brains!

So more power to the elbow of fellow larks – everywhere.

There is just one small problem. That dreaded foe time shift can pitch even a zealous lark into owl territory. This very evening I have to be on a conference call at midnight, linking me into a presentation on the West Coast.

I shall have to kid myself that it is not very late... but exceptionally early!

Blog extract

It takes Owls, Pussycats, and all sorts

In my previous blog I was doing a bit of chest-beating on behalf of larks.

Whether I am right or not in my belief that they (we!) are the master race, I think it's fair to say that owls are never going to be as well placed until the day your diary is full of meetings from 6 pm, 7 pm, 8 pm, and so on.

As it turned out, my yesterday turned into today on a conference call with California, so I have had a taste of being an owl. However, owls don't then have to drive to London at 5.15 in order to resume life as a lark!

Personality is a big influencer of decision making – as in all business activities. Of course our personality profile is determined by a lot more factors than relative effectiveness at different ends of the day. Let's look at other elements of our make up. Apart from the Headline system:

- There is the Driver, Expressive, Amiable, Analyst spectrum, developed by Peter Urs Bender and others:

- Drivers (Eagles) are leaders and achievers.
- Expressives (Peacocks) are extroverts and visionaries.
- Amiables (Doves – or Pussycats!) are team players and patient.
- Analysts (Owls) are thinkers and rigorous!

● And we all know about Myers Briggs, who gave us:
  - Extroverts (wide world) versus Introverts (my world).
  - Sensors (take information on board) versus Intuitors (interpret and add meaning).
  - Thinkers (logical, task driven) versus Feelers (emotive, people-focused).
  - Judges (quick decisions) versus Perceivers (need more information).

● On both scales we are combinations of characteristics, rather than being one or the other – but it is more helpful to understand the primary factor than to become lost in cocktails.

Importantly we know from the work of Meredith Belbin that winning teams (especially teams responsible for making decisions) need to have a balance of personality types. Next time you are sitting in a meeting (you won't have long to wait!), do a bit of personality profiling around the table:

● Are you top heavy with Drivers and Expressives?

● Or moving pretty slowly with Amiables and Analysts?

● Are the Judges becoming frustrated with the Perceivers?

● Is it tricky getting the Introverts to take a broad view?

● And are the Intuitors getting fed up with the Perceivers?

● Finally – and this is where we came in – are the Larks already running out of steam before the Owls have got into their stride?

The key is to know your own strengths and limitations, and to understand what all your colleagues are like, and what they are capable of. Sometimes we have to make decisions on our own. But most of the time it is a team game. A pure example of Behavioural Economics in action.

Hopefully with a basic understanding of profiling, you can prevent it becoming a contact sport!

Why do female tennis players grunt?

Google it, and you will find stuff about the need to inhale before a big physical effort (for example serving), and then exhale as soon as you've hit the ball. Interestingly Connors and Agassi were big grunters. But nowadays it is mainly the women, with the new World No.1 Victoria Azarenka shrieking so loudly at Wimbledon this year that you could hear her at Queen's! There is even a book on the subject by Professor Alison McConnell of Brunel University.

Some have credited famous coach Nick Bollettieri with encouraging the grunt – for tactical as well as physiological reasons. But I believe that we owe this noisy accompaniment to tennis, indirectly at least, to another of my heroes – Tim Gallwey (now 73), author in 1975 of *The Inner Game of Tennis*.

The scientific answer according to Gallwey would have been because Self 1 is using the grunt to tell Self 2 to get in the zone! What is all this about? Gallwey was a good enough tennis player to captain the Harvard team. He went on to become a professional, and later a coach. He studied under Guru Maharaj Ji, and became fascinated with the psychology of tennis. He wanted to understand why the greatest players could make stupid mistakes despite having immaculate technique and being super fit. Also why coaching for beginners and club players was often so ineffective. The player knew what he or she was supposed to do, but failed on court.

His discovery was that we have 'two selves'. Self 1 is the thinker and teller. Self 2 is the listener and doer. Self 1 knows what to do, and can't understand why Self 2 is so inept. Trouble is, Self 2 would be fine, left to his/her own devices, but freezes when Self 1 says 'break point' just as Self 2 goes for a cunning drop shot!

Gallwey's Inner Game is what sports commentators and psychologists now call the 'zone' – the state of concentrating hard and shutting out the external influences and thoughts that can distract the player from peak performance and faultless decision making.

He was a true pioneer, and wrote subsequent books about skiing (1977), golf (1981), and music (1986). Unsurprisingly sports-mad businessmen then clamoured for his motivational services, and Gallwey wrote *The Inner Game of Business* as a focus for his burgeoning consulting and executive coaching business.

Having studied considered decision making, and been puzzled at how teams of competent and intelligent people can use such poor process, I am constantly impressed by the efficiency of short-order decision makers, who usually have only seconds to decide. I am not just talking about the professionals here. It applies to us as well, as we drive our cars and walk the pavements well enough to avoid collisions. It has to be down to training and experience. It is also, as we discovered in Chapter 4, because of neuroplasticity, and our remarkable autopilot facility.

All of them (and us) must have Inner Games and well-trained Self 2's. When I hear you grunting at the wheel or walking down Regent Street, I'll know for sure.

Bright Eyes

Recently a procurement client sent an SOS for material to help him write a board paper on a significant industry issue – the tension between marketing and procurement. I found what I thought was a perfect backgrounder – a deck of charts produced by my US partner for an ANA webinar.

My client's response was a bit of a surprise. 'Very interesting, but very logical', he wrote. 'The most interesting aspect in my eyes is getting over to marketing teams that we can add skills when they think they are doing everything well.'

I guess I am predominately a left-brain kind of person, so logic is where I start. Yet so often persuasion is best achieved by ensuring a balance between rational and emotive thinking and language. I had made a trite assumption that left-brain thinking would work better with procurement. If a marketer had made the request, I would have probably tapped into more of a right-brain approach.

So obvious and so uninventive.

I want to share a related thought triggered by this episode, and also by having sat through some final agency presentations in my day job as a client adviser on agency selection. My observation is that there is a physical characteristic common to most successful people, most good communicators, most effective problem solvers – and, I suspect, most good decision makers.

I call it Bright Eyes. It is a gloriously unscientific description. And here I am talking about people, not rabbits! As far as I know there isn't an 'ometer' to measure ocular luminosity. But I am sure you all know what I mean. People with bright eyes are just so much more convincing, more appealing, more likeable, and easier to follow and agree with. They tend also to manage meetings better.

It is an emotional appeal, not a logical one. Yet it helps us single out winners, good potential recruits, people we want to work with and for. In a logical left brain world, dominated by data, numbers and rational arguments, how refreshing to think that we can sometimes put the criteria and subcriteria on one side, and instead be swayed by a look and a feel that some people have, and others don't.

Viva Bright Eyes. There is even an anthem about it.

Happiness is what we want, what we really want

'Happiness is the meaning and the purpose of life, the whole aim and end of human existence', wrote Aristotle in the fourth century BC. Two millennia later Descartes said, 'Everyone seeks everything else as a means to the goal of happiness, while no one seeks happiness as a means to any other goal.'

Four hundred years after Descartes, the TCA agency (the guys who did the remarkable Bob Monkhouse Prostate Cancer campaign) celebrated their 25th anniversary by commissioning a study by Melanie Howard of the Future Foundation on what happiness represents to 25-year-olds. I went to the presentation yesterday by Melanie and TCA Planning Director James Champ.

As I took notes on what are and what aren't the drivers for happiness in young adults, it suddenly occurred to me that it is very easy to talk and write about decision making (as I am prone to do) without mentioning happiness, which is clearly at the heart of emotional motivation.

Hence the quotes from two great philosophers.

Hence grateful thanks to TCA for reminding me of what should have been staring me in the face.

Hence a new determination to interpret much of Behavioural Economics in terms of the pursuit of happiness.

Hence two new filter questions when we are analysing the risk–reward equation on the cusp of making a decision:

- What upside would make me/us happiest?
- What downside would bring the greatest risk of unhappiness?

Is experience the be all and end all?

I was in a meeting selling our wares. (Yes, we have to compete as well!)

The client said very fairly, 'You certainly have made your point about all the experience you have.' She was right. Our presentation leans very heavily on so many illustrious clients, so many tough assignments handled successfully. Don't we naturally assume, in whatever field of endeavour, that it is persuasive to talk about past achievement? Indeed in all the books on decision science, there is an emphasis on feedback and learning as essential ingredients for the next decision process.

But I gave some thought to how we should value experience. Is it a no-brainer? Or is it just one asset among others? In decision making, experience is valuable, but so is good process and technique. It's also vital to pick the best team and to manage them well. It's essential to solve the key problems. It is vital to develop a suite of options and pick the one with the best upside, avoiding serious downsides.

I also thought about public worlds like politics, sport and entertainment. Sure, experience is important. But every ex-Cabinet Minister, every former footballer, and every one-time leading lady had plenty of experience at the precise moment that they left office, hung up their boots, or failed an audition. Life moves on, and the new Cabinet Minister, striker and female lead will all have been selected on potential as much as on performance.

Every list of winners, and every honours board records achievement, but also the inevitable passage of time and changing of the guard.

My conclusion is that it's crucial not just to have experience, but to use it. We also learn as much from failure as from success. That's a different kind of experience.

I wish people would remember that when they write their CVs. Am I the only person who would prefer to see an honest career resumé? No real person has been associated with an uninterrupted catalogue of glorious success, let alone personally responsible for all the high points.

Let's celebrate and respect experience. But at the same time we should particularly honour and reward those who have the ability and honesty to turn that experience into future success. That's why in our business, we still try to come up with new formulae, new techniques and new ideas – even after 24 years!

A big insight into the way business leaders behave: causals and effectuals

I want to start the exploration of people factors with a powerful piece of thinking that was new to me when my friend Serge Nicholls brought it to my attention.

It is about two types of reasoning – one that starts by setting a goal and working rationally towards its achievement. The other does not begin with a specific goal. It starts typically with a group of people, and allows goals to emerge contingently. This came out of a study into 30 entrepreneurs in the US, and what makes them tick. The author of the study *What makes Entrepreneurs Entrepreneurial* (2008) is Saras Sarasvathy of the University of Washington Business School. She calls the goal-driven reasoning 'causal', and the more lateral, discursive sort 'effectual'. It is effectual reasoning, or effectuation, that is characteristic of almost all entrepreneurs.

Apparently most entrepreneurs consciously or instinctively plan on the basis of three assets:

- who they and their friends are, and what they all bring to the party;
- what they know – education, training and experience;
- who they know – in terms of social and professional networks.

Sarasvathy contrasts a goal-driven warrior like Genghis Khan (objective: conquest of the known world), with the explorers like Magellan and Columbus who set out on voyages across uncharted waters, with confidence in their own abilities and not a lot else.

There are a couple of quotes from Sarasvathy that I particularly liked. The first was: 'Entrepreneurs... act as if they believe that the future is not out there to be discovered, but that it gets created through the very strategies of the players.' I suppose one of the great explorers would have concluded that it doesn't matter if you don't know where you have arrived, as long as you do something useful when you get there!

The other quotation was:

> Expert entrepreneurs explicitly stated that being in a market that can be predicted was not such a good idea, since there would always be someone smarter and with deeper pockets who would predict it better than they would. But being in an unpredictable market meant that the market could be shaped by their own decisions and actions. Armed with effectual logic, we can cope better with surprises.

Steve Jobs – the most effectual thinker of our era

We knew that Steve Jobs had to be very ill to stand down from the helm at Apple. But to die so soon after. At the age of only 56.

Consider Saras Sarasvathy's seminal paper: 'What Makes Entrepreneurs Entrepreneurial'. In her study into what makes entrepreneurs different from everyone else, she highlights the way they think. She describes it as 'effectual' reasoning, and contrasts it with predictive and rational thinking, which she calls 'causal'.

For Sarasvathy, a decision based on causal reasoning is designed to cause an outcome that will bring you closer to your goal. Causal reasoning or decision making is about means to an end. Logical. Sequential. Linear. This is command-and-control behaviour.

Effectual reasoning is not about setting a goal and making decisions based on how to achieve it. Effectual thinking and decision making is about making things happen in a broader sense. Effectual decisions can work just as well in an indirect way. In marketing and advertising, we are very familiar with both approaches. Marketing plans are predominantly causal, relating actions and investments to financial and verifiable targets and data.

Advertising, on the other hand, particularly in the brave new world of consumer conversations, tends to be based on strategic thinking and insights into consumer behaviour, and what might influence it. Planning and creative are inherently effectual, while media, direct marketing and promotions are causal.

Which brings us back to the amazing career, influence and sheer creativity of Steve Jobs. Not only an innovator par excellence. He was also a true visionary in that he was able to conceive, make and market a legendary line of products under the Apple, Mac and 'I-' labels, which his loyal followers adopted as if the branding was actually theirs.

Effectual is of course the exact opposite of ineffectual. Jobs was effectual and influential to an extent unmatched by any of his contemporaries. We can cite a distinguished list of pioneers from former generations: Stephenson, Brunel, Hargreaves, Ford, Marconi and so on. Or the early consumer champions who built giant companies like P&G, Unilever, Nestlé, Cadbury and co. But the mechanics of manufacture, distribution and selling in those days were much more straight line. People were still customers. They had not yet learned to become consumers.

Jobs has been the most effectual leader and champion of the consumer revolution – understanding that entertainment, leisure, friendship and fun are just as important as producing documents and making phone calls. Pixar and the App Store are as much a part of his extraordinary legacy as the Apple Mac and the iPhone. His inventions haven't just given us great products to buy. He defined, shaped and framed the empowered world we now take for granted.

Calver, Cassani and Vasiliev on enterpreneurs and managers:

Simon Calver of Lovefilm:

Entrepreneurs are not risky decision makers. They are the least risky decision makers you will ever come across, because it's their own money. Again, that's something about decision making that not a lot of people think about.

When I look for people and I look for my direct reports, I often look for people who have been in large corporations who know what good looks like. I also like people who have tried something different or entrepreneurial – whether they have succeeded or failed. It doesn't matter. They have tried it, but not hit that home run and are still hungry to achieve. They've been in a causal environment, they know that you've got to achieve goals, you've got to operate, and that process matters. Having an appraisal with somebody is a good thing. But there are some entrepreneurs who would never have an appraisal with anybody from one day to the next. Everybody in this organization is on a quarterly performance plan, which means they are set goals every 13 weeks, they are measured against those goals, and they get an element of pay based on how well they perform against their goals on a quarterly basis.

Cassani on being a manager:

" I really like working with people to enable them to get better at their jobs. Being super smart and going to an Ivy League school does not mean you could manage people. I think it is probably a barrier, because they are accustomed to being around people with whom they can speak in shorthand. Once you can't speak in shorthand, you've got to find a way of communicating complex and simple ideas in such a way that people will accept them. You can't fake whether or not you feel condescending towards someone, or if you really do feel that way, they aren't stupid, they will pick it up, and you will be affected. Once I found out I liked being a manager, as opposed to being a strategic boffin, which is where I started out, I thought, wow, this is very cool. Because the other thing I worked out is that all the power lay with the managers, but a lot of them were the people who refused to implement my great ideas when I had been a consultant. So I thought, this is very, very cool; if I still have the ability to think things through like a boffin does, but with the skills of a manager and the power of a manager, hot dang, I can really do stuff. So that was why I liked being in business.

Vitaly Vasiliev from Gazprom on people and cultures:

" There's a huge difference between the definition of the manager and entrepreneur. So in terms of the classic decision-making process, this is typical manager behaviour. They are managers, so basically they're meeting, they're discussing, they're saying okay, this is our forecast, and this is our view of the world. They're just discussing, and they're building something. Their decisions are based on their view of the world. Then actually it doesn't work. So they come and say okay, it doesn't work, but let's understand why it doesn't work. Okay, it didn't work because the world changed and then they explain to everybody and to themselves why it didn't work, because they have the explanation. We thought that the world would be like that, but then we found there are Black Swans which you can't see. These managers are very peacefully explaining; this event happened, that event happened, so basically it didn't work. And they are pretty fine with that.

But an entrepreneur is different. He has no choice, because he will be dead if it doesn't work. So what he's trying to do is to try to build the options. He does this, and he does that, but he knows that some of what he tries won't work. It's important for him to try this route, even if he hits the wall, and can't go on. For him the failure is actually the learning experience. The entrepreneur is trying quickly to build some options for his decision making process, because he knows that out of ten possible solutions, eight will not work. He says to himself that he will learn from them, and if two work, then the entrepreneur has achieved his objective.

I advocate a dolphin culture. You see I have a dolphin in my office. Everybody gets dolphins. There are three distinct cultures: dolphins, sharks and carp. Let's start with carp. If you look at carp behaviour, they are usually hiding and sheltering by the rocks. When there's any food left, for example from a big shark fight, the carp just quickly leave their shelter, pick up the bits of food and go back. It's an opportunistic kind of culture. They say, I'm not picking a fight, but I can always get something which has been left on the table.

But sharks have a predatory culture. It's all about winning. If I'm doing business with you, and I'm a shark, I just don't care about you. I just want to win. I want to get what I want. That makes me successful.

Dolphin culture, I describe as more like win to win. If I want to win, I need to make you successful. So if you're successful, and I'm successful, that's a good basis for long-term cooperation. I think that the win–win approach is very important. People usually believe that dolphins are very friendly. They think they're nice, and so on. But actually they're one of the only mammals that actually can attack sharks. Here's how dolphins attack sharks. They know that the shark actually has a weakest point on its belly. So if a shark is attacking somebody, the dolphin swims under the shark and uses its nose to hit the shark at its weakest point in the belly. And the shark dies.

So the dolphin is our symbol, rather than a shark or a carp. Our company's philosophy is that we want to cooperate, and we want to win to win. But when it's necessary, we can be the hunter. We can attack if something is behaving aggressively towards us. And dolphins are exactly this type of animal: they're friendly, they're cooperative, but if they feel a threat, if somebody is attacking them, they can attack back. In terms of what we're doing in this company, in terms of our role and our vision, I believe this is the right culture for us.

But if your company's core values are much closer to the carp, that's fine, because this is a big ocean. There need to be different fish out there. It would be very sad if everybody was a dolphin. It would also be very sad if everybody was a shark. People are different. You need to understand whom you are joining, what you're doing. I always say that there are two choices for everybody, for all of us: we either need to do what we love, or we need to start loving what we're doing. Otherwise it's very difficult to wake up in the morning, put our clothes on, and go to the office.

Chapter Seven
Choice is three-dimensional decision making

Choosing is different because of the way the brain – and committees – work

> *Choice is relative to what you can have,*
> *not absolutely about what you want.*
>
> **(BEHAVIOURAL ECONOMICS: RED HOT OR RED HERRING?**
>
> **IPA 2010)**

I suppose it is not surprising that choice fascinates me. I love TV programmes like *Strictly Come Dancing*, *The Apprentice* and *Masterchef*, not, sadly, the *X Factor* – I have tried. But I am warming to *The Voice*, and particularly to the idea of only turning round to face a candidate when I'm actively interested! After nearly 25 years facilitating the search and selection of advertising and communications agencies, I am fascinated by both the search criteria (how were these guys picked?), and the selection rules (how are they going to choose a winner?). I am riveted by the weekly drama of who is going to be eliminated. I sympathize with the contestants. I emphasize with the judges. I want supreme talent to triumph, but inevitably I become caught up in the sheer human drama of it all. Living a dream on national television every week, and working really hard to improve your skills is no small thing. Watching people getting better at something is inspiring.

Here is an unusual search and selection story.

Daniel Topolski on selecting oarsmen

I asked Daniel about the time he started coaching the Oxford University Boat Race crew in 1973. What action did he take to make sure that the selections were based on fact – current fact, rather than reputation or anything else.

David: 'I mean, as somebody who's a mad keen follower of five or six sports, it's hard to think of one sport where selection is done on that basis. So often you see a cricket team or a football team or a rugby team that's been picked on reputation. You read the journalists that you respect who say it can't be right to keep picking him and he doesn't make the runs and he doesn't score the tries.'

Daniel: 'Are you saying that in those sports they pick on reputation, rather than current evidence? They shouldn't.'

David: 'And there should be a huge learning from what you've done because at the end of the day anyone who reads the book *True Blue* [1989, about the mutiny by American oarsmen in 1986–87] understands that that was your trump card.'

Daniel: 'It gave me confidence to be able to confront those guys.'

David: 'And it's something that you developed years before. It wasn't something that you dreamed up to prove the point. I mean, it was an established selection methodology which had worked consistently.'

Daniel: 'The trouble is that complacency creeps in all the time. People assume that they'll outperform on the day. You know, don't worry about it; we'll be there on the day.'

David: 'But your experience has not been that?'

Daniel:

"No. In my very first year when I first took over, that's a good example. Andy Hall was the president and wrote to me when I was travelling in India to become the coach and asked me if I would come back and be chief coach and coach them, and I said, yes. There were about four or five guys from the year before who'd lost and really had five years of losing. Andy had been in the year before. So he'd lost three boat races and I started to lay down this training stuff that we were doing. We had a camp in Putney, in January and I needed to see if Andy or Dave Willis – a big strong freshman from Hampton School – would come through the tests I laid down for them.

I mean, it was pretty horrendous this stuff, it wasn't that scientific, but it was the best way I could find to put a lot of pressure on Oxford. I had to get them to overcome obstacles, so there were some sprints. We did 400 metre sprints, we did 200 metre sprints, we did 100 metre sprints and it was between Dave Willis, this 15 stone dream athlete, and Andy Hall, the president who got in the crew. So in January, doing these tests, Dave hadn't been performing and he should have. I had them doing a lot of single sculling. That was terribly important in the way I was assessing my guys. I wanted them to race each other, I wanted them in national races, in all the Head of the River races – they had to do all of those races – racing all the time. Just watching their own progress, learning how to move a boat on their own, how they were competing against each other and if they couldn't scull to start, they'd bloody well be able to scull by the end of it. I did all these tests all the time, and then on the Tideway, two Head of the River race tests, over the four and a quarter miles, two odometer tests, running tests, gym.

I mean, everything was tested and I remember they were doing these 400 metre sprints, I was at the end, somebody was starting and I would time them in waves of about four or five guys. During the day I had put Andy and Dave into the B boat – because I wasn't very impressed with their rowing. So I put them into the second boat, the B boat, and on these sprints they were running and neither of them were great runners, but Andy Hall was just fighting. He was president and he'd been humiliated – both of them had. He was fighting for the line and every time he finished he would be ahead of his group. He wasn't in the top group, he wasn't the fastest runner, he said he hated all this kind of thing. He'd say f... you, and run back down to the start again. Do it again four times. Every time. Dave Willis came in at the back trotting because he was very angry with me. So within two days I'd put Andy back into the A boat, Dave was still in the second boat and a day later he resigned and left the group. And that was one of the first decisions I had to make on that sort of level.

Dave wasn't prepared to fight the way that Andy did. Andy really laid himself on the line – humiliated, but fought back. Dave was humiliated and thought, I'm not going to push myself. You either put me in the boat, or I go. This is just a training camp. He could have easily fought back, but he retired himself.

Choosing agencies

When major advertisers select their ideal agency these days, it has become an increasingly complicated business. The advent of technology, digital and social media has made setting criteria much more difficult. There are more agencies. There are more types of agency. Expertise is far more differentiated, with a bewildering variety of specialisms, and inevitably more ambitious admen and all-rounders, always looking to add strings to their bow. As facilitator of the selection process, and importantly the talent hunter who unearths the potential stars, my colleagues and I carry a significant responsibility, which we try never to forget or diminish. We have to do an outstanding job for our clients, who pay us. We also have to be completely fair and understanding with the agencies, who don't.

The traditional Agency Assessments International (AAI) approach and search and selection process was explained (with diagrams) in Chapter 4. That is how we systematically managed group choice situations in a commercial context.

Three dimensions of choice

I see choice as three-dimensional, in contrast to decision making, in two separate senses. First, because we have to search as well as select. Decision making normally consists of a series of options. Do we act now, or not? If we are going to decide, do we say yes or no? If there are a number of options on the table, which one are we going to go with? Decision making is normally about taking options on board, ranking them, and deciding.

It is different with choosing. Before we can select or choose, we need to have searched for possible candidates. With choosing there is a vital preliminary phase: whittling the candidates or options down to a handleable number. How do we do that? By elimination, not ranking. And all that has to take place before selection (the real decision making) can begin.

Selection is different – and easier, because any list of options can be reduced to a series of binary comparisons. Here are my Five Laws of Choice:

1 Choosing is a strategic activity. Be very clear about needs, goals and framing the decision.

2 There is no point in looking at options until you have firmed up criteria – which will depend on needs and goals vs what's available in the marketplace.

3 Choosing is inherently risky. Draw up a list of options – looking at the gap between perfect choice and the worst-case scenario. Define risks.

4 Don't rank Long-list. Eliminate till you're down to, ideally, three, by discarding the worst option, one at a time.

5 Pick winner by three binaries (A vs B, A vs C, B vs C). Validate choice by getting buy-in and ratification – the mutual decision.

Formalized – or at least semi-structured – choosing is all around us. Choice determines a frightening proportion of our lives. This brings us to three dimensions in the second sense: choice affecting us in three distinct ways. We choose things for ourselves. Things are chosen for us. We are chosen – or not.

There is a life phase aspect to it:

- We do not choose our parents, where we are born, where we live as children, the shape of the family unit, our circumstances – affluence, hardship, and so on. Some of these choices were made consciously by our parents. In other cases, the outcome was determined by outside factors.

- We don't by and large choose where we go to school or what we study, but as we get older, we can influence the choice by performance and argument.

- At the same stage we don't have ultimate say in who our friends are, but we become increasingly influential, and with social media, children and young people can build friendships and networks across a much bigger geographic spread than was possible in any previous era. This is a very important change. Future choices, which as we shall see are far more within the young person's power, can be significantly shaped not just by friends, but by *connected and informed* friends.

- We can decide whether we want to go to college or university, and (within family financial parameters) whether we want to go away, and if so, where. Again ability and performance are going to be big factors, but so is our will. Nonetheless for university we have to be chosen.

- Theoretically we can choose what kind of career we would like, but sadly (and ironically given the sheer numbers of graduates on the market) the opportunities in attractive fields are probably proportionately lower than at any time since the dark days after the First World War. Putting this right doesn't seem to be a major priority for this government (any more than it was for its immediate predecessors), but it should be. Look at Chapter One, 'Dreams and determination'. Restrict opportunities, and there is a danger you will strangle success at birth.

- Assuming health, an income and bright eyes, the young adult now embarks on a feast of choice:
  - Where to live?
  - Rent or buy?
  - Career, job?
  - Partner?
  - Friends, social life, clubs, pubs, restaurants?
  - Sports, hobbies, pursuits?
  - Holidays?
  - Car and other major purchases?
  - Fashion and style?

- There are agents, agencies, expert advisors and facilitators to help us with all these choices – even of the ideal partner (see Chapter 10).

- Once the partner has been chosen, there are then important choices to be made: children, family, lifestyle, schools.

- At various stages there will be sharp reminders that we haven't completely grown out of having things chosen for us (jobs, doctors and health facilities, schools, by a partner), nor of being chosen (again in the world of work, socially in terms of friends and maybe new potential partners, and in competitive sport).

- As we get older, we become subject to a whole range of things that are chosen for us, or which we would not have chosen to do. We can fall ill. We can be sacked, made redundant or retired early. We can be deserted or left alone by partners or other family members. We can become dependent and need care. We die.

I am not intending to be depressing – just realistic about the way choice rules our lives. There is an aspect of choice that has dominated my whole working life – from marketing research at Nielsen to advising advertisers at AAI (from the Harold Wilson era to David Cameron, if you want to date it by Prime Ministers!). I am talking about consumer choice, the world of marketing, advertising, and now increasingly multi-screens and consumer dialogue. It is a world that has changed fundamentally from what I grew up with – the command-and-control and propaganda hangover from wartime. It is now a world with the consumer confidently in charge, and manufacturers, retailers and the marketing fraternity desperately trying to influence choice.

Consumer choice is a highly sophisticated business nowadays

I hugely enjoyed working with Rory Sutherland on his Behavioural Economics task force, during his stunning presidency of the Institute of Practitioners in Advertising (IPA). He had been inspired by reading *Nudge* (Thaler and Sunstein, 2008). In the 1960s when I started work, academics like Ernest Dichter and advertising practitioners like Stanley Pollitt (PWP and later BMP), Stephen King (JWT) and Stephen Broadbent (Leo Burnett) were coming to the fore with exciting ideas about what consumers (*aka* people) thought, and why they behaved as they did. It is probably too sweeping a statement to say that almost 40 years passed (*pace* some excellent and dedicated account planners and some good papers submitted to the IPA Effectiveness Awards) before this curiosity resurfaced in a big way. The IPA has published some useful papers. Probably the best was one called, quite simply, *Behavioural Economics: Red hot or red herring?* (2010). Under the leadership of Rory and Nick Southgate, a number of concepts were identified which, even in brief, go a long way to explain why fundamental thinking about the way the consumer chooses and makes decisions is alive and well:

- Loss aversion. People will work harder to avoid losing something than they will to gain it.
- The power of now. Consumers engage more with current events than with future events.
- Scarcity value. If we think something is scarce it has greater value. Equally, if something is plentiful, its value falls.

- Goal dilution. When multiple goals are pursued, they are less effectively achieved than goals pursued individually.

- Chunking. Parts are easier than wholes. The way a task is presented affects people's willingness to take it on and complete it.

- Price perception. The price demanded for something makes us value it.

- Choice architecture. Choosing is relevant to what you can have, not absolutely about what you want.

Behavioural Economics is a persuasive subject, but it is easy to get carried away. Here is a blog post I wrote about people (in this case government scientists) possibly making one assumption too many.

Behavioural Economics isn't a one-way street

We have become accustomed to positive stories about how the application of decision science has helped companies, government departments and other organizations influence behaviour in a beneficial way. There was a news story that reminded me that it doesn't always work like that.

The story that fascinated me was about a study that paediatricians have conducted on the increasing levels of Vitamin D deficiency in babies born in Britain. One of the authors of the report agreed that sunshine is a significant source of the vitamin for mothers and their new-born children. Obviously by world standards the UK has a disappointing lack of sunshine, but that situation has not changed. So how to explain the increasing level of deficiency?

The report thinks that one of the factors could be mothers using substantially more effective sun-screen products.

If true, this makes sun cream, which we have been told to use to prevent skin cancer, a potential 'culprit' in putting babies at risk of rickets and infections. This is the Behavioural Economics of well-meant medical advice giving with one hand and taking with the other.

Another example might be the widespread practice of parents taking their children to school by car. The motivation is clearly the peace of mind that comes from making sure the children are safe. But I can think of at least five actual or potential negative consequences:

- children who are less active and fit (less walking, cycling etc);
- children who are less self-reliant;
- congested roads;
- less use of public transport;
- carbon-negativity on a grand scale;

you can, as so often, argue it both ways.

Money isn't the only currency

The central tenet of Behavioural Economics is that people are motivated by a lot more things than just financial considerations. Yet how many decisions are announced with a financial spin, and little else? Closing down a factory will save so many millions. Launching a new product or expanding into a new market will make the company even more millions. Governments are as bad. Every policy announcement (and particularly the ones that have clearly been hastily cobbled together) carries a price tag.

So yesterday's announcement by GSK Chief executive Officer (CEO) Andrew Witty that they are offering to supply developing countries with an anti-diarrhoea vaccine at a discount of 95 per cent on the market price in the west hit the headlines. Was this, as Mr Witty claimed, an example of corporate social responsibility (CSR) in action? Or is it, as Andrew Hill in the FT's Business Blog said, CSV (creating shared value –

as recommended by Michael Porter and Mark Kramer, the founders of the FSG social impact consultancy)? Hill argues that for drug companies, tiered pricing makes commercial sense as well as earning plaudits:

- You act philanthropically by supplying impoverished populations at or near cost price.
- You act commercially in mid-income countries by charging enough to build markets, but price competitively to expand volume.
- And you build in big margins in rich countries to fund your voracious research and development (R&D) budget.

The motivation issue is really important in decision science. As individuals, families and parents we take a broader view than just financial self-interest in terms of making decisions driven by considerations like lifestyle, balance, health, education, enjoyment, culture and leisure. Equally the companies and organizations we tend to admire appear to respect employees, communities and the environment in making their decisions.

Also on the financial dimension we need to retain a balance sheet view of things (building and nurturing assets for the future), as well as the limiting short-term view that annual accounting – or worse, quarterly reporting in the United States – dictate.

As a footnote to yesterday's GSK story, I listened to a radio interview with a heavy duty fund manager, who simply did not buy that any CEO who used the phrase 'people before profit' (as Witty allegedly did) could be taken seriously by their shareholders. I can possibly understand 'people and profit', but 'people before profit'?

Never. It really is hard to take seriously any commentator saying that in 2011, when they have lived through a last 12 months in which dictatorships and mighty corporations have paid awesome penalties for decisions that put people last.

Neuromarketing

One of my most riveting interviews was with Charles Spence, Professor of Experimental Psychology at my old University, Oxford. He is one of the pioneers of neuromarketing – the application of psychology and neurology to marketing and communications techniques.

To start with, here's a blog post I wrote, somewhat breathily, when I returned to my desk from two hours with Charles.

Blog extract

Uncommon sense

For weeks now I have mainly been writing about decisions in business, politics and sport. It is high time to return to the area of decision making that has been the focus of my working life for over 40 years – how the consumer decides, and what influences those decisions.

On Friday last week I had the opportunity of an interview that did a great deal to get me back inside the consumer's head. I spent a riveting two hours with the Professor of Experimental Psychology at Oxford University. Charles Spence is one of the world's leading experts in the science of neuromarketing. Unsurprisingly he is in as much demand from marketers as from his students and research assistants.

I am sure that in his private and family life, Charles has a healthy supply of common sense. But when it comes to the application of his academic training as a psychologist and neuroscientist to understanding and stimulating his fellow humans as citizens, patients and consumers, he is truly the master of uncommon sense.

During the course of sessions in his spectacularly untidy office and the Aladdin's cave beneath that is his laboratory, I learned an extraordinary amount about how we experience products, brands and marketing communications through our senses, and how marketers and others can influence consumer behaviour by simultaneously impacting on more than one sense at the same time.

Importantly, I also learned how much I don't know. We are dealing here with the principles of synaesthesia: the interconnection between stimuli to our five senses: vision, smell, taste, touch and hearing.

For instance:

- We are well aware that appreciation of the taste of wine is enhanced by its smell – or 'nose'. But as we look for inspiration in Majestic, how consciously are we influenced by the colour of the bottle, and its shape and weight? Do we realize the impact of the shape of the label?

- How susceptible are we to the smell as well as the feel of a garment treated by a fabric softener...

- ... or to the noisiness of a packet of crisps, which 'says' crispness just as much as the contents deliver the taste we expect?

- Does strawberry jam taste better out of a jar with a red label?

- Has the sound coming out of an iPod been as important as the taste of the ingredients in turning 'Sound of the Sea' into Heston Blumenthal's signature dish at the Fat Duck?

I will be exploring more aspects of how consumer decision making and behaviour can be influenced by communicating with the senses as opposed to just using reason and emotion. I have a hunch that neuromarketing might throw even more light on Behavioural Economics in the *Nudge* or Rory Sutherland sense, and give us some powerful new examples of ingenious and hyper-effective ideas.

I would also like to see if considered or macro-decision making in the corporate or institutional context is also capable of being enhanced by appealing to the senses. We already know how important the evidence of the different senses is to people in the armed forces, emergency services, Accident and Emergency (A&E), on the flight deck, and even referees and umpires – who are all tasked with making decisions in very short order.

Could it be that we are just touching the surface by only applying reason and logic to big decisions in business and public life? Maybe we should be factoring in seeing, smelling, hearing and tasting, as well as touching!'

I probed Charles about his experiments in synaesthesia, and in particular his work with Heston Blumenthal:

> The ones that have been a big success have been with sound. So, there's been the 'Sound of the Sea' seafood dish at the Fat Duck, originated in the lab here on some experiments with Heston. That's had a very big impact and is still influencing people. What my lab tries to do is think about how the brain works and how the senses come together and take the latest in neuroscience and then say how does it apply and how can you translate psychological paradigms and test the best of the stuff in the laboratory. How do you put that into a real world context to assess the fragrance of a new washing powder, or the sound of a Lynx deodorant spray, or the taste of a food?

An awful lot depends on what happens when the consumer is in the shop. For somebody who was trained in extreme long-range marketing and communications planning (brief delivered at an off-site meeting in April – campaign finally goes national 18 months later), there's something appealing about watching what the consumer actually puts into her or his trolley. That's real-time consumer decision making, and I love it.

Charles Spence interview

I found talking to Charles Spence really interesting. Here are some more excerpts from the interview. I asked him if he had the slightest idea when he was training as a psychologist that he would ever be immersed in the forensics of consumer choice:

> No. I wanted to be a big earner in the City, in banking or management consultancy. It was the time when word processing was only just coming in, and I sent off all my CVs by hand one night to all the companies with about nine spelling mistakes in each one. Then the recession of 91/92 came along, and that was that.

The City's loss was marketing's gain. We discussed the different senses in turn, starting with sound.

Sound

> Look what happens in wine stores, look what happens in restaurants, look what happens in bars, when you change the music. And if you believe that, you have to try to tell me why it wouldn't work in clothing [for his big jeans client]. But all that comes out of our work with restaurants, because in a way big brands and companies can take such a long time, whereas chefs are more often than not their own boss, and they can actually try things out and then say, okay, it works there. The 'Sound of the Sea' has been a signature dish in the Fat Duck for about 18 months now.

> We were working with Unilever on the sound of food, and doing Pringles. We won the 2008 IG Nobel prize for Nutrition for showing that if you eat a Pringle and you change the sound when you bite into it, then it changes the texture and the taste. Pringles are about 15 per cent crunchier just by changing what you hear.

> Intuitive marketers know about this. If you take the Magnum advert at the moment, that crack of the chocolate is enhanced and for several other brands they've used the sound of the product, the sound of the packaging and emphasize it. But what they haven't done is extend it to other market sectors. This is where the neuroscience comes in. We can say this is the reason why changing the sound changes the taste of Pringles,

and for that reason we can predict it could also affect how smooth the shave is, or how soft the fabric is after the wash. Because in these cases, our brain uses all the senses, brings them together, and these are the rules that combine the senses. So there are obviously general principles, for instance there must have been a marketer who said it's not physically necessary to have a noisy crisp packet for a noisy product, but somebody thought that was a good idea and it worked. If you're selling tissues, then you want to make it a quiet and soft sound. You can change the sound the person hears as they pull each tissue from the box. So every product has a sound and here are the techniques that will allow us to quickly say which sound is the best one. Let's change it and see how people respond and if that doesn't work, we'll change it again.

So you get a slow design process: test, change, test, change, test. This way we are able to, for people like Unilever and Nestle, say, okay, with your product, without having to cook it differently, let's just play with all the sounds you could get your food to make, see which one people prefer, or which is best associated with your brand, and then you can go to your development kitchens and say, can we actually make our biscuit or breakfast cereal sound that way? And maybe sometimes you can, sometimes you can't, but at least you know where to go and you can innovate much more rapidly.

Sight, in terms of shapes

People associate sweetness with roundness, bitterness with angularity (eg, think stars and triangles). Well, it's not really triangles; it's angles. And it turns out we've just been doing a whole series of experiments on tastes and packaging and abstract imagery on food packaging and came to basically the same conclusions as Ernst Dichter forty years ago.

Gladwell quotes from Madison Avenue marketing magician Louis Cheskin about a skin creme product that women liked more when it had circles rather than triangles on the pack. The same principles apply to cheeses and chocolates and sparkling water, hence all the stars on San Pellegrino bottles and cans. They're all using shape and symbolism.

I've been working on the senses and then also on application, thinking, at least if we're doing interface design, I'm just blinding people with numbers and models that are all based on their intuition. There's no real rigorous science underneath it and ever since I've been trying to put these two things together and applying science to real-life problems, be it car design or packaging. It's really interesting and it's really scientific, or it can be.

Wine: taste, touch, look and smell

I've just written some stuff on the weight of a wine bottle. Two kilos versus one kilo for exactly the same amount of wine, so much higher apparent value. It worked out that the price went up for each extra eight grams in weight. It turns out the same thing goes on with lipstick.

Once you start playing with different-shaped bottles, you can very cheaply create angular labels, or rounded labels. There's so much to do. You can't really do anything to the bottle or the volume, then there's so much interesting psychology already there on the labels. You have to analyse it and see if what you see on wine labels can be extended to soft drinks or to spirits. All of the principles you'll find being used to make one brand stand out against another. Here's a £180 bottle that has a cap that's just so incredibly heavy, so much heavier than you'd expect, to give the illusion of quality through the weight of the cap.

Subliminal

It could be the case that lots of our decision making goes on under the radar subconsciously, so making it difficult to actually explain it logically. How do you improve something that's often happening without us being aware of it? We think we're consciously making decision, but maybe a lot of those decisions are actually happening subliminally, before we know about it.

Synaesthesia

"I can make your life easier by combining all the senses and saying, I'm getting four estimates of what's out there. I can smell it, I can see it, I can hear it, I can feel it, what is it really? Your brain seamlessly integrates what it sees and what it hears. Vision scientists argue about it on something called CVNet, which is like a vision scientists' discussion forum. I'm not sure whether there was a paper that started it or whether it was just somebody who'd done some research, but there is a theory about people with particularly sharp eyes, who exercise their eyesight to make it even more acute. It is also worth looking at wine expertise. Some of the latest work suggests that wine experts are able to actually pull things apart. Their expertise is actually to separate out to a greater degree than anybody else, the taste from the flavour, by nosing.

I'm halfway through a book on psychology in the kitchen, and the bottom line would probably be that over half of what we think of as taste or flavour or food or enjoyment of wine is actually not in the wine, not in the food we put in our mouth, it's everything else. And you can't believe it, but physical experiments prove that case.

Analysis and synthesis

"The wine buffs are much better at analytic perception than they are at synthesising it all together. Some cases suggest that in fact if you're an analytic frame of mind trying to keep everything separate, then you don't enjoy it as much. You ask these experts, 'Well, how was the wine? Was it good? Did you like it?' And they say, 'I don't know.' They are too busy segmenting it.

Doctors, detectives etc

I asked Charles whether any of this learning might explain how people like doctors and detectives work. Are really good diagnosticians able to do that, because it is painfully obvious to everybody that GPs aren't. They're too busy, they see too many people, they're probably not that brilliant at it anyway. They are completely unable to spot a symptom hiding under another symptom. Yet it's astonishing how really good physicians can see two patients, both presenting apparently the same symptoms and having that feeling that there's something more profoundly wrong with one of them and yet to even a GP's eye, let alone a layman's eye, there was nothing. And it goes back to the things that they're taught, look in the eyes, look in the toes, look at the hair, just look for something that isn't quite right. Charles mentioned smell:

> It could be that in a multi-sensory case, often what our brains do is pick up very faint cues, a very faint smell and a very faint taste can give you a very strong flavour. Expert lip readers will pick up lip movements that aren't very useful by themselves. Then a very faint sound at a noisy cocktail party, and put those two weakly effective cues together and get something much bigger. So part of one's skill might be in the brain's ability to combine very subtle information in different channels of different sorts.

Smell

> A lot less of our brain is given over to smell than with animals like dogs. Some would say, it is connected with our going on two legs that allows us to see further, but smell less. Vision's more useful to us, whereas if you're at ground level, no matter how well you see, you can only see as far as the next bush.

People are finding all sorts of things about smells, even smells that we don't know we're smelling, and its effect on decision making and behaviour. We're doing lots of work at the moment with an international fragrance company on the way we can use fragrance to make people look more attractive, and seem as if they have softer skin.

Charles's Lynx story

> 'Spray then bonk' is the three-word summary of the product promise. It hasn't been announced but we did the work with Lynx to see whether that claim was really true. Could we validate it? The advertising agency BBH devised to support the claim, that young women rate men more attractively when they have a pleasant fragrance. Lynx has a special fragrance, so it's slightly nuanced. We then did a brain-imaging study to see which parts of a woman's brain light up more when they see a man's face while smelling a pleasant odour such as Lynx, and it showed us which bits of the brain at the front code facial attractiveness. Just by looking in here you can see how attractive a woman finds a man, and in the part of the brain that code's facial attractiveness, you can see we have this pleasant fragrance that shifts the brain activity just that little bit towards the more attractive guys.

Charles showed me the area of the laboratory where this testing was done. It reminded me of a sort of battery hen unit, where he installed the women who were being scanned as they were exposed to the multisensory interaction of Lynx and pictures of guys!

How the brain was built

So the gut response, instinctive response, area would have all been the old bits of the brain, primitive bits of the brain, which are in the centre; and all the clever-thinking stuff and rational stuff has been built over and outside.

There's a little bit at the top of the spine because that'd be the first part of the brain, so it's a bit further forward and right in the centre. That would be the gut instinct just like that. That would be a blink thing rather than 60 seconds.

I then asked Charles:

> Suppose you were asking say a marketing director about a very important 60-hour decision – shall we launch such and such a product? Competitors have come up with something that is

apparently very similar. Shall we go ahead with the launch? We've got really three days to think about it. And then his cousin, the firefighter, goes into a building, looks up and sees flames and everything and then the classic case, feels the heat through his feet and realizes that the dangerous fire is not the one he can see up there, but the one below, which nobody's actually noticed. The basement of the building's on fire. Would the scan show activity in different parts of the brain?

Charles replied:

> For the gut response, it should be much more the primitive central brain areas. There's much more visceral response of bodily danger. For longer-term decision making, you are doing something very different. There's much more rational analysis, weighing up relative options, looking for analogies.
>
> I would think 60 seconds versus 60 days wouldn't be any different. When you're given 60 minutes or 60 days, then you will spend more time sending blood to the outsides of the brain to think more rational thoughts, or look in long-term memory, see what were some of the situations you were in in the past and try and do some statistical analysis. But whether at the end, you actually end up still just going on gut feel is an open question. Maybe you rationalize to yourself. You might wonder whether in fact it's all done on gut feel. What 60 minutes or 60 days buys you is just the rationalizing to yourself or to others why I chose that. I chose it because the projections were better, or did you really choose it just for the gut feel? Antonio Damasio's book *Descartes' Error* is all about making decisions on gut feel and using the body instead of the mind.

The consumer can't tell the difference

> Many products are virtually indistinguishable to the consumer. You actually can get them to discriminate if you have a trained panel and they're in the same room with the same lighting doing one then the other, then they can discriminate, but in the

real world they have product A today and then product B tomorrow morning, tomorrow evening, different time of day, different lighting, different mood, different state. Maybe it's all about the marketing and the branding and the labelling.

The jam test: post-rationalizing

I could show you a video of a jam-tasting experiment. Put people into supermarkets, have two pots of jam, one in the red container, one in the blue container. Researchers ask shoppers to try these two pots of jam, we're interested in seeing which one you like and which one you prefer. 'I like the red one from the red container.' The containers go away, they come back out. Just take another spoonful and tell me why you like that one.

We actually used double-ended jam jars and, so we switched it. They're post rationalising. We switched it from the one they didn't like a second ago, now they're justifying why they like it. Less than 1 per cent of the brain is given over to taste and maybe 4 per cent to smell, 50 per cent to vision, so maybe it's no surprise that in fact it's all been driven by the non-factual.

How suggestible are we?

I asked him whether people are almost infinitely suggestible:

To some degree, yes. Obviously there must be limits to it. But you can do it when you're on the internet looking at houses or cars or things on Amazon. All those attributes – how do you compare? Which car? It's got four wheels and it's blue versus one that's got four wheels and grey, but with a CD player. Which of those cars do I want? Which of those books? Which outfit? I think I'm making a rational choice. I've weighed up the pros and cons, and then when I choose this one, why? You've got two apparently identical offers and you're more attracted to the one where the price keeps going up because you think that people must have spotted something. Same laptop, but you have the USB ports on the front rather than the back, if you make them into the shape of a smile rather than a frown, people like the computers more.

Colour coding

We've been in Colombia looking at colour, meanings of colours and shapes and image forms and packaging. Put something in a green crisp packet and they're convinced it's sour cream or it's lemon flavour. Whereas in England it's cheese and onion or it's salt and vinegar, depending on if you're a Walkers fan or not. So these things are cross-cultural. There are differences in the triggers that get combined optimally by culture. You've probably got the same rules being applied no matter where you are, it's just the particular combination of stimuli that really get your brain going on different depending on what you've been exposed to, or what your mother ate when she was pregnant with you.

Beer Taste

I asked Charles about the taste of beer. When I was young, the beer wasn't cold, whatever beer it was. It didn't matter at all. Now we've just adopted the rest of the world's preoccupation with coldness. And I worked on Guinness for a long time. Since those days Diageo have developed Guinness Extra Cold. There's an interesting one. What's the rationale?

Charles: 'It's the only feature that you can change that's discriminable.'

David: 'But it tastes of nothing. I'm a Guinness drinker and Guinness Extra Cold doesn't taste like Guinness. It tastes like dark lager because you lose all these notes and you lose a lot of the texture in it as well.'

Charles: 'Taste doesn't work at cold temperatures, but that's the only thing you can discriminate.'

Is anyone else doing this kind of work?

No. I look at the journals, I'm citing some papers at the moment and it falls somewhere between business schools, psychology and design. There are one or two other people, but very few. There's Baba Shiv in California at the business school, and the great work that is going on at the Delft University of Technology. We're all actually doing the same experiments, but in completely different departments, looking at how consumers... how packaging and products affect consumer decision making and liking. It's going to explode, I hope.

I was at a neuro-economics and neuro decision-making conference in Miami, 2009, in May, a big tri-annual thing and it had Ariely and it had lots of these other great researchers there and we had a session on neuroscience and how it's going to change. Neuroscience itself is very exciting, but it's pretty disappointing that there have not been more applications of neuromarketing and neurodecision – making to business. There are few amazing papers that were so well cited like the price of wine, and a few other Ariely examples, but, it just hasn't come off in the way that people were hoping four, five years ago.

Two moments of truth

This is the point where consumer decisions meet marketing decisions.

Definitions vary. The First Moment of Truth (FMOT) is either when you put a product in your trolley, or when you check it out. The Second Moment of Truth (SMOT) is when you eat it or use it. In a bar FMOT is the bar call, SMOT is the 'cheers' moment.

Research has shown that shopping lists overwhelmingly consist of products, not brands. Also that just over 75 per cent of in-store purchase decisions are on impulse, and that it takes between three and seven seconds to choose the item you want.

For those of us who spent the best years of our lives planning ad campaigns, these stats are pretty depressing. Nor are they very reassuring for a veteran pitch consultant. All that time and process to find the best agency in the world for your dairy client, and

Mrs Cameron in Notting Hill chooses an own-label yoghurt in five seconds flat.

Even Professor Spence must shudder. Some of the best minds in Oxford have advised the wine company on the shape and weight of the bottle, the design and colour of the label, even on the flavour and nose of the wine itself... and Mr Osborne has selected half a case of Chile's finest at £4.99 a bottle.

But that's how it is with decisions. You can be very influential in the ones you contribute to yourself. But a stressed customer in a hurry and a cash flow crisis can decide against logic and reason, and your best laid plans are frustrated.

None of this means that marketing and advertising decisions do not need the greatest care, and informed inputs. Of course it is worth finessing product formulation and packaging by building in sophisticated calculations on how it impacts on the consumer's taste, touch, sight, smell and hearing. It is everyone's task to make the product deliver at both FMOT and SMOT.

Traditional and digital advertising and marketing communications are as vital as ever to set up the desire. Just as long as we never forget that the real consumer isn't in a focus group or lab. She's left herself just three to seven seconds to load her trolley with a brand (yours, someone else's or an own brand).

Marketers have to make their decisions with all the limitations of consumer decision making in mind. So why don't they invest more money at or near the point of sale? Good question. Those clever people at P&G have upped their spend by four times.

Costco: Behavioural Economics in the raw

You need strong nerves to shop at Costco.

The first moment of truth is not about choosing between Heinz and the own label. It is about space in the trolley, space in the boot, and ultimately space in the home.

And that's before we get to comparative pricing. Are the profiteroles better priced than the cat litter? That vast chocolate fudge cake looks great value. But is it a better buy than 120 giant peeled prawns?

Then moments of rationality: 'Do we need 24 cans of tuna? How long will it take us to get through 120 pittas? I know we are always running out of soy sauce, but can we put a 2 litre pack of the stuff on the dining table?'

And also temptation by durable: the massive TV sets, the laptops, the golf clubs, the kitchen appliances, hobs, fountains. Even the wheel-chairs, for goodness sake.

Costco assaults behavioural sensitivities in every aisle. A psychologist with a clipboard would be jotting down:

- bargain hunting;
- economy of scale;
- planned saving on a one-off big buy;
- stocking up ahead of the next natural disaster;
- but above all... impulse purchasing.

These warehouses are temples to impulse purchasing on the grand scale. You yearn to interview the people pushing the most interestingly stacked carts. 'Why? What made you do it? What do you know that I don't? Are you reassured by the Kirkland brand?'

The whole experience reminded me, a Costco virgin, of the Cheltenham Festival. Familiar-looking people in an unfamiliar environment. Making decisions between this unknown and that unknown. 'Is Snug as a Bug in a Rug going to beat Popcorn Pie?' 'Is it better to buy four kilos of pizza or a year's supply of loo rolls?'

It strikes me that the Kirkland brand performs the same function as an each-way bet. In a choppy sea of uncertainty, they both sound reassuring – even if they do nothing to reduce risk.

I must go back to Costco regularly. Not so much to shop. I can't afford too many visits like that. But to watch, to observe binge shopping, and to work out why consumer behaviour can sometimes defy analysis.

But do you know the cleverest bit of sales promotion? It's the labels on the medicines saying 'Trade only'. That's the stimulus to loading the cart with even more stuff that you are allowed to buy!

Chapter Eight
War

What we can learn from the way nations fight

War deserves its own chapter, because the stakes are so much higher:

> That first evening I made a particular point of going up to the airport (in Pristina) to see Viktor Zavarzin, who was the Russian Commander. Russians are a wonderful mixture of stubbornness and sentimentality. It was a bit frosty to start with but I greeted them in Russian, pulled out a hip flask, gave them a slug of whisky and Zavarzin cheered up hugely. (General Sir Mike Jackson, later Chief of the General Staff, then – 1999 – Commander of KFOR in Kosovo)
>
> When a decision has to be made, make it. There is no totally right time for anything. (US Army General George S Patton, 1885–1945)
>
> Staggering irrationality can beset the thinking of otherwise highly competent, intelligent, conscientious individuals when they begin acting as a group. (Norman Dixon *On the Psychology of Military Incompetence*, 1976)

War

The Dixon book is compelling, and deserves a wider audience, given the fact that conflict in the 21st century shows no positive signs of any learning from history. Norman Dixon was a commissioned officer in the Royal Engineers before becoming Professor of Experimental Philosophy at UCL. He is highly critical of the way in which wars have been conducted over the centuries. His view of military incompetence is that it has shown itself repeatedly in the following ways:

- serious wastage of human resources and failure to observe one of the first principles of war – economy of force;
- fundamental conservatism and clinging to outworn tradition (inability to profit from past experience, and the tendency not to use available technology, or to misuse it);
- tendency to reject or ignore information that is unpalatable;
- tendency to underestimate the enemy, and overestimate the capabilities of one's own side;
- indecisiveness and a tendency to abdicate from the role of decision maker;
- obstinate persistence in a given task despite contrary evidence;
- failure to exploit a situation gained and 'pull punches';
- failure to make adequate reconnaissance;
- predilection for frontal assaults – often against the enemy's strongest point;
- belief in brute force rather than the clever ruse;
- failure to make use of surprise or deception;
- undue readiness to find scapegoats for setbacks;
- suppression or distortion of news from the front;
- belief in mystical forces – fates, bad luck etc.

Dixon emphasizes just how important it is to look at military history for examples of how disastrous bad decision making can be. Incompetence occurs everywhere, but military incompetence is far more costly:

- Military errors cost hundreds of thousands of lives and untold misery to civilians and soldiers.

- Armies attract people who might be a menace, and the nature of militarism will accentuate these traits.

- We can't get rid of generals the way we can refuse to re-elect governments or fire Chief Executive Officers (CEOs).

- What he calls 'decision pay-off' (effectively the downside of a failed decision) is far more costly in military organizations than, say, companies.

He is uncomplimentary about the performance of 'hopeless' generals:

- crippling passivity;

- lack of aggressive spirit;

- overweening ambition coupled with a terrifying insensitivity to the suffering of others (for example that famous Napoleon quote, 'a man such as I am is not much concerned over the lives of a million men');

- stupidity;

- lack of rigour in military schools and anti-intellectualism;

- preference for physical strength over brainpower.

Dixon blames 'noise', for interfering with the smooth flow of information. For him, noise includes static on a radio link, incompetence of staff, short-sightedness, defective memory, brain disease, neurosis, alcoholism.

Generals are channels of limited capacity. Dealing with more information takes longer. But if you don't take longer, you will make mistakes.

Dixon's thinking recalls three of our Decision Traps from Chapter 2:

- Analysis bypass – too much information or not enough time to analyse it properly.

- Anchoring – being overinfluenced by the first information or view we receive.

- Confirming evidence – we believe in and agree with people who think like we do.

He writes: 'Having gradually accumulated information in support of a decision, people become more loath to accept contrary evidence. And the greater the impact of the new information, the more strenuously it will be resisted.'

More quotes from Dixon:

- 'Pontification' is aiming to make nasty facts go away by the magical process of emitting loud noises in the opposite direction, for example Sir Ronald Charles, Master General of Ordnance at the time of Hitler's accession to power: 'There is no likelihood of war in our lifetime'.

- Pontification is also one of the ways in which people try to resolve their dissonance. Once the decision has been made and the person is committed to a given course of action, the psychological situation changes decisively. There is less emphasis on objectivity and there is more partiality and bias in the way the person views and evaluates the alternatives.

- 'Dissonance Theory' refers to the cognitive dissonances when a person possesses knowledge or beliefs that conflict with a decision he has made.

- Decision making may well be followed by a period of mental activity that could be described as at the very least somewhat one-sided.

- The oldest theory of military incompetence: namely that inept decisions occur through intellectual disabilities.

- Individuals who become anxious under conditions of stress, or who are prone to be defensive and deny anything that threatens their self-esteem, tend to be bad at judging whether the risks they take, or the caution they display, are justified by the possible outcomes of their decisions.

- A proportion of people will make irrational decisions whose riskiness is unrelated to reality because, being neurotic, they will strive to maintain an image of themselves as either 'bold and daring' or as 'careful and judicious decision-makers'.

- The apparent intellectual failings of some military commanders are due not to lack of intelligence, but to their feelings.

- Fear of failure rather than hope of success tends to be the dominant motive force in decision making, and the higher the rank the stronger the motive because there is farther to fall.

- Military decisions are often irrevocable. They often involve large pay-offs. Much hangs on their outcome, including the reputation of the decision-maker. The least rational will be the very ones least able to tolerate the nagging doubts of cognitive dissonance.

- Four of the worst military disasters in recent American history are directly attributable to the psychological processes that attend group decision making:
  - Bay of Pigs;
  - Pearl Harbour;
  - Korean War;
  - Escalation of Vietnam War.

It is worth asking whether there has been an unfortunate transplant from military to business, in that after the war many businesses imported the command and control structure wholesale into their cultures. Furthermore some of the faulty decision-making processes described above are recognizable in contemporary corporate life. Going back to the importance of the mutual decision in Chapter 4, it is frightening to see how decisions can turn out to be disastrous when there is no referral or ratification.

All Hell Let Loose by Sir Max Hastings (2011)

Moving on from this critique of military history, I recently read a compelling and terrifying book – *All Hell Let Loose: The World at*

War 1939–1945, by Max Hastings. It is Hastings' compendium about the Second World War, having previously written a number of books about specific aspects and campaigns. It is quite shocking in its depiction of the full horror of many theatres – particularly Russia, China, Germany, Italy, the Balkans, Greece, South East Asia and France. I strongly recommend this enormous tome – both as vivid history, and as a terrible warning about what can happen on a global scale when extremists take power, ideology obliterates democracy, and mass brutality takes over. As well as writing about the monstrous human cost of war, Hastings writes interestingly about decision making. Here is a blog post I wrote about it last December.

Blog extract

The veneer of civilization

It's Christmas time, but allow me some sombre thoughts.

Sometimes I stop to wonder how extraordinarily different our lives are to those of our parents and grandparents. I may be a fully paid-up citizen of the 21st century, but I actually arrived on earth a generation late. I was born towards the end of the Second World War. My father and six uncles fought in the First World War. Both my grandfathers were born in 1860. So in my family ties and memories go back a long way.

Wise decision making is essential on the micro scale that encompasses our personal and business lives, as I have tried to illustrate in this blog during 2011.

But read *All Hell Let Loose*, and you will convince yourself how vital it is that Britain and our allies decide at almost any cost to avoid war over Syria, Iran, North Korea or whichever flashpoint happens to be dominating the news bulletins. The Iraq, Afghanistan and Libya involvements have been bad enough. But at least – terrorism aside – they have been more or less contained. The Second World War was notable for the contagion, not just of war, but also the casualty rate, destruction, misery and degradation it caused in its wake.

The book I'm waiting for? Hastings' *The First World War: 1914–1918*.

The Great War was after all the War that failed to end all wars.

Happy Christmas.

The fog of war

BBC Radio 5 Live is doing full justice to the tenth anniversary of 9/11. This Saturday morning (10 September 2011) I caught an excellent interview by Phil Williams with Tony Blair's Chief of Staff, Jonathan Powell.

In it he used the phrase 'fog of war' to describe the immediate aftermath of the news of the attack on the Twin Towers reaching London. 'No one had any idea what was going on', he said. All the other European Union leaders were calling Blair for news, and Bush was unreachable in Air Force One, flying back from Florida. If Blair and the Europeans didn't know what had happened, they could hardly make any sensible call on what to say or do. For all decision makers the fog of war (at least as a metaphor) is a significant hazard. Not having enough information on which to base a decision is unsettling. Too much data can be confusing – as we have discussed before – but too little is dangerous.

Powell came up with another graphic phrase to describe what happens in the middle of the fog: 'everyone just sits down talking to each other'.

I'm reminded of many meetings I have attended over the years. We are supposed to be meeting to decide what to do next. There are probably at least two options on the table. Inevitably some of the discussion will be running ahead to how we execute the decision, and what might happen after that. Will it work? How will the competition react?

But suppose we don't know for certain what the situation is now. We may still be lacking key facts and data. If we don't have enough information, or we don't have the right information, what chance do we have of getting it right? Dangerous stuff fog.

Decision making – it's a contact sport

I'm not just talking about rugby and boxing. Nor even about the armed forces. All decision making – to be effective – relies on a degree of anticipation of how people are going to react to your decision. Which people? In a commercial context, you have to be thinking about your own staff, competitors, the distribution chain, authorities, regulators, pressure groups etcetera. In a military situation, it is going to be allies, neutrals, enemies, the media and so on.

Education has led us to rely on our intellectual ability and mastery of process and planning techniques. A lot of the academic material on decision making assumes that it is like Sudoku – something we do, and get better at with practice. But it is really a form of chess, with a resourceful and experienced opponent standing for all the elements out there who don't want you to win, or have the capability of acting in a way that can influence the outcome of what you are trying to achieve.

So did Obama take the decision to have Bin Laden killed, despite the strong likelihood of retaliatory action and reprisals? I believe that in a real sense he was not taking a decision at all, but executing, in both senses, one taken on behalf of the US people by his predecessor George W Bush in the aftermath of 9/11. The Abbottabad raid was part of decision implementation, and in the original thought process that put Bin Laden on the United States' 'most wanted' list in October 2001, the US Government clearly prioritized retribution over caution.

There's an important lesson for students of decision theory here. We can easily confuse the practicalities of carrying out a decision already taken, with a priori decision planning. I would submit that in marketing (rather like politics) what passes for decision process is often the detailed action planning for implementing policy statements and manifesto commitments. That is why, I believe, there is such a high failure rate in marketing planning. Decisions are often made in a gung ho fashion without due risk–reward analysis. Even detailed attention to implementation cannot make up for poor prioritization and insufficient cognisance of data and intelligence that does not support the chosen path. Even the best execution plan is unlikely to rescue a decision that wasn't properly made and validated.

The contact sport aspect has another implication. Not only do you need to take opponents and enemies into account when you plan decisions, they are also capable of provoking you to make decisions:

- In plotting 9/11, Al Qaeda knew that the United States would pledge an all out war on the organization. It must have been part of its plan to become more famous and escalate the scale of its activities.

- When the Japanese bombed Pearl Harbour, they knew it would provoke the United States into declaring war. What they didn't anticipate was the United States' resolve and the weapons of mass destruction (WMD) they were developing.

- When Hitler invaded Russia in June 1941, he knew it would end the Molotov–Ribbentrop Pact, and turn the Soviet Union into an implacable enemy, but he gambled on speed and surprise and by December had inflicted 4.3 million casualties on the Soviet Army and captured 3 million prisoners, as well as reversing most of Stalin's land grab. But Hitler had not fully calculated three factors:
  - the rigours of the Russian winter;
  - the extent to which Germany having so many resources tied up in Russia made it easier for Britain to keep going on the Western Front;
  - the fact that the United States was going to be brought into the war by Pearl Harbour (also in December 1941).

Interestingly historians have now established that Stalin also entered into the Pact to buy time – having been in no position to fight a war in 1939. Bluff and double bluff.

Britons and Americans – Part 1: the Gulf, 1988

Former Rear Admiral David Snelson gave me valuable insight into how Brits and Americans can see things differently – this time at sea:

> In the Vincennes incident [when the US guided missile carrier shot down Iran Air flight 655 – an Airbus A300 – mistaking it for an Iran Air Force F-14 Tomcat, and killing 290 passengers and crew] the Americans thought they had electronic indicators of a potential warplane, fighter plane or whatever. They had the thinking time to say, hang on, can this be? Because the evidence was there that it wasn't. The target was big and it was climbing and if it's big and it's climbing, it's probably an airliner. And the command team in the Vincennes didn't take all the bits of information that were available to them. Now, if you're really experienced in living and working in operations rooms, working with electronic sensors, it is easier to realize those things. This is a slight criticism of the US Navy the Royal Navy always has. In the US Navy commanding officers and other officers move around from logistics to engineering to warfare and back and so on, so they're not specialists. They're Jacks of all trades, and probably master of none. Actually when they get to command – and I spent a lot of time with the Americans during my career – they do not necessarily have that intuitive feel for their core business when the chips are down. I cannot remember if I ever knew what the captain of the Vincennes' career history was, but he probably was not an experienced warfare officer. And that's why sometimes the Americans will take decisions by rote and so they had this indication from what they call an IFF (Identification Friend or Foe?) signal that

this was a hostile aircraft, without thinking it through.

I saw a bit of this at first hand. I was involved in the invasion of Iraq. The Americans on the second or third day of the invasion of Iraq shot down a Tornado of ours. That's largely forgotten now. It was returning from a sortie.

Britons and Americans (and Russians) – Part 2: Kosovo, 1999

In my interview with General Sir Mike Jackson we spent relatively little time on the Kosovo Crisis of 1999, because he felt (quite correctly) that he had given a very full account in his book *Soldier* (2007). During his leadership of KFOR (NATO's peacekeeping force that entered Kosovo following NATO bombing of Serbia and Milosevic's acceptance of cease fire terms), he had an uncomfortable relationship with US General Wes Clark, the Supreme Allied Commander Europe (SACEUR). Jackson's account of the tension that could even have led to a Russia–NATO military confrontation is grippingly told in *Soldier* (pp. 276–351). Clark was convinced that the Russians would take Pristina Airport (the only way in or out of Kosovo by air) and after a great deal of sabre-rattling issued Jackson with a series of orders, culminating in one to block the runway. Jackson was very disinclined to do this after coming to some sort of understanding over a bottle of whisky with the Russian General Zavarzin, as mentioned at the beginning of this chapter. Jackson's exchange with Clark says it all:

> 'Clark was unmoved by my arguments, and insisted that we should block the airfield. I won't do it, sir, I just won't do it, I said heatedly.
>
> 'Mike, these aren't Washington's orders, they're coming from me'
>
> 'By whose authority?'
>
> 'By my authority as SACEUR.'
>
> 'You don't have that authority.'

'I do have that authority. I have the authority of the Secretary General behind me on this.'

'Sir, I'm not going to start World War Three for you. I'm a three-star general, you can't give me orders like this. I have my own judgement of the situation and I believe that this order is outside our mandate.'

'Mike, I'm a four-star general and I can tell you these things.'

Jackson insisted on contacting his boss in London (General Sir Charles, later Lord, Guthrie) and George Robertson, the NATO Secretary General. He offered to resign, but was strongly supported. A delaying tactic was found to avoid the direct contravention of an order from a superior officer, London played the red card. Clark was thwarted in what would have been an extremely dangerous course, and two months later, he was recalled. Meanwhile tension with the Russians had reduced to the point where they and KFOR achieved a working degree of cooperation. Jackson's judgement and decision making had been vindicated.

As Jackson said to me, 'Time was very short and I think my initial reaction could be described as a gut one... the stakes were quite high at that point.'

Britons and Americans (and Serbs) – Part 3: offshore Montenegro, 1999

David Snelson told me of an incident during the Serbian crisis:

NATO Navies were offshore preventing oil tankers getting into a harbour in Montenegro, which could have provided oil to the Serbian forces. I was part of Standing Naval Force Mediterranean. We were running a classic naval blockade off the coastline there, and a colleague of mine was the Commodore in charge. They intercepted a small tanker that had been coming into the Adriatic. And the tanker was claiming that he'd got a steering gear failure. He was going to put it up on the beach, but if a tug could be found to salvage him, then that would be fine. Sure enough, a tug came haring out from the harbour to tow it. This was all part of their plan to get the tanker in, so with the tug came some Serbian Navy missile boats.

The Serbs were clearly under orders to try and help this tug to get this tanker in. Things got tense and as the warships got closer, the Serb captains with their fairly ancient missile systems, opened the doors of the missile tubes and that was always a standard thing in Cold War rules of engagement, that if you saw the missile doors opening, it was a sure sign of an intent to open fire. The American warship in this group then said, right, that's it, we're shooting, and my colleague said, no, I think they're bluffing and he was right and he didn't engage.

They were just grandstanding. He was reading the whole political situation as well as what was in front of him at the time. Would the Serbs really engage NATO? Answer? No.

He was right and they didn't. But he would've been thoroughly justified in the rules of engagement and the American wanted to do it, say that's it, tick in the box, engage, sink, and he didn't. And that's where an element of the gut feel conditioned by political understanding and knowledge, when you become a senior commander, becomes extremely important.

Jackson on decision making

The question I asked was whether in the British Army the 'James Robertson Justice principle' (that the boss makes the decision, even if members of the team have reservations) is well and truly dead.

'Yes. Hopefully. We'll get a common sense of understanding of the problem and a common outcome in terms of choice of actions. It is very foolish to assume you're infallible.'

I asked, 'Was it always that way? Or is that an aspect of the modernization?'

Yes. I think there was some of that at high command level. But where you've got a complicated situation, particularly in today's operational world where you always have a political context which is bound in with it, there will be debate. There will be discussion. There will be an examination of the merits or demerits of this and that course of action. Now, it's perfectly up to the Commander to say, oh, I don't buy any of that. I've heard plenty about course of action A and B, but, we're going for C. And, yes, at the end of the day, if that's what he decides, that's what will happen. But he would have to think, I think, extremely carefully go in the opposite direction to the staff.

Now, sometimes there are explanations for that. If the staff are being too cautious, the Commander may decide to take a bold course of action, and accept the greater risk in the belief that it's going to damage the enemy in a more dynamic way than the more cautious modes.

There's a member of the team whose sole job it is to look at the political aspects of things. These days, it would be unheard of, I think, for a major headquarters to deploy without a political advisor; normally an MOD source, but could be foreign office, as well. They are advisors. They're not in the decision making direct chain but they form part of the debate and help to paint that political picture. As Clausewitz said, and he was always right: the use of force is politics by another means, which really says it all.

Snelson on gut feeling and training

"You raised the business of gut feel. I've quite often used gut feel as a major factor, but actually I think I've largely been conscious at the time that the gut feel is informed by a whole lot of training and experience. And interesting, when I got to the stage of being a ship's Commanding Officer, and I went through the training for that three times before going back to sea as a CO for three times, quite often one of the messages that came through from those who were more experienced and those who were mentoring me was, if you have difficulty over making a decision even if you've had time to weigh things up, in the end go for your gut feel. But they thought your gut feel will be pretty good, not because your gut is good in itself, but because your gut has been trained to be good.

I asked General Sir Mike Jackson about intelligence and hierarchy

David: 'When you have slightly more time, when it isn't quite so stressed on time, and you get more and more information and more and more intelligence, can you get too much? Can you get so much that it actually makes it more complicated?'

General Sir Mike: 'Well, that's a good question. If the machine is working properly, the Commander, the decision maker, his intelligence staff officer will go to some lengths to avoid that. It's the staff officer's job to sort, prioritize, weigh, so that the Commander's intelligence picture is collated; he is not just given all the raw information, but it's interpreted and collated so that he gets an integrated intelligence picture, so much as intelligence is available. But in the situation you've just indicated, whereby there is too much thrown at one decision maker, there is a staff process by which that large amount of material is, as I say, analysed, prioritized.'

David: 'And, in that sense, even though hierarchy obviously plays a huge part, it is a team game?'

General Sir Mike: 'Oh, God, yes; hierarchy doesn't play a great deal of a part in a major headquarters. You have obviously a Commander, sometimes a Deputy Commander – that varies and there's a good debate about whether it adds or doesn't – Chief of Staff, crucial, and then you have the staff branches. It's very structured. The operations branch is, of course, primus inter pares. Every function that is needed, to make an army in the field work, is replicated at the headquarters by the relevant staff branch and, in a way, you can almost look at the Commander as conductor of the orchestra. That's what he does and his Chief of Staff is the first violin.'

Should we use wartime decision making in dealing with terrorism?

Is war a completely unique set of circumstances? Is it only in war that we can predicate the abandonment of morality and the subordination of all other goals to winning and/or survival?

Should we try to apply peacetime criteria to terrorism? On the criterion of cheapness of life, terrorist groups are thinking and acting like soldiers in a war. Would that and the adoption of wartime thinking help governments or secret services anticipate and head off terrorist acts – as well as fight and retaliate?

Where military meets politics, a government is going to be incredibly cautious before they make a change. The battlefield is completely different, because in a battlefield environment he who hesitates is lost, and you simply have to do it. In peacetime – even in a peace significantly threatened by determined and sometimes devastating terrorist activity – it would be a very big decision.

Chapter Nine
Sport and other games
Serious lessons from evenings and weekends

> When I'm playing White in chess, I like a really open board, I like open diagonals, open columns and files and those other things, and I will look at a board and go, that is beautiful, and to make it more beautiful, I should try and do the following things, like opening up the right flank or close the left flank, or pushing all the pieces back to the top of the board, or whatever.
>
> As Black I will generally only be occupying a third of the board, you'll be occupying two-thirds, you'll be expansive, all this kind of stuff, and I will wait for you to over reach yourself and then I will kill you at some point, and that's how I will be playing that. That isn't the only way to play and win as Black; it's just one of many different aesthetics but it is my natural one. **(NIGEL JONES, ONE-TIME CHESS PRODIGY; NOW CEO OF THE LONDON ADVERTISING AGENCY, PUBLICIS)**

Nigel was answering my question about how professional chess players can plan seven or eight moves ahead. He said, they don't really. It's all visual.

Let's start with a game – an ancient game

Chess is around 1,500 years old, but thanks to insights from Nigel Jones, it seems to me to provide a valuable analogue to life itself:

> I suppose the thing that I find most interesting and most non-chess pros find most bizarre is the thought process that goes on in chess, because everyone says to me, 'oh, that must be really difficult – how do you think so many moves ahead, and how do you keep all the combinations in your head?' And the answer is you don't really; that is not how you play chess to a really, really high level. I genuinely believe that the really good chess players play chess, I would say aesthetically, and they see chess and the board as a picture or a series of diagrams or drawings, and they either train themselves or they are born to see the board as beautiful or ugly.
>
> So if I was playing you at this moment, I could stand behind my position and I would immediately without even thinking know whether that is a beautiful or an ugly position for me, and if I went and stood behind you, I would see exactly the opposite. And if I walked up to a game that I had not seen before and someone else was playing I would immediately think, that is ugly or beautiful or beautiful or ugly, depending on where I was standing. And generally, when I'm playing chess, I'm trying to create a more beautiful picture, and that is what I'm trying to do.
>
> So you then get personal style involved in it, because everyone has a slightly different personal perception of what is beautiful in chess, but there are some fundamentals that you can't stray away from. But, you know, when I'm playing as a White player in chess, I like a really open board, I like open diagonals, open columns and files and those other things, and I will look at a board and go, that is beautiful, and to make it more beautiful, I should try and do the following type things, like opening up the right flank or close the left flank, or push all the pieces back to the top of the board, or whatever.

I will think mainly like that, and then at some point during the thinking process, maybe the last 10 per cent, I will think, right, if I actually move that piece there, what will happen next? But most of my thinking is, I would say, on that aesthetic level, and then there's two interesting consequences: first of all, it means you can actually play much faster than most laymen would think; I would say I'm 99 per cent as good at lightning chess (10 seconds to move) as I am at playing ordinary chess.

So I'm not as good as I am at normal chess, but I am nearly as good, and that is because I'm thinking aesthetically, and aesthetics are a sort of quick emotional connection with your brain, rather than a long-thought-through rational process. It also means, you know, you just memorize things without thinking, so, you know, if I was playing you at chess and you knocked the pieces over halfway through the game, I could replay the entire game from scratch, and/or set up the board exactly as it was without even thinking.

I then asked Nigel whether he had a photographic memory for other things. For instance, could he visualize offices he's had in the past?

No, I have a terrible memory, I think, for the most part. I do think in terms of diagrams and pictures rather than words, but I haven't got a very good memory in the normal sense. If I'm being really serious, I've spent most of my life refusing to memorize things. I'm a mathematician but I hate formulae, so when I was at school I was always in the lower sets at maths because I refused to memorize formulae. So if we were doing a test on trigonometry, I would take twice as long as everyone else because I would have to work out each formula for myself before I would use one. I would draw a right-angled triangle, work out the formula that I wanted to use, and then use it – I would not memorize them. I think filling your brain with memory-type things is a bad idea. I'm much more about understanding than memory. But of course when you really understand things like that then you do start to know or remember them. You can't help it despite refusing to remember things in the traditional sense.

Let's go back to chess, because I think the analogy's appropriate: let's assume I'm playing as Black, because playing as Black is completely different from playing as White. The difference is as extreme as receiving or serving in tennis. If you're Black, and you're playing professionally, you are trying to draw.

If you're White, you are trying to win. You are expected to win, as White; you are expected to just about draw, if you're lucky, as Black. So that one move advantage is phenomenally important, so your aesthetics as Black and White are completely different. Let's just assume I'm playing as Black: I have a different aesthetic to many other really good chess players as Black. My aesthetic when I'm Black I could describe it as a sort of porcupine approach. I like a cramped position, I'm going to keep everything very close to my chest, I'm going to wait for you to overreach as White. Because you think you're going to win – you think you ought to try hard to push the White natural advantage – you're going to eventually overextend a bit, and I'm going to just hide behind a wall of shields, and eventually you're going to overstep the mark and then I'm going to pounce and kill you, and that's going to be it. It's a spider-waiting-for-a-prey-type thing.

What I'm trying to do is create a shielded area on the board where I can move my pieces around. But they are quite cramped, so it's all about stepping over each other and all this kind of stuff, and I'm waiting for you to overextend and open some lines and gaps. That's the picture I've got. So I will only be occupying a third of the board, you'll be occupying two-thirds, you'll be expansive, all this kind of stuff, and I will kill you at some point, and that's how I will be playing that. That isn't the only way to play and win as Black. It's just one of many different aesthetics. But it's my natural one.

There is clearly more than one aesthetic that can work for you in chess, both as Black and as White. And it is an interesting life model as well, I think. I'm not saying there's only one aesthetic at all, or only one gut feel, or only one thing. That's quite a conundrum for me. How do you reconcile that with life and decision making, because I know from chess there is more than one aesthetic.

It would be hard to come across a more articulate description of plasticity and the influence of the subconscious mind on decision making. Chess is a particularly interesting area for study. Simon White, Planning Director of Grey Advertising in London, told me that teaching delinquent children chess can make them better behaved. Nigel Jones and I also discussed whether there might be learning also from other board games – both those purely skill-based, and those requiring intervention from dice. I suspect that video games (a genre I know almost nothing about) might give us some useful learning about decision making. I am sure that pastimes like crosswords, Sudoku, and other paper and pencil and word games would yield rich information on plasticity and the way the subconscious intervenes without us realizing it.

Sport matters

In an increasingly hectic and stressful world, people look for distraction and pleasure away from the stresses and strains of concerns about family, health, finances, work, political tensions and so on. All over the world sport provides that release. It equally provides enjoyment and a beneficial health and fitness dividend for those who play and compete. But if professional sport matters (and it is big business apart from being high interest – largely thanks to saturation TV coverage), it is equally important that it is a satisfying spectacle, as well as being well run and professionally officiated.

Top sportsmen and sportswomen need a great deal of decision making to achieve peak performance. Sport also requires as near to impeccable decision making by officials as can be achieved, often by a combination of human ability and the use of supporting technology. If you start a discussion on decision making in a canteen or bar, it will take less than five minutes before someone is criticizing the decision of a referee or umpire. In this chapter, we will turn shortly to important aspects of decision making in sport. The huge betting industry offers another kind of distraction, and feeds principally off sport.

Decision making by sportsmen and women

Competitive sport, and especially professional sport, is a decision voyeur's paradise! We have to rely on the media, gossip and inside track to know what decisions are being made in government at all levels, the civil service, the armed forces, the emergency services, companies, voluntary organizations, pressure groups and so on. We will probably never know how most of those decisions are made. At the higher levels of sports governing bodies (for example IOC, FIFA, ICC, IRB, F1), and indeed in national organizations and clubs, the decision making will probably be equally rarified, and hard to comprehend.

How different it is in sport itself. From team selection to winning strategies, from kick-off to the final whistle and beyond, we can watch decision making in action. We see long-term, medium-term and fast decisions. We see endless autopilot (some executed more faultlessly than others). We see decisions and counter-decisions on the spot. We see how competitive pressure makes decision making much more difficult. We watch gambit and counter strike. We see boldness and caution, risk-taking and caution. We see success and failure in all their forms. I relentlessly blog about sport, because it is a personal interest area that is both accessible and shareable. With so many sports lovers everywhere, we can debate, celebrate, criticize, gnash our teeth and hope for better days.

Echoing the flow of this book, we have dreams and determination all around us, particularly following the home Olympics. For every triumph there are several nightmares – winning supporters celebrating greatness, and the losers wanting to know what went wrong. There are opportunities aplenty and problems galore. So much is decided in fractions of a second. The 60 seconds time frame is unrealistically generous here. For the considered decisions of 60 minutes, hours, days and weeks, there are many decision-making approaches, but many will echo the mixture of reason, emotion, gut feel and subconscious that I have tried to capture in Smart Decisions. There is a massive people factor. Selection is choice on a stage, with as much multivariate analysis as you can wish for, especially with cricket teams. There is war and peace, there is love and passion, and plenty of gamesmanship! Read on, and see how sport echoes life and life echoes sport.

Daniel Topolski on how bad decisions can drag down even proven winners

This is a Boat Race story, but not the famous Oxford mutiny of 1987 (another Americans versus Britons tale) that led to an unlikely triumph against all the odds. The story of the 1987 race is described in detail in Topolski's book *True Blue* (with Patrick Robinson, 1989). The race Daniel is talking about here is 10 years later in 1997. By this time he was a consultant to the Oxford University Boat Club (OUBC), with the task of recruiting the best possible coach:

I was trying to find a coach to take them on to the future. I got the coach of the Dutch eight who'd just won the gold medal at the Olympics, Rene Mijnders. Fantastic coach, but he didn't quite believe the stuff about the boat race being a different sort of race. He said that if we know we're the faster crew; we will win. He had proved it. 'We see it on the times that we do; it's a very fast crew and, you know, we'll be fine.' And I said, 'Well, Rene, you've got to come out on the launch, let's spend time.' He was out on the launch, but he didn't really take any of that in and he said, no, you look after them with the course and stuff.

I wanted to take the coxes over the course, but he said they will win; they're a good crew. On the day of the race I just wanted to brief the cox about the course and what he was going to do again once we got there. He really didn't want me to. He said don't, you'll make them nervous and anxious. So they went into the race. The umpire warned the Cambridge cox 120 times, and the Cambridge cox took no notice at all. He just pushed the Oxford cox off the faster stream and Rene had briefed the cox. He said don't get into any trouble at all, just keep out of the way, you are faster, you will win. So just don't get entangled in any struggle. So, Oxford were level through to the last half mile, but always rowing in slower water and having to race further. The Cambridge cox would have given way if he started clashing, but Oxford just kept giving way.

We lost it on the last bend, because we were on the outside. Rene didn't want to come down onto the Tideway that much. He only came down for the last week. He took them off to Amsterdam to race in a big regatta, where we beat the French national eight, just missed beating the Olympic Champions. Oxford were a very fast crew, rowed beautifully, and lost the boat race.

That night at the dinner we, Rene and I, were talking and along came the Cambridge coach who was a New Zealander called Harry Mahon, who's now dead. Harry Mahon was a sort of guru figure, helping Cambridge, and had coached the New Zealand eight that won a gold medal in 1972. He was just a lovely, calm sort of man, but talked really good sense and was able really to say his bit. Harry said, when I got here I'd been out nearly every day when we were on the Tideway. I ran the course. I ran it right up to the finish and back again because I wanted to feel where the wind changed on my face as I turned the corner. I wanted to feel exactly where they were going to feel the tailwind, and how strong those corners were that they've got to row around. Rene's eyes were just …

Because you're the fastest crew doesn't mean you're going to win. Rene's a strategist, he's very nice. He plans things out, but this was an area that he wouldn't listen. It was his decision to tell the cox to give way all the time. Terrible decision.

Colin, Lord Moynihan, Chairman of the British Olympic Association (BOA)

"You cannot expect to have gold medals from the athletes unless you provide the services and support to those athletes from the coach to the 'ologists to the governing bodies and the National Olympic Committee. They have to step up to the mark and be gold medal support services. You have to do that. The attention to detail, a focus on a clear goal that there isn't a single extra thing that you could have done for any one of the 550 athletes to help them deliver their personal best – that is the driving determined ambition of everybody who works here.

I will tell you a story. I've had lots of pillowcases printed with 0.545 on them. Just 0.545. If you go back to Athens, which was the Games before I arrived, if you took Kelly Holmes, she did 800 and 1,500 metres, gold medals in both; and the men's 4×100 and they got a gold, and Chris Hoy, his first one ever for the 1 km time trial; and the great coxless four that always delivers. So we won five gold medals and their collected time if you add all their finals together was 12 minutes and six seconds, and the difference between all five being gold and being silver, was 0.545 in aggregate for all of them – just over half a second all up. The winning margins were that tight. It is a really powerful incentive to everybody here to work for the athletes, because they know they can make the difference. They respond under huge pressure. You've got press looking for divisions and problems, and you've got the government with its own agenda sometimes, which doesn't necessarily agree with ours, especially on sports legacy, and you've got us fighting very hard for the athletes and we know that 0.545 is a great motivator because it's so tangible. It's so clear an objective that you go that extra mile, you go that extra hour of work, you drive yourself that bit harder to help those athletes and you will achieve your goal. My first Games at the BOA was in Beijing. We had a great BOA team, and very strong financial support, which we campaigned hard for, from the Lottery. We got great governing bodies of sport, who were modernizing all the time, looking after athletes and securing the best coaches, and we went out there and we did better than we've done since we hosted the Games in 1908.

We came fourth, got 19 gold medals and now we face very strong competition from countries that have come up since then, like Germany and Australia. To deliver fourth at a home Games would be an amazing result and what we aspire to do; to win more medals from more sports. We were very reliant on what we call the sitting-down sports. We were very good at sitting down. We weren't so good at standing up!

The Inner Game of Tennis, Timothy Gallwey (1974)

We looked at Tim Gallwey's insights in Chapter 6. Nearly 40 years ago he had brilliantly described the autopilot phenomenon without having access to neurological science that wasn't available at the time. The book is well worth revisiting. Two quotes from *The Inner Game of Tennis* still seem to be highly relevant when we are looking at decision making in sport:

> Every game is composed of two parts, an outer game and an inner game. The outer game is played against an external opponent... neither mastery or satisfaction can be found in the playing of any game without giving some attention to the relatively neglected skills of the inner game.
>
> Most people are talking to themselves all the time... But just who is this 'I' and who the 'myself'? Obviously the 'I' and the 'myself' are separate entities or there would be no conversation. So one could say that within each player there are two 'selves'. One, the 'I', seems to give instructions. The other, 'myself', seems to perform the action. Then 'I' returns with an evaluation of the action. For clarity let's call the 'teller' Self 1 and the 'doer' Self 2'.

Quieten the negative thought in your head

Sir Matthew Pinsent used this phrase in an interview on Radio 5 live on Saturday 18 June 2011. He was asking what advice he would give to Rory McIlroy, as he stood 6 ahead of the pack at the US Open after 36 holes.

It struck me that it is also a good mantra for that crucial moment (could be an instant, could be a month) after taking an important decision.

Consider all you have to do before making the decision:

- setting and resetting the goal;
- making sure that you have the right problem in your sights;
- analysing different problem-solving options;
- weighing up attractive upsides and worrying downsides;
- carrying out the reward–risk assessment;
- painstakingly arriving at the decision.

It is introspective. It is cerebral. It is not what you associate with action heroes. But the constant framing and reframing has to be done if you're going to be sure.

But having decided, you then need to be resolute. Have confidence in the decision. Act accordingly. Quieten the negative thought. You may subsequently need to react to changing circumstances, mistakes or disasters on your side, or enemy action. These are unavoidable influences on the implementation of your decision. These factors may be life and death issues. They may be the loss of an important outlet and a brilliant ad campaign from the brand leader. They may be your dropped shots and an eagle by your closest challenger.

Not to change aspects of your plan would be folly. But you cannot and should not change your decision. Or the conviction that it was the right one. Nor the determination to win.

"

As Pinsent said
'Quieten the negative thought in your head'.
It rhymes.
Remember it in difficult times.

Federer – master decision maker

We have concentrated almost entirely on considered decisions. But there are so many decisions that have to be made with little or no premeditation. In my research I have taken particular interest in decision making in medicine, the forces, the emergency services, flying and driving.

But it is sport which enables us to study short-order decision making in a very public context.

Let's start with tennis – a game that mixes proactivity and reaction, with very little time to think. From a wonderful vantage point on Centre Court I was able to wonder at Roger Federer's remarkable ability to control a match. His approach was so different from that of Novak Djokovic who followed Federer on court. Federer has had a lean time of late in the Grand Slams by his standards, whereas Djokovic enjoyed a remarkable 43-match winning streak until Federer beat him in the semi finals at Roland Garros.

Yet from the knock-up onwards, it was obvious that Federer had a game plan. He exudes confidence, but also has a serenity about him. Under pressure he has an uncanny ability to narrow the eyes and secure crucial points. Nalbandian is past his peak, but good enough to reach the third round. Federer's decision making ensured that he would progress no further. It was not just his technique and stroke making, which are both awesome. It was his mental strength. It was his determination, in defiance of the seeding, to win a seventh Wimbledon title this year.

Watching Djokovic later it was hard to believe he has only lost once this year. Crushing serve – yes. All the shots – yes. But against Baghdatis (another awkward opponent like Nalbandian) he didn't exhibit Federer's confidence and cool. You just didn't feel he was in control in the same way.

Blog extract

Lessons from Augusta

(Where Rory McIlroy lost the first major he should have won.)

There's something about the US Masters that seems to captivate not just golfers, but millions more besides. Augusta National makes a wonderful stage, in terms of beauty, tradition, and its extremely demanding course. But the actors! And the drama they play out – especially this year, with so many golfers in contention, starring Rory, the principal boy, and Tiger, now cast as the villain.

Having recovered from an inappropriately late Sunday night, dried our tears for Rory, and congratulated Charl Schwartzel on a deeply impressive victory having birdied the last four, what are the lessons we decision making students can draw from four amazing days in front of the box?

First we have to remember that golf is a good example (like most sports) of a mixture between conscious decisions (strategy, perfecting technique, planning the playing programme etc), and the myriad instant decisions, which take place in a different part of the brain altogether. Just think of the number of decisions (choice of club, high or low shot, draw it or fade it, lines on the putts, hit it normally or baby it... that a golfer has to make over the course of 72 holes. Then there are factors like adrenaline and stress that can lead to both 'wonder shots' and disastrous mistakes.

But to understand what happened yesterday, we also need to look at other interesting elements in the McIlroy story:

- Experience (or rather lack of it): how much of a contributory factor to McIlroy's extraordinary collapse was his youth?

- Partnership (often a key to successful decision taking): what on earth was McIlroy's caddy doing? Surely he could have helped the young man to steady the ship.

- Ambience: was McIlroy less comfortable playing the last round in the company of Cabrera, a much older man, with very poor English and a pretty grumpy mien? (The poor guy had been off games for a while with major dental problems). Rory had looked very much at home for the previous 54 holes with Jason Day, an Aussie of his own age.

- Lasting damage? Will McIlroy be able to shrug off his nightmare round?

Then there's Tiger. Was he really in a mental state to win? He showed his old brilliance in both his second and last rounds, but the consistency still hasn't returned. Will it? Has tinkering with his swing made matters worse? And importantly, the Schwartzel story. Is it a coincidence that two not very well-known South Africans have won two of the last majors? Were Oosthuizen and Schwartzel driven to win by greater desire, and a less comfortable home environment in South Africa than that enjoyed by the European guys? Is not having the Ryder Cup motivation a spur to winning big in the Majors? Look also at the fact that Charl was chased home by three Australians and Cabrera, who also aren't eligible for the Ryder Cup.

I will leave you with a final thought – and golfers will be talking about that last round for years to come. Is part of golf's appeal the fact that, unlike football, rugby, and cricket, you just have the players, with no umpires or referees to interfere and steal their thunder?

Lessons from Congressional

Where were you when Rory McIlroy learned to win?

As golf fans struggled into work having sat up to all hours watching McIlroy win his first Major, it is worth asking what lessons there are to be learned from his extraordinary performance.

Most important must be the vivid demonstration of the strength of his character, finishing off in such style having collapsed from a strong third round position both at the Open and the Masters in April 2011. It is axiomatic in decision theory to learn from previous episodes, and feed the learning back into future opportunities.

It will be interesting to see whether Dustin Johnson (US Open 2010) and Nick Watney (US PGA 2010) are capable of emulating McIlroy the next time they are in the lead at a Major, having squandered apparently winning positions. Interviews this weekend with McIlroy, Watney and Johnson were revealing. All three players admitted to 'speeding up' under pressure. 'It all happened so quickly,' said Johnson, 'I was walking faster, playing faster, and didn't leave myself time to think.'

The interviewer said that all three golfers admitted their mistake was not 'staying in the moment'.

There is a lesson for all of us there. Pressure can disrupt equilibrium and thought patterns. Decision makers in the 'reflex' or 'instinctive' category – soldiers, pilots, firefighters, police, nurses in triage, referees etcetera – know that their only chance of taking good decisions in a nanosecond is to think straight, breathe deeply and let their training click them into autopilot.

If we don't stay in the moment, disaster awaits. The language we use says it all:

- Don't get ahead of yourself.
- Focus on one thing at a time.
- Concentrate / keep in the zone.

Frustration, impatience, annoyance, even panic – these are natural reactions to pressure, crisis or looming disaster. But all emergency service workers and combatants are trained to rely on what their training has taught them. Programmed response is as much a part of short-order decision taking, as is weighing up options and factoring in more data when you have time to take a considered decision.

Sport – and particularly individual games like golf – can teach us a lot about pressure and the best way to react to it. McIlroy's triumph yesterday tells us as much about his mental toughness as his phenomenal ball striking.

Sports fans know that the moment a player gives into pressure, technique will falter, with the result that first consistency and then victory will be lost. That's just as true in the day job.

A caddy and a coach – what every Chief Executive Officer needs?

Apart from huge enjoyment and fun, what have I gained from this year's Open? Two principal learnings of particular interest to the decisionomane:

1 That even the world's finest golfers need to make constant changes of tack as they plot their way around testing links like Royal St George's.

2 That the tournament pro's dynamic duo of coach and caddy would almost certainly work beyond the realms of golf.

Let's start with the relentless sequence of decision making that confronts each competitor, whether they have shot 65 (lowest yesterday) or 82 – the highest score. As ever, sport is a valuable analogue to life. For each shot, you have to:

- work out the maximum upside outcome, and then go down the scale from perfect to adequate;
- work out maximum downside outcome, and scale from catastrophic to liveable-with;
- do the reward–risk analysis, and settle on your strategy;
- select a club;
- aim it;
- decide how hard to hit it;
- grip club and take stance;
- backswing + downswing -> impact.

Obviously short putts don't require as much thought as a drive at a par 5 hole with out of bounds on the right (like the 14th at Royal

St George's). But the pressure is on the brain all the way round, just as you are being tested in terms of physicality, dexterity and stamina.

Life's like that. Every day requires endless decision making. Not all these decisions are equally difficult. But some need more effort and technique than others. In life, as in golf, you also have to adjust for luck and competitive action.

Now for what I think is an even more important thought. Top golfers, like all professional athletes, need coaches (psychological as well as technical). But the golfer has the priceless asset of a friend, counsellor and gofer – namely the caddy. A round in the Open at Sandwich is nothing like as lonely as, say, that of a tennis player. Batsmen have partners. Footballers and rugby players have team mates. But the latter also have to be primarily out for themselves. The caddy is for you. To help in every way. At the minimum a second opinion. At best a crucial line on a putt or the counsel to play a safe shot with a seven iron, rather than trying to hack a wood from deep clag. Even more important: someone there, someone to talk to.

Wouldn't Chief Executive Officers (CEOs) and other business leaders do better with caddy or Man Friday constantly at hand? And regular coaching?

If I was the CEO of a big outfit, I'd far rather rely on a great coach and a good caddy, than all the direct and indirect reports in a matrix organization. And think of the thinking and deciding time you would have, freed up from all those meetings!

A CEO (or anyone else who has to make important decisions) would be a better decision maker with inputs from one adviser and one constant companion, than relying on the normal diet of meetings, presentations and documents. A number of people have said to me, 'I could do with a caddy'.

Actually I seem to have been guilty of a bit of a solecism in the spelling. You can use either, but if the Rules of Golf say 'caddie' for the singular of the species, I will go for that. After all a singular caddie is what you want, not what we golfers call a 'bag puller'. Cynics would say there are enough bag pullers in the corporate world, as it is.

But let's look at the coach aspect. All the top golfers use a coach either all the time or from time to time. Why? Because there are faults or involuntary changes in the basics (grip, stance, alignment, tempo) that you simply can't see for yourself. An expert watching you swing a club, and importantly comparing what they see now with what they remember from before, is going to provide far superior counsel to anything you can work out for yourself.

That is important, because most CEOs, while acknowledging corporate democracy and listening to what their executives tell them, still value their own opinion more highly. If you believe in personality profiles, you know that most CEOs are 'Drivers'. According to **www.Personality100.com**, Drivers are:

- action-orientated;
- decisive;
- problem solver;
- direct;
- *assertive*;
- *demanding*;
- risk taker;
- *forceful*;
- *competitive*;
- *independent*;
- *determined*;
- results-orientated.

I put the 'self-reliant' characteristics in italics. To take just a few of them, if as a CEO you are independent, assertive, determined and forceful, are you going to take a great deal of notice of those below you in the hierarchy?

But you might listen to your coach! With an expert to call upon, why wouldn't you listen and take their advice on a strategic decision? As well as coaching on the physical and technical side, the Darren Clarkes of this world also work with sports psychologists to make sure their heads are in gear. Think of the pressures faced by business leaders. That might work for them too.

The caddie? He or she (don't let us forget famous Fanny or the beautiful Brenda Calcavecchia) may not be the best choice as strategic counsellor, but for practical advice in the execution of a decision – none better.

Rugby and Decision Making. What I learned from being mugged at Lansdowne Road on Saturday

Saturday 19 March 2011 was a strange final day in the Six Nations Championship. England and Wales, the two countries with a chance to win, were heavily defeated by Ireland and France respectively – sides that had previously performed poorly. Italy, who had beaten France and only lost at the last gasp to Ireland, were brushed aside by Scotland, who they might have expected to beat. So England did win the Championship, but not the Grand Slam, nor the Triple Crown.

I was at the Aviva Stadium in Dublin, confidently expecting revenge for the defeats England have suffered on their last three visits there. We were humiliated – almost as badly as on that emotional, wet afternoon at Croke Park in 2007. Sorrows having been drowned, I tried to find rational explanations for what I had witnessed. Did Ireland play exceptionally well? Did England perform very poorly? Undoubtedly 'yes' on both counts. But why?

Was a younger, more inexperienced team overawed by the occasion? Did the roar, the bloody drums and the sea of green flags disrupt planning and thinking? How else can you explain Flood and Wilkinson missing straightforward kicks? England's passing and discipline were both way below standard.

But in my day job I have always believed pitches are won and not lost. There is a control freakery in most of us that wants to believe events are in our hands, until alien factors intervene:

- 'We lost because of the ref.'
- 'We lost because we had the after-lunch slot.'

It is never (in our own minds) because we weren't as good as the opposition.

Yet at the Aviva on Saturday we were thrashed. We played as well as we were allowed to, which was not at all. Declan Kidney and his team out-thought us as well as outplayed us. Andy Robinson and his Scottish team (hardly as talented as an in-form Irish side) had disrupted us and given us a hard time the week before at Twickenham.

If we had had half a mind, the Aviva debacle shouldn't have been a surprise. The old hands in the magnificent Lansdowne FC clubhouse before the game were extremely confident. Why? The Irish had worked us out. Videos had been studied minutely. Attack the half backs. Don't let the back three play. Exploit the weakness at centre. Neutralize the back row. Dominate the line out. Give no quarter in the front row. Don't give away penalties with a pernickety ref in charge. Wait for England to infringe as they always do. And on the emotional dimension? You hate losing to England. You love beating England more than anyone!

It actually was not rocket science. Ireland had built their battle plan around disrupting and destroying England's plan – which was exactly what it had been in the previous four outings. England did not anticipate the disruption. They used the same blueprint as before – and there wasn't a Plan B.

Warfare's like that. Marketing is like that. Decision making has to be dedicated to outwitting the competition as well as pursuing our own plans. Deciding is one thing. Implementation is quite another. And that is a contact sport in marketing, just as much as it is in rugby.

The RFU – we all know what FU stands for

What happened during the World Cup was bad enough for those of us who are keen England rugby supporters. The constant flow of leaked stories since the team returned from New Zealand hasn't made it better, but yesterday's spectacular in The Times makes everything much worse. You have to ask if transparency is all it is cracked up to be.

The whole world now knows that the Rugby Football Union (RFU) was completely unable to organize our participation in the World Cup, and that the RFU Council, the Director of Elite Rugby, the manager, the coaches and players, all in their different ways, let down their supporters, their backers, and most of all themselves.

Who could possibly have had access to all three reports (the RFU's own, and those commissioned by the Rugby Players' Association and the Aviva Premiership Clubs)?

What was the motivation for not just leaking them, but handing them over wholesale?

What has been achieved with the Six Nations just over two months away?

As a study of organizational decision making it makes both the Charge of the Light Brigade and corporate governance at Enron look like textbook case histories for MBA students.

It is hard to know where to start in terms of analysing which decision traps were particularly disastrous. Here are my starters:

1 Any commercial organization (and just because the RFU is the governing body of a sport, it doesn't make it immune from working to business world rules) needs a viable structure, with defined areas of responsibility and accountability. The RFU's management structure is totally ineffectual, and the team itself on the field (think factory for a manufacturer or store for a retailer) was out of control.

2 The golden rule in decision making is to consider options before making any big decision, and in doing so to eliminate all options with a dangerous downside, however attractive the upside. The RFU, and its individual managers, clearly don't even know the basics of risk assessment. Any decision maker has to ask 'how is this going to look if it goes wrong?'

3 'Group failure' is when experienced, qualified people convince each other that black is white.

4 As noted here last week 'condemned to repeat the experience' is the refusal to learn from mistakes.

5 'Outcome blindness' is the failure to accept bad news when you see it.

6 'Delusion' is convincing yourself you won't be found out.

But on top of everything else, the decision to commission three instant reports on what is already acknowledged to be an unmitigated disaster, while you are looking for new managers and coaches, and renegotiating sponsorships defies belief. Did whoever decided this (singular or plural) believe it would stay tight? Did they really imagine that interviewees and respondents to questionnaires (many of whom are already discarded and bitter) would keep it to themselves?

Any sensible organization (let's say one with a Chairman, a CEO, a board with non-executive directors, and a management structure) would have written off World Cup 2011 as a failure, made swift management changes, picked a new squad and moved on.

After this nightmare, played out in public and in the most unsavoury way, moving on is going to be difficult. I also have news for the baying pack of journalists: firing Rob Andrew might be seen by his detractors as justice, but by itself it will achieve nothing.

Does it matter if refs and umpires make mistakes?

Millions of sports fans will say 'yes'. How frustrating to watch your favourite team go down to a disputed penalty. Nothing worse than a disallowed try. And how frustrating if all your LBW appeals are turned down.

But in any decision-making situation where the official has a nanosecond to see what has happened, analyse it, and make a call, is it surprising that mistakes are made? Fortunately Rugby League led the way in using technology to determine whether or not a try had been scored. Rugby Union followed, and then the cricket authorities came to the aid of hard pressed umpires with a cocktail of gadgets: Hawkeye, Snicko and Hotspot. Hawkeye has also made a big difference to line calls in tennis.

So why has football – our richest sport by far – fallen so far behind, without even basic goal-line cameras? It is tough enough being a football referee without having responsibility for spotting whether the ball has crossed the line. Let's assume in a halcyon post-Blatter world, football at least uses technology to confirm the scoring of a goal. Will that mean that technology-equipped refs won't make any mistakes? Of course not. Why? Because they are human and therefore fallible. And what is more their fellow humans on the field and in the stands (not to mention in the commentary box) will not be making it easy for them.

But that wasn't my question. My question was: does it matter if sports officials make mistakes – incorrect decisions, if you like?

Call me a heretic, but I don't think it does matter. Referees and umpires are there to officiate and keep the game moving within the spirit and laws of the game. Ideally refs will call infringements correctly. I spoke to a rugby referee yesterday who admitted he probably makes the wrong call two or three times in a game. But his decisions will probably even themselves out.

Ideally cricket umpires will adjudicate correctly the first time at real speed. Ideally tennis umpires will know when to overrule calls and when and when not to allow or disallow trainers and bathroom breaks.

But I see no reason why officials should not be allowed to make mistakes when the players they are supervising make many. They are after all supported by a team (assistant referees, third umpires etcetera). We are understanding of other people who have to make really serious decisions quickly and under pressure, for example:

- policemen and women;
- the other emergency services;
- fighting men and women;
- commercial pilots;
- doctors and surgeons.

In nearly all cases there is again a team in support to put things right if the first decision was wrong.

So... don't shoot the ref! And by the way, would you really want to be one yourself?

Umpires and referees

I looked at the five sports I follow most closely: rugby union, football, cricket, golf and tennis. There's big money in all of them. The stars are household names. Each attracts massive media coverage, and the officials in charge – referees and umpires – could hardly operate in more different ways:

Rugby union

Players treat referees with great respect. Nearly all referees are ex-club players. The referee operates with two touch judges, now called assistant referees. Touch judges just used to signal where the ball had crossed the touch line and whose throw in it is at the line out, and judge whether kicks at the goal had passed between the posts and above the bar. Now, although the referee is the sole judge of fact and law, the assistant referees can not only draw the referee's attention to foul play or other offences, they can also indicate the appropriate action to be taken (penalty, yellow card etc). I interviewed Paddy O'Brien, who is the world's top referee, as head of the International Rugby Board (IRB)'s referee board. He feels that respect for referees stems from the fact that they get so many decisions right, and that the referees are almost all former players (and were historically mainly teachers and policemen). Because players are comparatively disciplined (compared to football), and supporters also better behaved than at football there is less pressure. But the game is not easy to referee:

- The laws are complex and constantly changing.
- The game is extremely fast and intense.
- With 30 players on the pitch at any one time, a great deal is happening, particularly in scrums, rucks and mauls, which is both violent and hard to see.
- The referee is expected to prevent foul play as well as punishing it, and a kind of running commentary scenario has developed – unknown in any other sport.
- The scrum is beset by rules (particularly in the set up: 'crouch, touch, engage'), with the result that basic fouls like putting the ball in crooked is seldom punished.

As O'Brien told me, 'You can't go through a game without making a mistake, it's impossible.' He said referees hate making mistakes, but can't beat themselves up, because there will be so many more decisions to give.

Football

Players treat the referee with very little respect, and indeed referees continually have to run the gauntlet of criticism and abuse from players, spectators, managers and media. The referee forms a team with two referee's assistants (formerly known as linesmen) on the field and a fourth official off it, who mainly deals with infringements in the technical areas, with timekeeping, and with substitutions. Very few of these officials have played football at any significant level. Astonishingly football employs no technology whatever in support of the officials. Decision making for football referees is difficult on a number of levels:

- The pace of football is as demanding on referees as it is for the players. Keeping up and being in the correct position to see if an offence has been committed is not easy.
- The referee has no technology, but everyone else has, thanks to television and big screens.
- Players continually cheat (diving, fouling out of the referee's vision). They also appeal and put pressure on the officials.
- Supporters are exceptionally partisan.

Cricket

In international cricket there is now a team of four umpires – two on the field, as has always been the case, the third umpire who is in charge of interpreting the technology (Decision Review System or DRS) and a fourth umpire who is in charge of admin and logistics. There is widespread respect for umpires, and generally a good relationship on the field between players and umpires, who in the UK have nearly always been ex-Test or first class players. It is interesting that very few of the non-British umpires on the international panel have first-class cricket playing experience. I interviewed two retired and highly experienced first-class umpires Ray Julian and Vanburn Holder. Ray was a former Leicestershire wicketkeeper and Vanburn a West Indies Test fast bowler (40 caps), who subsequently played county cricket for Worcestershire. Both have umpired in one-day internationals.

Decision making for umpires is difficult, but much less so in international cricket, now some form of DRS is in use almost always. But there is not yet any consistency in what aids are in use in different companies. Also below international level, no technology exists except for big finals etc. It is difficult because:

- All forms of the game except Twenty 20 take at least one full day, thus putting the umpires under pressure to maintain concentration. A five-day test match is a very tiring ordeal for umpires.

- It may look like a leisurely game from the stands, but once the bowler starts to run up, everything happens very quickly, and the fastest bowlers are delivering a ball at 90 miles an hour.

- Cricket is another game with complex rules. The umpire called upon to adjudge a catch or an LBW dismissal has had to check the bowler's front foot position for a possible no ball an instant before.

Vanburn Holder told me:

> It is stressful with the cameras on you all day. Not many people have to go to work with that pressure. The DRS (Decision Referral System, now in use in international cricket) takes some pressure off, but not every decision can be referred. Umpiring is very good today, and the DRS proves it. But players will cheat even when they know what really happened. We used to give the benefit of the doubt to batsmen, but that's not possible any more. Umpiring is a job where you have to make decisions all the time, and if you get one wrong, you mustn't try and even things up.

I asked him about maintaining concentration all day. 'You have to be physically fit now. I eat sensibly and do a lot of walking and swimming.'

Ray Julian spent 50 years in first class cricket – 21 as a player and 29 as an umpire. He loved playing, and he is so keen on umpiring that he is still doing it for fun more than 10 years after he retired.

He told me:

> I was an 'outer', and that's why I didn't get Test matches. I always gave someone out if I thought he was, and they thought I could have reduced a five day Test to three days! The third umpire (who has to interpret the technology) is now more influential than the guys in the middle. I know the DRS works, but I'm worried that it takes away from the field umpire's decision making authority.

Golf

Officials in professional golf are almost invisible. Golf is a game with an almost unique player code of calling rule infringements on yourself (snooker is the only other sport of which this is true). Golf is also a simple game with no complicated rules. Either the player has taken four shots or he hasn't. Either the ball went in the hole, or it didn't. There are no disputes like, 'Did the ball hit his glove?' or 'Did he ground the ball? or 'Did the ball cross the line?'. No offsides, no problem with no balls, no disputed line calls.

Tennis

The umpire in tennis is the official score-keeper, presides over the 'Hawkeye' line review system, and can over-rule line calls from his or her team of six line judges. A tournament referee is in the background, and will only be called upon when there is a serious (and disputed) weather, injury or disciplinary problem.

Randy Haynes is a leading expert on sports betting

Randy told me about the lasting impact on the sports betting industry of the famous 'Dettori Sevenfold', when Frankie Dettori rode all seven winners on a card at Ascot in September 1996:

I had initiated what is now probably the biggest revolution in the industry, which is what they call in-play (betting on an event after it has started, as opposed to ante-post). I helped to develop the business of a bookmaker called Stan James in Oxford. Steve Fisher, who runs it, would say I was an important part of their move into in-play, which helped them differentiate themselves.

The Dettori sevenfold did a lot of injury to the betting business in general, but in particular to Stan James. My hat goes off to the Fisher boys, because whilst some of the bigger bookmakers were refusing to accept their responsibilities, they stood up and they made sure that all the people who were taking their odds were able to hedge their bets. That left them with a huge liability, which they took on the chin. They survived and prospered. Bookmakers in total lost £50 million thanks to Dettori's seven out of seven. To lose £50 million on one day meant that with 10 per cent margins, they'd have to take £500 million and then pay taxes and so on to get it back. Punters had 10p accumulators that were coming in to life-changing sums. The Dettori Sevenfold meant that bookmakers had to raise their sights and change their game.

The sports betting and gaming market now has the potential to mirror the size and complexity without hopefully the headaches, and with a lot more transparency, of the financial markets.

What you will get, as in the financial markets, are experts who will say, I am an expert on Premiership football. Not an expert in everything but on Premiership football I'm the man. I will make the market and when I make the market I'm not therefore 1,000 euros, I'm 100,000 euros, a million.

Chapter Ten
Love

Deciding with the heart and not the head

It took me two years and 25 trips to Korea to convince her parents.

Vitaly Vasiliev, CEO of Gazprom
– a true love story

It was in London. We were on this study trip from Stanford, with Harvard Business School and Wharton Business School in London. I had noticed her the first time at the Morgan Stanley office in Canary Wharf. This inner voice, you know, talked to me and said 'This is your wife.'

She was a Korean lady. When we met, it turned out that she is from the same school. She was on a different programme – the two-year programme, while I was on the one-year programme. I was the kind of person who dated, I didn't have any problem with the girls. I can't say that I was popular whatever.

She and I started dating when we got back to the US. It was a very difficult decision making process because she said no all the time, you know. Koreans tend to stick with Koreans, that's Korean culture. And she's really like from Korea, Korean

Korean. Not American Korean. And Koreans marry Koreans. Her family's a very traditional family.

So it basically took me two years and 25 trips to Korea to convince her parents. She told me that if my parents say no, I can't marry you. So I understand that now my target is not so much her, but the parents, who don't speak English. And I don't speak Korean at all. So communication is a little bit difficult. My wife says nowadays that maybe it was an advantage that I didn't speak Korean, because I was constantly sitting silently with them. I didn't understand what they were saying, but they thought I was very respectful. I was not hurt because I did not understand what they were telling me – which was basically, why are you here, just go away. In the end we got married, we've got two kids now, so very happy. It was a great decision.

Karl Gregory – MD of Match.com

When I met Karl, I asked him the fundamental question for me about finding a partner. Is the old adage true – do opposites attract?

To my amazement, he told me that no one had ever asked him that question before.

> Opposites do attract, but I also have seen strong evidence that people from the same background, vision of life, and values also attract. Thinking in practical terms, it could go either way. We would not put two control freaks together because we know that that is going to be problematic. We wouldn't put an individual who loves to go out travelling and is sporty, with somebody who just wants to watch TV on the couch because that would be a problem. They're really distinct.

I didn't want to tell him that that sort of 'distinctness' probably accounted for about half of all UK marriages in years gone by! I asked Karl what he liked about his job.

> What's great about my job is that when I go out – a wedding or I'm out for dinner, or I'm sitting with a group of people

– and they say, where do you work? I say, I work at Match. com. There is always someone at the table who has met their partner or knows somebody who has met their partner on Match. So, we've become a significant factor in society. When you ask people who they are and particularly how they found their partner, they light up. They want to tell you their story.

In the last five years, we have created 92,000 marriages in the UK, and 517,000 relationships. A relationship is defined as somebody who has left our site because they've met somebody and been together for more than three months. Our research report Lovegeist tells us that people are fussier today than they were 10, 20 or 30 years ago. Just think about the amount of information we consume today versus somebody 30 or 40 years ago, and for instance how easy it is to travel. Most people met their loved ones, because she was the girl down the road; the girl in their village or town. Or somebody you met in the office.

Today, we are so much more demanding. Our horizons are so much broader. We're so much more willing to travel and we're fussier. When you sign up, we ask you to give us quite a bit of information about yourself. When we're matching you, we start basing it on the information you gave us. But the great thing is, you look at somebody's profile and say, do you know what? That person is not for me because their value system is different, or what they enjoy is different.

I asked Karl whether his clients get a photograph at the same time as the information.

They do and it's a very valid question, and one which hugely surprised me, and was a big learning for me. It came out of the focus groups. I always thought that men would be based on chemistry and pictures and women would be more emotive, and deeper in looking at the information. But actually, men and women, at all ages, would always look at the photo first to see if there is going to be any chemistry.

I had a focus group which was women 50-plus and what was fascinating to me was the fact that they absolutely wanted to see the photo first. He didn't need to be good looking, he didn't need to be a star, but there must be chemistry. Also, in their words, he mustn't be mean.

And here's one you'll enjoy. One of the ingredients of our success is our focus on product and matching people. We then realized that what women in particular were telling us they are looking for in a man wasn't always what they originally had asked for. So, in a profile she explicitly tells us what she is looking for: a banker, not older than 40, maybe Jewish or Catholic. Very specific. Wants to have kids in the future... absolute must. Such and such a height. Must be a non-smoker.

Then we see that this lady is actually looking at profiles of hippies who absolutely never want to have kids, don't have a secure job, and who have got a very carefree life. What she said she wanted, and the profiles she is looking at are very, very different.

What we started doing was serving profiles of people that they actually didn't explicitly request, but based on their behaviour. It's been a huge success. The whole dating game is all about ice-breakers. It's about confidence and having the confidence to go up in a bar and talk to somebody. Online, it's exactly the same. We give you the opportunity to wink at somebody. So, it's non-committal and, if they don't reply, that's fine. People are in fear of rejection. So, in some ways we circumvent the rejection part. Then, from there, they start looking at profiles. The process is still a long process and the time and effort that they need to put in place is quite a lot.

We have people who have married the first person they met online. There's a couple who have been trying six or nine months. We say, you know, give it time. Go out and kiss some frogs.

Thoughts on Karl Gregory's description of how the dating industry works

I spotted the similarity with choosing ad agencies. Chemistry sessions are fine if you've got to do it quickly, but for most clients it's more successful if we keep them away from seeing agencies until they have determined what they're really looking for, and what went wrong last time and what the ambitions of the company are. Then, we can help them.

Decision making in love is probably a book in itself. What is clear is that it is definitely an area where a mixture of logic, emotion, and that clever subconscious mind of ours is the only way to go. Nightmares and decision traps abound for anyone who relies just on logic, just on emotion, or just on the subconscious. Those in search of a partner will also do well to remember that list of conditions to avoid at the end of Chapter 2!

Karl generously shared with me *Lovegeist 2010*, the annual report Match.com produce on what we might call the nation on the couch with the lights turned low. Some highlights follow at appropriate moments below.

Are there any rules for decision making in love?

How interesting that romance and sex are conspicuous omissions from most books on decision making! In Chapter 4 we saw Benjamin Franklin advising his nephew to choose a wife by doing a kind of SWOT (strengths, weaknesses, opportunities, threats) analysis on the two contenders.

In his 2004 book *The Paradox of Choice* American psychologist Barry Schwartz describes the dilemma of a former student Joseph, who had fallen in love with a fellow graduate student Jane: 'With his career on track and a life partner selected, it might appear that Joseph had made the big decisions. Yet, in the course of their courtship, Joseph and Jane had to make a series of tough choices':

- Should they live together?
- Should they get married?
- If so, under his religion or hers?
- Should they keep their finances independent, or merge them?
- Should they have children?
- Should they each go for the best possible job – even if that meant living apart?
- She came from the East Coast, he from the West. Where should they ideally live?

'They thought that they had already made the hard decisions when they fell in love and made a mutual commitment. Shouldn't that be enough?'

It's a good point, and possibly explains why it is harder to categorize decisions in personal relationships. *Lovegeist* gives some context to this in contemporary Britain:

It is clear that finding love is a priority for many of the UK's daters – nearly half (46%) feel that having a successful relationship is more important to them than their career; and once again we see an interesting comparison between men and women, with 52% of men prioritising their love life over their career, compared to 42% of women. Perhaps this is another indication of the toll the recession has taken on men, as they seek the comfort of a loving relationship in contrast to the pressures on them in the tough economic climate?

A healthy proportion of singles (59%) are also aware of the importance of maintaining a good balance between one's work and personal life and finding time for love, with women more likely (63%) to attempt to strike this delicate balance than men (55%). However, more than half (54%) feel that they are simply not able to dedicate enough time to finding or maintaining a relationship, with time pressured 40-something men most likely to feel the strain (60%).

The LoveGeist Report has uncovered a new breed of dater – Pragmantics (or pragmatic romantics) – 25–40 year old singles who tread a delicate balancing act between the realities of everyday life and the desires and aspirations of finding true love.

Love ranks a healthy third in a list of nine life priorities, beating friends, social life, career and personal ambition, and just after family and health (first and second priorities respectively). The Report indicates a strong desire among the UK's dating community to find and nurture long-term love. Some of the key findings include:

- 93% of daters are looking for a long-term relationship – rising to 97% among the 18–30s. Love is clearly an aspiration for the vast majority, particularly for those just starting out on the road to a long-term relationship.

- Despite the plethora of negative news coverage about the state of marriage in Great Britain today, only 13% of daters say they actively don't want to get married in the future – and once again, younger daters are most positive about matrimony, with nearly 80% of singles within the 18–36 age group expressing a desire to get married in future.

- Interestingly, having children together (37%) is seen as a bigger symbol of commitment than marriage (33%) for the UK's daters. We would argue that this is in many ways reflective of a new era, with more options and choice for long-term relationship formats open to singles today.

In *Paradox of Choice* Schwartz also prosaically tackles what he sees as the 'sunk cost' effect in long-term relationships:

> Many people persist in very troubled relationships not because of love or what they owe the other person or because they feel a moral obligation to honour vows, but because of all the time and effort they've already put in.

He compares this to other examples of the same phenomenon:

- The pairs of expensive, but uncomfortable shoes that you hang on to.
- The shares that you don't sell because their price has now fallen below that at which you bought them.
- People who pay more for a ticket are more likely to use it.
- Finishing your plate in a restaurant when you are actually full.

He may have a good point here, however unromantic it sounds. Agony aunts tend to take a moral or ethical tone in giving advice on the snags that afflict long-term relationships. They are free with value judgements and often appeal to altruism. But the sunk cost theory is an important aspect of behavioural economics. The same thinking often triggers conservative responses to questions about changing job, moving house or even changing a bank account or energy supplier. We might imagine our decision making is primarily motivated by future considerations, but so often it is a function of how present circumstances relate to the past.

It would be a mistake though just to consider decisions in love on such a practical and rational level. In his 2008 book *Predictably Irrational* Dan Ariely, who is Professor of Psychology and Behavioural Economics at Duke University, writes about his research into sexual motivation. Some excerpts:

1 The 'decoy effect'. Chatting up will be more effective if you hang around with someone a bit like you – but less attractive, less articulate, or less funny.

2 The battle between social norms (for example the courtship ritual) and market norms (like money for sex). Obviously 'free sex' in a social context is on an altogether higher plane than commercial sex. But how many dates are you expected to fund before something more than a peck on the cheek can be reasonably anticipated? If the man is unwise enough to share these thoughts with his girlfriend, mayhem may follow. Ariely quotes Woody Allen: 'The most expensive sex is free sex.'

3 Ariely had (he claims) an academic interest in why sexual behaviour does not always align with sexual attitudes. Why do people who claim to disapprove of unprotected sex, and are fully aware of the dangers of catching AIDS and sexually transmitted diseases (STDs), sometimes fail to take precautions, and indulge in wild excesses they would normally condemn? The answer (unsurprisingly) is the effect of sexual arousal. His experiments were conducted on 25 participating 20-something male students at Berkeley. Ariely makes an interesting case for researching only men: 'In terms of sex, their wiring is a lot simpler than that of women (as we concluded after much discussion among ourselves and our assistants, both male and female). A copy of *Playboy* and a darkened room were about all we'd need for a high degree of success.' Oh yes? I hear you cry. A conversation between Ariely and Charles Spence, based on the latter's Lynx work (see Chapter 7) might prove interesting!

Ariely's study on decision making under sexual arousal showed conclusions that were, as he writes:

> consistently and overwhelmingly, frighteningly clear. In every case, our bright young participants answered the questions very differently when they were aroused from when they were in a 'cold' state, Across the 19 questions about sexual preferences, when the participants were aroused they predicted that their desire to engage in a variety of somewhat odd sexual activities would be nearly twice as high as they had predicted when they were cold... Across the board, they revealed in their un-aroused state that they themselves did not know what they were like once aroused. Prevention, protection, conservatism, and morality disappeared completely from their radar screen.

Ariely feels that these findings have enormous significance in teaching safe sex. Telling teenagers, for instance, not to indulge in unprotected sex is unlikely to work if you are relying on them to take the message on board rationally, and store it away for the future.

But he also says that they point to a wider significance than just the influence of sex. He suggests that we need to protect ourselves from ourselves in other ways:

- by not pinging off e-mails when we are angry;
- by not buying a sports car with the adrenaline still surging after a test drive;
- better life decisions; for example not forswearing painkillers in childbirth ahead of the event.

What match.com's *Lovegeist* report tells us

Much of *Lovegeist* is dedicated to the rational, the objective, the economic and the balanced. But I found it reassuring that even today, a) men and women see the world differently, and b) they, even when 'cold', are interested in physical characteristics as well as personality and fit:

> Drilling down into anonymised partner preference records from match.com, we can build up a picture of the women and men looking for relationships across the UK, what they want from a partner, likes, dislikes and much more.

The Female of the Species

Love comes in every shape and size! But looking at a cross-section of over 75,000 recent female match.com members, the 'average' female dater

- Is between 25–30 years old – making up 22% of the sample
- Is around 5'5" tall (15%)
- Has dark brown hair (31%) and (40%) blue eyes – and rates her eyes as her best feature (53%)
- Views her body type as average (36% of the sample)

- Sees herself as easy going (32%) and sociable (14%)
  Is intelligent – 53% have a degree (compared with 13% of the wider UK female population)

- Enjoys travel above all other activities, followed by movies, conversation and cooking

- One of the most common occupations for female daters on match.com is within the field of medical, dental and veterinary (11%) – these are often hectic jobs, perhaps outside major cities, leaving daters little time or opportunity to meet new people. Medical professionals looking for love are most likely to live in Northern Ireland and the Republic of Ireland, Scotland and Wales. Female daters in London are most likely to work in financial services (11%). When it comes to what women want from men, we analyse the multiple choice responses of female match.com members and discovered that women are looking for a guy who terms his body shape as 'average' (90%), with short (97%), dark brown (89%) hair, blue eyes (84%) and an easygoing manner (86%).

It would seem the blond Brad Pitt look has rivals in the hair stakes – 59% of the female sample would choose a blond man, 75% would go for a smouldering black-haired look, 73% like light brown and 38% lust after the George Clooney salt and pepper shades. In addition, 56% like a man with cropped or shaved hair, and 26% would go for a bald head.

The male waif look is out – only 38% would choose a slender man, almost the same proportion as would choose a man carrying a few extra pounds (34%).

The eyes have it – 78% of women like attractive eyes in a man. Also high in the popularity stakes are an attractive smile (77%), a good bum (35%) and good arms (27%). Only 4% choose a man based on his feet. 86% of women want an easygoing man with a good sense of humour. 75% yearn for someone thoughtful, 74% admire a man who is sociable and 73% look for reliability.

When it comes to enjoying their spare time, women tend to be most interested in a man who enjoys eating out and travelling, with very little age differential – these interests appeal to women of any age. Younger women prefer men who are into movies and music, while women aged 50+ are more likely to go for a man who shows an interest in gardening.

Boy, Oh Boy.

And taking a look at a similar sized sample of the male dating population, we see that the 'average' man on match.com:

- Is between 25–30 years old (24%)
- Is 5'10" in height (16%) – 22% of the sample is over 6ft in height
- Categorises his body type as average (46%) – more than a quarter (29%) say they are toned and athletic
- Has dark brown hair (31%) and (40%) blue eyes
- Is also easy going (43%), although perhaps less sociable than women (4%)
- Is intelligent – 53% have a degree (compared to 15% of the male population of the UK)
- Enjoys travel above all other activities, followed by movies, conversation and eating out
- Is most interested in movies and videos and travel
- 16% of the sample of male daters on match.com are in the field of computers or technology, while 14% are self-employed and 13% are in management roles.

The multiple choice options of recent male daters sample reveal that they are looking for a woman who is average in build (86%), with shoulder-length (93%) blonde (87%) hair and blue eyes (88%). Easy-going women are attractive to men (89%), as are those with a good sense of humour (80%).

While it would seem that gentlemen do prefer blondes, dark brown and light brown brunettes (85% and 78% respectively) also feature highly. 79% like a raven-haired woman and 59% like a redhead.

The flowing locks of celebs like Cheryl Cole and Penelope Cruz have inspired a penchant for long hair – the majority of men like a woman with shoulder-length (93%), long (90%) hair or very long (65%).

85% of men like a slender body type, and 80% love a toned, athletic body. Happily, 65% would be content with a lady carrying a few extra pounds.

As with women, men go for a lovely pair of eyes first (77%). Also high on the 'like' list are smile (76%), a cute bottom (54%), nice legs (52%) and 13% like a nice belly button.

Looking at what men want from a partner's interests, they are most likely to seek out a woman who is interested in eating out, with music, gigs, cinema and spending time at the pub all also ranking highly.

Chapter Eleven
My 20 best decision tips

> *Whenever you see a successful business, someone once made a courageous decision.*
>
> **(PETER DRUCKER, WRITER, MANAGEMENT CONSULTANT AND SAGE. BORN 1909 NEAR VIENNA, DIED 2005 IN CALIFORNIA)**

There are many brilliant academics in decision science. Good books have been written on the subject by experts in many different disciplines. But there seems to be remarkably little help available for the man and woman in the street – who all have to make hundreds if not thousands of decisions in their lives.

Decision skills are the biggest differentiator between success and failure: more influential than intellect, academic qualifications, energy, hard work, personality. More powerful even than political savvy or low cunning.

To be a success in life we need to be disproportionately determined. That could be why so many successful people are particularly good at making decisions. 'Great deciders' are often inspired by dreams or influences in early life, and are also able to pull off dramatic changes of career direction. Make the most important decision of your life: take decision making seriously, and become seriously good at it.

My Number 1 decision tip is that every decision – even one we have to take quickly – is a journey, not a single step. The journey looks like this:

- Set a credible achievement goal.

- Is the challenge mainly about exploiting an opportunity, or solving a problem? Indeed, has opportunity been identified? Very little progress is made other than by realizing opportunities.

- Avoid at all costs the 'early decision', where the problem still hasn't been solved.

- Problem solving and decision making are different things – and you have to approach them in that order.

- Make sure you are answering the right question. Define the 'meta decision' – the real crux of the issue – and be completely clear about the goal, or desired outcome.

- Gather evidence greedily, and analyse it dispassionately.

- Work out the best available options.

- Decide only when you have weighed up the downsides as well as the upsides of each option.

- Give the decision itself all the concentration you are capable of – which may involve sleeping on it, and letting your subconscious play its part.

- Make the decision a mutual one by getting buy-in, selling it up or whatever you need to do.

- Communicate it clearly (which is often the moment when the decision 'happens').

- Implement it, and make as many more decisions as are necessary.

- Always 'follow through'. Learn from every important decision you make by doing a simple written summary of outcomes against objectives. Feed this back into your experience bank, so you can learn from it next time.

Here are my other 19 tips:

2 Anticipate all the problems you can think of and work out a possible solution to each – like Ellen MacArthur before a race.

3 Put as much effort into minimizing the downsides of options, as maximizing the upsides.

4 Always remember the 'limiters' that reduce our choice. Wanting something does not necessarily mean that we can have it.

5 Rationality is vital – especially in setting up the decision process (deciding to decide). Rationality is crucial too in terms of collecting intelligence. But choosing options, and carrying out reward–risk assessment on each one is going to harness the subconscious mind as well. Emotion and gut feel are important triggers to evaluating the options and coming to the decision itself.

6 If you have a visual mind like Nigel Jones (the beautiful board at chess), use it to see your way through decisions, while others can only think.

7 Understand your own 'autopilot' system, and use it as much as possible; not instead of your conscious brain, but alongside it. Great decision makers use their right *and* left brains.

8 A key consideration for any decision is how long we have to make up our mind. Remember the magic number 60. There is a huge difference between having:

- 60 seconds (or a lot less: instant reaction time, or life and death);

- 60 minutes (the average length of a meeting);

- 60 hours (over a weekend, or start thinking Monday, decide Thursday);

- 60 days (a two-month project);

- 60 weeks (a one year assignment, with a little allowance for slippage).

9 Learn to take fast decisions. It is not just trained professionals in the military and emergency services who have to move very fast. You sometimes have to as well. Think about situations we take for granted – like driving a car.

10 Ubiquitous communications, and especially social media, have changed the world. Nowadays everyone and every organization in the public eye *has* to be able to make fast decisions and communicate them.

11 Being wrong is OK. That's how we learn. What is disastrous is not knowing how to put things right.

12 There is no excuse for ignoring the obvious danger signs that tell us when a decision might go badly wrong. Inevitably we will make mistakes, but if we don't avoid the obvious decision traps, we are likely to pay a price.

13 Choosing is also different from making other kinds of decision. Deciding is about validating the likeliest option. Choosing is a function of searching for candidates, and then selecting on a comparative basis. We can only find a winner by eliminating the options that don't work. But the choice itself is highly likely to be influenced by the subconscious, particularly in consumer choice.

14 The people factor is crucial. To make effective decisions we have to be able to understand our own personalities and those of everyone else involved. Profiling is also key to predicting how allies and enemies will behave and react.

15 Team decision making will inevitably involve lots of meetings. It often seems that the entire business calendar is taken up with meetings – with sometimes unfortunate results. We have to get together regularly with colleagues and associates, but bad meetings are often counterproductive. It is only by understanding the pitfalls of the meeting culture, that we can learn how to use meetings to make better decisions, and make sure that all key players buy in to what has been decided.

16 Don't be fooled by language. 'Decisive' is a compliment and 'sitting on the fence' an insult – but there are times when it will pay to stay on that fence a little longer, and not rush in. Equally 'changing my mind' sounds like an admission of weakness. But far better to change your mind and succeed in the end, than be consistent – and wrong. 'Going back' doesn't sound too positive, but Shackleton did, and lived to fight another day.

17 Deciding to give up something or someone is often much harder than deciding to start or do something for the first time. Remember that 'loss aversion' and 'sunk cost' are vicious decision traps that can block progress.

18 Two problems or decisions are easier to deal with than just one. If you're agonizing over a big decision, give it a break, and try to resolve a lesser problem. Sorting that out will often clear the way to solve the big one.

19 Switch off the brain at night. Get some mind rest. Sleep on the decision if you can, and hand over to your autopilot. Start fresh in the morning.

20 Decide! Success comes from making decisions, not putting them off, or fudging them.

References

Ariely, D (2008) *Predictably Irrational*, HarperCollins

Baumeister, R and Tierney, J (2011) *Willpower: Rediscovering the greatest human strength*, Penguin

Belbin, M (1981) *Management Teams: Why they succeed or fail*, Belbin Books

Charan, R (2007) Conquering a Culture of Indecision, *Harvard Business Review on Making Smarter Decisions*

Colvin, G (June 2005) The Wisdom of Dumb Questions, *Fortune* magazine

Damasio, A (1994) *Descartes' Error: Emotion, reason, and the human brain*, Putnam Publishing

Damasio, A (2010) *Self Comes to Mind: Constructing the conscious brain*, Random House

De Bono, E (2009) *Six Thinking Hats*, Penguin

Dixon, N (1994) *On the Psychology of Military Incompetence*, Pimlico

Franklin, B *Advice to a Young Man on the Choice of a Mistress* (25 June 1745), Letter to his nephew

Gallwey, T (1975) *The Inner Game of Tennis*, Jonathan Cape

Gilbert, E (2002) *The Last American Man*, Viking

Gigerenzer, G and Goldstein, D (2004) Reasoning the Fast and Frugal Way: Models of bounded rationality, *Centre for Adaptive Behaviour and Cognition*, Max Planck Institute for Psychological Research, Munich

Gigerenzer, G (2008) *Gut Feelings*, Penguin

Gladwell, M (2005) *Blink*, Allen Lane

Hallinan, J (2009) *Errornomics*, Ebury Press

Hastings, M (2011) *All Hell Let Loose: The World at War 1939–1945*, HarperCollins

IPA (Institute of Practitioners in Advertising) (2010) *Behavioural Economics: Red hot or red herring?*, IPA

Lehrer, J (2009) *How We Decide*, Houghton Mifflin Harcourt

Kahnemann, D, Lovallo, D and Sibony, O (June 2011) Before You Make That Big Decision, *Harvard Business Review*

Kiyosaki, R (2011) *Rich Dad, Poor Dad*, Plata Publishing

Kleiner, K (Summer 2009) Review of *What Intelligence Tests Miss: The psychology of rational thought*, Professor Keith Stanovich (2009), Yale University Press. *University of Toronto Magazine*

Kneeland, S (1999) *Effective Problem Solving*, How To Books

Lehrer, J (2009) *The Decisive Moment*, Canongate

McConnell, Professor A (2011) *Breathe Strong, Perform Better*, Human Kinetics

McCormack, M (1986) *What They Don't Teach You At Harvard Business School: Notes from a street-smart executive*, Bantam

Miller, G A (1956) The Magical Number Seven, Plus or Minus Two: Some limits on our capacity for processing information, *The Psychological Review*, **63**, pp 81–97

Murray, K (2011) *The Language of Leaders*, Kogan Page

Nobre, A and Coull, J (2010) *Attention and Time*, Oxford University Press

Nutt, P (2002) *Why Decisions Fail*, Berrett Kohler

Russo, E and Schoemaker, P (1989) *Decision Traps: The ten barriers to brilliant decision-making and how to overcome them*, Fireside

Sarasvathy, S (2008) *What Makes Entrepreneurs Entrepreneurial?* University of Virginia – Darden School of Business

Schulz, K (2011) *Being Wrong*, HarperCollins

Schwartz, B (2004) *The Paradox of Choice: Why more is less*, Harper Perennial

Thaler, R and Sunstein, C (2008) *Nudge*, Yale University Press

Toda, M (1980) *Emotion and Decision Making*, Hokkaido University

Topolski, D and Robinson, P (1999) *True Blue*, Random House

Wirasinghe, E (2003) *The Art Of Making Decisions*, Shanmar Publishing

Wiseman, R (2009) *59 Seconds*, Macmillan

Index

(*italics* indicate a figure or table in the text)